T0291308

Financialization and Local Statecraft

Financialization and Local Statecraft

Andy Pike

OXFORD
UNIVERSITY PRESS

OXFORD
UNIVERSITY PRESS

Great Clarendon Street, Oxford, OX2 6DP,
United Kingdom

Oxford University Press is a department of the University of Oxford.
It furthers the University's objective of excellence in research, scholarship,
and education by publishing worldwide. Oxford is a registered trade mark of
Oxford University Press in the UK and in certain other countries

© Andy Pike 2023

The moral rights of the author have been asserted

All rights reserved. No part of this publication may be reproduced, stored in
a retrieval system, or transmitted, in any form or by any means, without the
prior permission in writing of Oxford University Press, or as expressly permitted
by law, by licence or under terms agreed with the appropriate reprographics
rights organization. Enquiries concerning reproduction outside the scope of the
above should be sent to the Rights Department, Oxford University Press, at the
address above

You must not circulate this work in any other form
and you must impose this same condition on any acquirer

Published in the United States of America by Oxford University Press
198 Madison Avenue, New York, NY 10016, United States of America

British Library Cataloguing in Publication Data

Data available

Library of Congress Control Number: 2023932532

ISBN 978–0–19–285666–1

DOI: 10.1093/oso/9780192856661.001.0001

Printed and bound by
CPI Group (UK) Ltd, Croydon, CR0 4YY

Cover image: Michelle Wood (seatern.co.uk)

Links to third party websites are provided by Oxford in good faith and
for information only. Oxford disclaims any responsibility for the materials
contained in any third party website referenced in this work.

For my late sister Helen; Michelle, Ella, and Connell

Acknowledgements

Curiosity about why local governments were being depicted by elected local politicians taking chances with taxpayers' money and jeopardizing public services in the 'councillors at the casino' narrative motivated this book. A more balanced view of what local governments and their politicians and officers in England were doing where, when, and why was needed. The ambition was better understanding of how financialization and local governance were playing out in different geographical settings.

Communicating the experiences of local government in England in the UK to an international audience was a further aspiration, extending beyond those working in the area and steeped in its idiosyncrasies and connecting research in municipal and commercial finance, governance, and territorial development and policy. The book seeks to convey the complex and technical nature of local government and its funding, financing, and governing in England to this global and multidisciplinary readership in an accessible way.

Gratitude is due to the people involved in the book's production. Throughout the process, thanks to Adam Swallow and Vicki Sunter at Oxford University Press. In the early stages, thanks to Neil Coe, two anonymous reviewers, and Andy Cumbers, Al James, Kean Fan Lim, Danny MacKinnon, Giles Mohan, Emma Ormerod, Peter Sunley, and John Tomaney for comments on the book proposal.

During the research stage, thanks to the contacts and interviewees for their advice, contributions, expertise, and generosity. Specifically, thanks to: Alistair Clarke (Newcastle University); Bevis Ingram (Local Government Association); Andrew Chappell (Public Service Audit Appointments Ltd.); Cait Robinson (University of Bristol); and Mark Sandford (House of Commons Library).

In the analysing, thinking, drafting, and writing stage, earlier versions of the arguments were presented at: a CURDS seminar, Newcastle University, May 2022; the 'Financialization, regulation, and the local state' sessions at the Global Conference on Economic Geography, Dublin, June 2022; the University of Cambridge, CURDS, and LSE workshop on 'What's happened to the local state in England? Local government, financialization, and regulation', LSE, June 2022; and the School of Geography and Planning at Cardiff

University seminar, December 2022. Thanks to the organizers and participants, especially Frances Brill, Laura Deruytter, Crispian Fuller, Mike Raco,
and Callum Ward, for their engagement, questions, and feedback. Thanks to
Allan Cochrane, Alistair Clarke, Andy Cumbers, Al James, Kean Fan Lim,
Jessa Loomis, Danny MacKinnon, David Marlow, Aileen Murphy, Emma
Ormerod, Terry Paul, Jane Pollard, and John Tomaney for comments on
draft chapters, and the external reviewer for comments on the full draft
manuscript. The ideas and their expression in the book are the better for all
your advice.

   In the final stage, thanks to Nigel Auchterlounie (knocky.smith@gmail.
com) for the 'councillors at the casino' cartoon and Michelle Wood
(seatern.co.uk) for the cover art.

   The colleagues and research ethos and culture in CURDS continues to
inspire and inflect my work. Dialogue with postgraduates in the Local and
Regional Development and Planning programmes in CURDS and under-
graduates on the Geography and Planning programmes at Newcastle University has contributed substantively to the arguments in the book.

   Referencing uses Richard Walker's (2018: xvi) 'Berkeley system' from *Pic-
tures of a Gone City* (PM Press, Oakland) because it 'provides references
(and comments) at a glance in footnotes along with the convenience of a
consolidated bibliography'.

   The usual disclaimers apply.

Contents

List of Figures

List of Tables

1

'Councillors at the casino'

The local public services gamble in financialized times

1.0 Introduction

Figure 1.1 Portsmouth City Council, town hall, 2021
Source: Photograph © Andy Pike 2023.

In a minority administration between 2014 and 2018, Conservative leader of Portsmouth City Council Donna Jones, a former finance executive, initiated a 'change of culture' towards a more commercialized and financialized direction to generate income and offset the impacts of reduced national government expenditure (Figure 1.1).[1] Deepening the previous leadership's

[1] Conservative Councillor and former leader Donna Jones quoted in BBC News (2018: 1).

Financialization and Local Statecraft. Andy Pike, Oxford University Press. © Andy Pike (2023).
DOI: 10.1093/oso/9780192856661.003.0001

strategy, innovations included: establishment of wholly owned services company Victory Energy; a £146 million commercial asset acquisition strategy buying properties in Portsmouth and across the South East, Midlands, and North West of England; and a £73 million income strip lease deal for the Wightlink ferry terminal in Portsmouth with international insurance company Canada Life.[2]

The city council's activities raised concerns about local government's purpose and financial strategy, its use of local taxpayers' money, and its implications for local public service provision and democracy.[3] Following political leadership change after the 2018 elections, the reinstated Liberal Democrat leader, Gerald Vernon-Jackson, commenting on the financial guarantees provided for Victory Energy noted: 'It is not the role of a council to be effectively acting as a hedge fund and playing roulette with public money.'[4] This telling episode demonstrates the difficult financial position of local governments in England since 2010, when national government expenditure reductions compelled them to make savings and generate new income sources.

Situated in different political-economic and institutional geographies internationally from the 2000s, local governments in such predicaments were characterized as naïve municipal actors engaging in finance capitalism against experienced commercial hands. Grappling with funding gaps, local councillors and officers are seen as taking a 'bet' by risking local taxpayers' money on financial arrangements with unpredictable outcomes and compromising local public service provision.[5]

Acknowledging and conceptualizing the institutional, legal, and regulatory differences that structure and shape differences on the ground, empirical instances are myriad. Municipal authorities—including Saint-Étienne, France; Pforzheim, Germany; and Milan, Italy—embraced financial innovations and became mired in 'large derivatives debacles'.[6] 'Creative financing options', including cross-border infrastructure leasing, drew municipalities in Germany into complex, long-term, and opaque deals with often 'nameless' US investors.[7] City governments in the US—including Atlantic City, New Jersey, and Chicago, Illinois—became embroiled in complex new financial arrangements, resulting in spiralling indebtedness, financial failure,

---

[2] Portsmouth City Council (2018), Buckley (2016).
[3] Cheverton and Sykes (2016).
[4] Quoted in Marrs (2018a: 1).
[5] Lagna (2016: 17).
[6] Hendrikse and Sidaway (2014: 22), Dodd (2010), Lagna (2016, 2017).
[7] Bülow (2004: 1).

and bankruptcy in Detroit, Michigan, and San Bernardino, Stockton, and Vallejo, California.[8]

Such local governments were depicted as being bamboozled and fleeced by financiers and the houses of finance capital. *The Economist* bemoaned 'cities in the casino' and how financial innovations and their risk have ended up with those 'least able to understand it' rather than those 'best qualified to hold it'.[9] On the other side of deals, banks were accused of 'selling hard to understand' and 'startlingly opaque products' with novel concepts, names, and acronyms to municipal authorities.[10]

These interpretations of local government financial affairs recall Keynes's identification of problems for national capital development if it 'becomes the by-product of the activities of a casino',[11] and Strange's *Casino Capitalism* of uncertainty, volatility, and risk generated by deregulated markets.[12] Local governments are portrayed as punters placing bets with taxpayers' money on complex games with outcomes determined by chance.

Such views reflect increasing concerns about national governments seeking efficiencies and reforms by compelling local politicians and officers to behave more commercially and engage with financial actors and markets in new, untried, and riskier strategies and arrangements. While local governments have long histories of financial innovation and experimentation,[13] anxiety has grown that activities in contemporary finance capitalism have especially uncertain and potentially damaging ramifications for local government financial sustainability, resilience, and public service provision.[14] At stake are fundamental questions about what local government is for and how it can be funded and financed.

A widening array of new and innovative arrangements hitherto alien to local municipal finance have been used by local governments in particular places in recent years. Differing from existing tried-and-tested and standard approaches, such novel financial strategies and practices have been formulated and deployed in attempts to make savings and raise income. Rather than only straightforward importation and duplication of vanguard concepts and instruments from the US, actors have sought and adapted ideas from wider international networks to work in their varying political-economic, institutional, and regulatory settings.

[8] Ashton et al. (2016), Davidson and Ward (2018), Peck and Whiteside (2016), Strickland (2016).
[9] The Economist (2010: 1).
[10] Hendrikse and Sidaway (2014: 203).
[11] Keynes (1936: 159).
[12] Strange (1986).
[13] Sbragia (1986).
[14] Hendrikse and Sidaway (2014), Lagna (2016, 2017).

For commercial finance actors, the local municipal finance market is underexploited and ripe for growth. Business opportunities exist in selling local governments innovations to make financial markets work more efficiently for them by clarifying market signals between participants and supporting their financial and risk management.

Replaying historical concerns about state fiscal crises and structural gaps between income and expenditure,[15] finance actors devised new instruments promising a 'financial "fix"' in attempts to 'reconcile the contradiction of ballooning expenditure needs with increasingly scarce resources'.[16] Reverberating unevenly through local governments situated in different institutional, legal, and regulatory settings internationally, changes include: investing cash in a growing range of financial products with a widening array of financial institutions; reorganization of in-house, outsourced, and in-sourced local service provision; establishing commercial trading ventures; and formulating new asset management strategies. Local governments unwilling or unable to undertake such activities are seen as out of step with their peers in embracing innovation and less capable of coping with fiscal stress.

A broadening mix of external advisors has been engaged for advice on saving money and generating income, especially through trading activities and commercial property investments. Unprecedented debt has been incurred, often using new, untried, and 'exotic' financial instruments including cross-border leases, interest rate swaps, and new loan products.[17] New investment strategies have been devised including and extending beyond local government areas to dispose of, hold, and acquire assets in efforts to generate income to offset fiscal stress.

In varying ways in different geographical settings, concerns have mounted that such strategies and behaviours risk undermining local governments' fundamental purposes and responsibilities. Many fear compromise of its central tasks of enhancing the prosperity and well-being of local residents and areas, providing essential local public services, addressing local voters and taxpayers' interests, and managing public money in transparent and democratically accountable ways.

Some worry local governments are becoming more like the financial institutions with which they are now increasingly working as they are exhorted by professional services actors to 'think like a bank' in supporting their local areas.[18] Others insist that local governments have a fiduciary duty to use financial innovations to secure value for taxpayers' money or

---

[15] O'Connor (1973).
[16] Kass et al. (2019: 1051, 1059).
[17] Pickard (2016: 1), The Economist (2010: 1).
[18] Coane and Brown (2020: 1).

else incur opportunity costs. A key concern is whether local governments' provision of essential local public services is becoming more of a gamble in financialized times.

1.1 Local governments in England returning to the casino since 2010?

COUNCILLORS AT THE CASINO

Figure 1.2 Councillors at the casino

Source: Original cartoon by Nigel Auchterlounie (knocky.smith@gmail.com), 2021.

Reproducing its position within the UK state and the fiscal crisis, austerity, and restructuring of the 1970s and 1980s,[19] worries about gambling with public money and local services have become acute for local governments in the specific setting of England since 2010 (Figure 1.2). Unprecedented

---

[19] Cochrane (1993), Cockburn (1977), Duncan and Goodwin (1988).

expenditure reductions, rising service demand, national government's local financial self-sufficiency agenda, and reduced central grant dependence intensified pressures on local government actors in England to close funding gaps by making savings and finding new income sources. This iteration of local fiscal crisis has been playing out in a different set of circumstances from the 1980s. Finance capital is more pervasive and powerful in contemporary political economy, and the UK was amongst other national states pursing austerity following the 2008 crash.

From the 1980s and accelerated by the 'Big Bang' deregulation, local governments were 'active participants' in financial markets, 'using the skills and inventiveness of City brokers and financiers' from London's business and financial services complex.[20] Fiscal stress saw local governments 'swapping prudence for risk', attempting to trade for profit rather than manage risk, and increasing their reliance upon external advisers to understand the sophisticated financial instruments they were signing up to; all largely 'without comment from regulators' despite its questionable legality.[21]

Financial innovation by local governments in England has, however, been limited since the London Borough of Hammersmith and Fulham swaps affair in the 1990s. The 'bad bets' made by the Borough on interest rate swaps created a notional exposure worth nearly £3 billion at the time.[22] The UK House of Lord's ruled its contracts were ultra vires or beyond its powers and illegal.[23] As the contracts were rendered void, the counterparty banks lost over £500 million. The way in which 'one arm of the [local] state' was 'given protection from its debts [to international investors] by another [national] arm' cast a long shadow.[24]

This financial hit and legal precedent effectively closed the UK local public sector market to financial innovations for many years. Activities perceived as 'playing the market' and 'gambling with ratepayers' money' in the 1980s, including borrowing and on-lending to nationalized industries and other local governments, were dramatically reduced or halted.[25]

Reverberations from the swaps affair continued into the 1990s as further legal rulings were made in local governments' favour. Islington Borough Council was allowed to pay simple not compound interest on restitution payments to its bank lenders. Allerdale Borough Council avoided liability for a

---

[20] Tickell (1998: 866, 874).
[21] Tickell (1998: 866, 872).
[22] Tickell (1998: 866).
[23] Campbell-Smith (2008).
[24] Tickell (1998: 866).
[25] Sbragia (1986: 335).

£17 million repayment because its borrowing was ruled ultra vires.[26] Amidst this turbulence and uncertainty, finance actors perceived acute 'sovereign risk',[27] exiting the market to focus elsewhere.

Local governments in England began to turn their attention back to financial markets following the prudential borrowing regime's introduction in the early 2000s. This code increased local government autonomy and responsibility for borrowing, prompting their consideration of new relationships with financial actors and innovations including Lender Option Borrower Option (LOBO) loans and cash deposits in Icelandic banks.

The situation from 2010 in England fundamentally changed local governments' financial predicament. In austerity, the UK government encouraged new ideas to reduce financial dependence upon central grants. Financial actors sensed a reopening and growing local public sector market for specialist advice, services, and products. Local governments in England were keen for ideas more actively to manage their finances and risk and to hedge and protect their investments amidst national funding reductions and increasingly internationalized and volatile financial markets following the 2008 crash.

Through austerity from 2010, local governments in England faced depictions as 'casino councils' engaged in a 'high stakes bid to balance their books' and taking a 'public service gamble'.[28] Suggesting their return to the casino, local councillors and officers are described as wagering national public funds and local taxpayers' money in the pursuit of financial gain on activities with uncertain outcomes. Such assessments are especially evident in charges of profligacy in using their unique access to UK government subsidized and sovereign guaranteed debt to play 'billion-pound property roulette'.[29]

In the *Financial Times*, Plender criticized local governments for engaging in a 'buying spree' and carry trade of borrowing 'at rates much lower than those available to private sector borrowers to invest in assets that show significantly higher initial yields'.[30] This 'bizarre two-way traffic' is in motion with local governments 'furiously selling assets to plug gaps in their budgets resulting from central government cuts', while 'simultaneously … accumulating property assets across the country' to generate revenue by borrowing at lower cost than commercial finance actors 'largely thanks to cheap finance provided by an arm of the UK Treasury'.

---

[26] Tickell (1998).
[27] Tickell (1998: 876).
[28] Davies (2018: 1).
[29] Davies (2018: 1).
[30] Plender (2017: 1).

Detter criticized local governments' limited commercial knowledge, savvy, and experience in 'taking huge commercial risks' and 'trying to be hedge fund managers' by engaging in 'dangerous arbitrage to bridge the gap in funding'.[31] Instead of embarking on this 'commercial adventure' and performing a 'role they're not set up for' because of their 'inability ... to manage commercial risk', Detter argued local government needed 'more professional management of all its assets, rather than a headlong rush into risky commercial ventures'.[32]

Further controversy followed. Reflecting the engagement of a local government in England with globalized commercial finance, Warrington Borough Council attracted criticism from local Member of Parliament (MP) Helen Jones for the organization of its £200 million purchase of Birchwood Business Park through offshore company Oaktree Capital Management. This arrangement allegedly avoided 'around £10 million in tax' and, while 'not illegal', the MP argued, 'paying tax is the price we pay for a civilised society. Not paying your dues sets a very bad example and I hope the council will think again and immediately activate the option which would bring the ownership into the UK'.[33] The national fiscal implications of such local government financial innovations raise profound political economic questions.

Other interpretations see local governments as 'gullible' and scammed in their search for savings and new revenue sources.[34] Sophisticated financial actors are explained as engaging local councillors and officers in deceptive schemes to cheat them out of public money or con them through tricks or lies. Local governments are interpreted as hoodwinked into believing in the magic of 'financial wizardry' and promise to acquire 'fool's gold' from off-the-shelf money-making schemes peddled by external advisors.[35]

Amidst concerns about corruption in financialization's contemporary episode,[36] evidence of 'misleading valuations' and 'outright frauds' has demonstrated where criminal deception has led to false and deceitful actions.[37] Such instances impacted the financial system and local government in England. Traders at Barclays Bank were found guilty of manipulating the London Inter-Bank Offered Rate (LIBOR) providing the benchmark interest rate for many financial contracts.[38] This rate rigging affected the LOBO loans worth £10.6 billion taken out by 155 local governments in England

---

[31] Detter (2017: 1).
[32] Detter (2017: 1).
[33] Quoted in Dhillon (2017: 1).
[34] Hendrikse and Sidaway (2014: 203).
[35] Hendrikse and Sidaway (2014: 195).
[36] Harvey (2015).
[37] Hendrikse and Sidaway (2014: 196).
[38] Ashton and Christophers (2015).

from the 2000s.[39] Legal action by UK regulators resulted in a £290 million fine for Barclays Bank.

Given the new legal territory in such complex innovations and 'financial shenanigans',[40] decisions lack precedent and are uncertain in outcome, typically resulting in expensive litigation local governments can ill afford. In the LOBO loan case, the UK High Court struck out a class action led by Leeds City Council against Barclays for mis-selling because the claimants could not demonstrate they had relied upon the representations allegedly made by the bank and had already affirmed their participation by entering the contracts.[41] The seven local governments in England involved were left to bear the undisclosed legal costs.

Local financial innovation since 2010 is a potential fix for local governments facing fiscal stress and lucrative for financial actors selling products and services. It is marked by the emergence of new and complex financial ideas and instruments alongside weakened local transparency, scrutiny, and accountability. In England and elsewhere, financial novelties provided a 'universe of accounting deception', whereby new arrangements 'provide opportunities for actors to avoid regulation', 'window-dress accounting rules', avoid oversight and scrutiny, and conceal the level and/or nature of risks.[42]

In this context, local politicians and officers have in some cases been compelled by fiscal imperatives to interpret creatively legal rules and regulatory guidance in ways that may have blurred into potentially unlawful endeavour. Integral in such situations are the differing national and local government understandings of the autonomy that legal and advisory frameworks afford local actors.

Formal investigations into financial dealings are proceeding at several local governments across England. Transparency campaigners are actively using the UK Freedom of Information legislation to promote openness in the public interest and challenge local governments withholding information as confidential on the grounds of 'commercial sensitivity'.[43]

Amidst such tumult in England since 2010, the spectre of financial failure has haunted the sector. As local government actors sought financial innovations to offset fiscal stress and manage risk, some have found themselves in further financial trouble, as these arrangements have compounded rather than resolved their problems. Specific local governments in England

---

[39] Mertens et al. (2020).
[40] Bhatti and Manley (2015: 70).
[41] Local Government Lawyer (2021).
[42] Lagna (2017: 210).
[43] Davies and Smith (2021: 1).

are 'in too deep' but, like a gambler chasing losses, have sought further novel approaches as stronger remedies for their financial plight.[44]

Local government experiences in England since 2010 echo the 1980s and 1990s. During this period, national government encouraged 'creative accounting', including: new 'exotic' forms of borrowing that capitalizes interest payments on capital assets; factoring; lease-and-leaseback and sale-and-leaseback deals; manipulating rules to maximize national grant revenue; 'prefunding' or 'advanced purchase' schemes with external development companies; premature realization of profit from development activities; reformatting loan repayments; and utilizing reserves and suspending replenishment.[45] Crucially, many such practices originated from municipal rather than only commercial finance.

The new financial strategies and instruments deployed by local governments in England from 2010 still struggled to resolve chronic deficits, leading actors to even more risky arrangements to address their predicament. Local councillors and officers were trapped into grappling with the ongoing symptoms rather than causes of their structural financial problems.

Since 2010, a growing number of local governments in England have issued Section 114 notices legally required when they are unable to balance their annual budgets. For the first time since the London Boroughs of Hackney and Hillingdon in 2000, several local governments issued such notices: Northamptonshire County Council (2018), Croydon Borough Council (2020), Nottingham City Council (2021), and Slough Borough Council (2021).[46] Many of which situations resulted from multiple factors, including accumulated financial stress, overextended and failed commercial activities, and municipal finance practices which contravened existing rules including breaking the ring-fencing on specific funds earmarked for other uses and miscalculations of minimum revenue provisions (MRP) to cover borrowing.

A further twelve local governments in England made capitalization requests to the national government department responsible—Levelling Up, Housing and Communities (DLUHC)[47]—for permission to use their capital funds or borrow against their capital assets for revenue purposes. Such is

[44] Hendrikse and Sidaway (2014: 199).
[45] Pinch (1995: 49).
[46] Housing, Communities, and Local Government Committee (2021).
[47] National government has changed the name of the department responsible for local government numerous times in recent decades to reflect policy priorities and organizational changes: Department for Transport, Local Government and the Regions (DETR) (2002); Department for Communities and Local Government (CLG) (2006); Ministry for Housing, Communities and Local Government (MHCLG) (2018); and Department for Levelling Up, Housing and Communities (LUHC) (2021–). Reference is made in the book to 'the Department' to cover the ongoing name changes.

the precarity of local government finances in England that DLUHC keeps an at-risk list of those on the financial brink. Pandemic, Ukraine conflict and climate emergency impacts are compounding the situation.

The sector press is replete with coverage of local governments across England having to 'grapple with multi-million pound deficits'[48] and 'at risk of exhausting cash reserves'.[49] Conditions create decreasing margins for error in financial management and expose an increasing number of local governments unable to balance their budgets. While the UK government has provided funding to support local governments' role in pandemic response and compensate for non-commercial income loss,[50] their finances remain acute.

Nevertheless, the UK government continues to claim instances of financial failure are the localized and particular results of rogue or badly governed and managed local governments with 'poor culture' and 'weak governance'.[51] Interpretations of actors trapped and trying to cope in an increasingly dysfunctional funding system under extreme duress since 2010 receive less recognition.

Local governments in England have been stung by criticism of their financial strategies. Against such claims, explanations cite the fiscal stress and lack of alternatives they confront in facing the 'perfect storm' of expenditure reductions, rising service demands, and income generation pressures since 2010.[52] Local councillors and officers have resisted being cast in the role of acting as financial institutions that would 'speculate with taxpayers' money'.[53] Rather than playing the casino and taking a local public service gamble with outcomes determined by luck, local government actors argue they have fast had to learn how to understand, manage, and mitigate the multiplying risks of their financial predicament since 2010.

There is much at stake if councillors in England since 2010 really are back at the casino; if balancing the books to deliver essential local public services has become a game of chance. The over 300 local governments provide a wide range of services to over 56 million people in England, often to the most vulnerable social groups.[54] The total of almost £100 billion of revenue expenditure handled by local governments in 2019–20 is around 10 per cent of total

---

[48] Ford (2021: 1).
[49] Brady (2019: 1).
[50] National Audit Office (2021b).
[51] MHCLG (2020a: 1).
[52] Ogden and Phillips (2021: 4).
[53] Howard Williams, former Conservative Councillor and Cabinet Member for Finance, Spelthorne Borough Council, quoted in Marrs (2018b: 1).
[54] The total number of local governments in England is constantly changing due to ongoing reorganization (Copus 2017).

annual national public expenditure,[55] albeit with around £50 billion beyond their control and ring-fenced or passported through specific channels. Many jobs, incomes, and livelihoods depend on local government, which employs around 1.4 million people across the country.[56] Local government in England is 'still very big business'.[57] What local government does, how it is funded and financed, and how it manages and governs its financial affairs are vital matters of national and local public concern and politics. As elsewhere, local government in England remains 'one of the most important institutions of democratic life'.[58]

Much differentiation exists in how local government actors in different places and financial circumstances across England have dealt with fiscal stress and pressure for financial innovation since 2010. A complex, evolving landscape has emerged. It is marked by peaks of high-profile innovations alongside hills of more widespread shifts, and plains where little appears to have changed. There is a pressing need to widen and lengthen the frame geographically and historically to capture, understand, and explain local government financial strategies and activities in the specific geographical and temporal setting of England since 2010.

1.2 The financialization of local statecraft

While the experience of local governments in England is a long-standing bellwether of public sector restructuring internationally,[59] further conceptual and theoretical development is needed to understand and explain the landscape in this particular setting since 2010. Change in England and elsewhere has been explained as the financialization of the local state: the growing role, power, and influence of external financial actors, logics, innovations, and markets in local governments and local public service provision.[60] The influence of cutting-edge practices and examples from the US looms large over conceptualization and theorization of financialization and local states in other very different geographical political economic and temporal settings. A need exists to build upon this existing work and address the emergent gaps

---

[55] DLUHC (2021a).

[56] ONS (2020a). This is a broad definition of job numbers, which includes jobs at Local Education Authority–maintained schools, and these are being reduced by Academy Schools moving staff to the national Department for Education.

[57] Wilson and Game (2011: 129).

[58] Lagna (2016: 1).

[59] Newton and Karan (1985).

[60] See, inter alia, Christophers (2019), Hendrikse (2015), Deruytter and Möller (2020), Deruytter and Bassens (2021), Lagna (2016), Weber (2015).

in our understanding and empirical knowledge. The differentiated landscape across England from 2010 and its effects and implications for people and places are incompletely known and poorly understood. Placing the particular experiences of local governments in England since 2010 within the broader relations and process of financialization at work provides the focus for these tasks.

The theoretical ambition confronts the involvement of local government as an integral part of the local state—encompassing a widening array of public, private, civic, and hybrid organizations—with financial actors, rationales, novelties, and markets in the international financial system. The task is more fully to account for how, why, where, and when local government and its related organizations are engaging in such new financial relations, rationales, and arrangements. Further, largely absent from existing accounts, where this process is being contested, stymied, and blocked needs explanation. Given the scale and nature of changes in the case of England since 2010, the outcomes and implications of financialization for local government financial sustainability, resilience, and politics require attention.

Addressing the period following the 2008 global financial crisis, the book's aims are twofold. First, to develop a theory of local statecraft to better understand and explain the involvement of local government and local state with financialization and its impacts and implications. Second, the book puts this theory to work to account for how local governments have navigated austerity and financialization in England since 2010. Rather than writing from 'nowhere', the arguments are written from the 'somewhere' of a particular political-economic and institutional setting in time and space. This temporal and geographical standpoint necessarily influences the interpretations of the more general actors, relations, and process involved.

In subnational studies, statecraft has been deployed as a potentially useful idea, but it needs further specification and theorization.[61] Inspired by work on the 'economic statecraft'[62] and 'financial statecraft'[63] of nation states, statecraft has been defined as the art of government and management of state affairs and relations with multiple actors and their geographies.[64] This conception advanced Bulpitt's original notion by making it more geographical, incorporating actors other than central and local governments, and connecting its political to economic analysis.[65]

---

[61] Ayres et al. (2017), Kutz (2017), Lauermann (2016), McGuirk et al. (2021), Moran et al. (2018).
[62] Baldwin (1985).
[63] Steil and Litan (2008).
[64] Pike et al. (2019).
[65] Bulpitt (1983).

Developing local statecraft theory aims to address gaps in its specification and operation for local government and the local state. At its least useful, statecraft is deployed as a vague catch-all category referring to the agency of state actors. Extending beyond national and urban scales, this book elaborates local statecraft's definition and conceptualization, grounds the idea in a theorization of the state, and distinguishes financial from local statecraft. It then identifies municipal and commercial worlds of finance and specifies local government commercialization in relation to financialization.

Broadening its conceptual reach and building upon recognition of local governments as agents *and* objects of financialization,[66] this new local statecraft theory seeks to understand and explain how local government councillors and officers are engaging with finance actors and the financialization process. They must confront as well as configure an array of differentiated funding, financing, and governing settings with various impacts and implications. The institutional, legal, and regulatory differences in certain places and times structure and shape their agency and variegated outcomes.

Moving beyond a binary and static understanding of whether local government is financialized or not, this local statecraft conceives of actors engaging commercial finance actors in dynamic relations of varying degree and extent; from stronger, closer, and more embedded to weaker, distant, and semi-detached involvements. It is also alive and open to instances of avoidance and non-engagement with the relations and process of financialization by local state actors. Whether financialization is remapping key functions and reconfiguring powers as local states attempt to govern *through* finance is a central concern.[67] The ways in which financialization in particular instances needs explaining *and* helps construct explanations are integral too. The ambition is to provide a more clearly conceptualized and specified theory, assessed and challenged in an empirical study. In doing so, the book aims to strengthen explanations of the specific case of the differentiated landscape in England since 2010 and, through the studies of others, cases elsewhere.

Addressing the book's second aim, local government in England since 2010 provides a fruitful case to assess and challenge local statecraft's analytical and explanatory power. Compared internationally, the UK has a liberal market-oriented and financialized political economy and variegation of capitalism.[68] The City of London is a globally significant centre of business and financial services. The public sector and local government are considered important and growing markets, targeted by firms in these sectors. Local government in

[66] Weber (2015).
[67] Ashton (2020).
[68] Davis and Walsh (2016), Peck and Theodore (2007).

England is long-established and large-scale, providing multiple functions and services across the country, and highly centralized in its funding, financing, and governance by national government.

Following the 2008 crash, the UK government pursued austerity from 2010, substantially reducing local government funding and seeking to increase its financial self-sufficiency. Local governments have been compelled to balance budgets by reducing expenditure and finding new income sources. Their strategies have involved municipal finance innovations and varying engagements with commercial finance actors and the international financial system. Intensifying the pressure on local public services, England has entrenched and long-standing geographical inequalities, rising provision demands, and increasingly differentiated local politics.

Rather than objectifying and generalizing local government experiences in England since 2010, this case is used to develop, challenge, and refine local statecraft theory by investigating a leading international laboratory for local public sector restructuring, with potential mutual learning for research elsewhere in the global North and South. A highly differentiated landscape exists amongst local governments in England, but accounts are mostly of limited examples of new approaches, arrangements, and instruments by leading actors in specific places. Important contributions have been made to understanding changes in England in financial strategies and activities, local government borrowing, commercial property investment, housing, trading activities, urban development, and responses to austerity.[69]

Building upon this existing work, a broader examination of the extent, nature, and forms of local government financial strategies, activities, and instruments *across* England since 2010 is lacking. The system is 'diverse'.[70] Investigation is needed of the key characteristics and rationales as well as the different types of local governments and local state organizations with varying powers, resources, sizes, locations, and political and officer leaderships. Explanation is required of how such dimensions shape the thinking and strategies of local councillors and officers and their relations with financial actors and the financialization process. Consideration is overdue of the outcomes and implications for local financial sustainability, resilience, and politics across England. Underpinned by the theoretical advances able to explain similar phenomena in other settings, the new empirical research of this critical case helps develop and refine this theory-building.

---

[69] See, for example, Dagdeviren and Karwowski (2021), Mertens et al. (2020), Muldoon-Smith and Sanford (2021), Beswick and Penny (2018), Christophers (2019), Penny (2022), Andrews et al. (2019), Raco and Souza (2018), Gray and Barford (2018), Hastings et al. (2015), Lowndes and Gardner (2016).

[70] Copus (2017: 8).

1.3 The arguments and organization of the book

The main arguments and contributions are fourfold. First, local statecraft provides a meaningful conceptualization and theorization for explaining local
government and the local state's engagements with the relations and process
of financialization. Local statecraft is the art of local government and management of local state affairs and relations by local statecrafters[71]—politicians
and officers—with multiple national state, private, civic, and public organizations working across and between different spatial levels and with varied
geographies.

Grounded in a theorization of the state as a social relation constantly being
remade through the agency of state personnel,[72] local statecraft is situated in
ongoing state formation as actors seek temporarily to cohere and stabilize
its structures, imaginaries, strategies, and projects in particular geographical
and temporal settings. This local statecraft conception sees local governments
as endowed with distinctive attributes of local statehood in their authority,
powers, and resources to act within their territories and, to a degree and in
specific ways, beyond their jurisdictional boundaries. Local statehood largely
determines local statecrafters' agency in engaging financial actors and the
financialization process.

Local statecraft is distinct and broader than narrower financial statecraft
given local government's wider purposes, functions, and responsibilities.
Municipal and commercial worlds of finance intersect and blur, bringing into
contact certain actors, relations, aims and objectives, accountabilities, frames
of action, and geographies. Rather than a clear-cut transition to a new or
coherent local governance form, each world is relating in spatially and temporally variegated ways to create differentiated local statecraft engagements
with financialization-in-motion. Financialization is understood as socially,
spatially, and institutionally variegated relations, rationales, and a process
established and shaped by participant actors. Through municipal and commercial finance's intersections, such financialized relations and rationales are
being internalized and embedded in at least the leading local governments.
Commercialization is evident in local statecraft but not wholly synonymous
with financialization.

Increasing risks are generated in local statecraft's varying engagements with
financialization. They manifest in varied forms and originate from multiple

---

[71] Thanks to Allan Cochrane for coining the 'statecrafter' term at the 'Infrastructural futures across
cities of the global North' seminar, Manchester Urban Institute, September 2019.
[72] Jessop (2016).

sources in the state *and* municipal finance rather than only from commercial finance. Local statecrafters are now compelled into spending more time and resource trying to manage and mitigate the distribution, transfer, and potential impacts and implications of such risks.

Addressing the who, why, where, and when questions, the theory identifies and examines specific and related realms where local statecraft is exercised: financial strategies and risks; external advice; borrowing and debt management; and the geographies of in-area and out-of-area activities. Underpinned by the local statehood of specific configurations of powers and resources in particular national governance and funding systems, local government actors in England devise visions for place-making and local service provision within their areas, exercise their authority to levy and collect local taxes and charge fees for local services, borrow underpinned by the UK sovereign guarantee, and invest within and without their areas in pursuit of balanced budgets. These activities are the substance of their particular local statecraft in this specific geographical and temporal setting.

The second contribution reveals and explains the differentiated landscape of local statecraft engagements with financialization across England since 2010. Examining these local governments' experiences enables the use, challenge, and further refinement of this local statecraft theory. Rather than the risky and speculative financial innovation rampant throughout the sector portrayed in the 'councillors at the casino' narrative, the picture is characterized by vanguard, intermediate, and long-tail behaviours in specific activities.

Vanguard approaches in England since 2010 involve active introduction of and experimentation with new ideas and instruments, often testing the legal basis and guidance framing local government autonomies. In the majority of cases, however, financial novelties remain relatively small-scale activities in overall finances. Intermediate behaviours are characterized as less active, largely using existing strategies and instruments, and delving into new areas but in limited ways. Copying and adapting approaches used elsewhere in vanguard approaches are evident. Long-tail actions rarely include innovations and, where pursued, are very small-scale in overall financial strategy and management.

Identifying more active financial and risk management in local governments in England since 2010, local statecraft provides a means of explaining this differentiated landscape. Evolving geographically, the picture is accounted for by combinations of five dimensions: (i) specific local government types with varying powers, responsibilities, and resources; (ii) differing local politics, political and officer leaderships, and prior experience determining visions, strategies, and risk appetites; (iii) organizational models, expertise and capacities; (iv) knowledge and openness to external advice and commercial finance; and (v) local economic assets and liabilities, conditions, growth potential, and tax bases. While each dimension is evident across local instances to varying degrees, they combine in particular ways in specific geographical and temporal circumstances.

The third argument is that UK government policy and, where evident, engagements with financialization are unevenly rewiring and rescaling local statecraft and displacing and relocating risks onto local government and the local state. Objectives and incentives were modified as the UK government restructured the funding system and its regulation in England from 2010, changing how local governments operate and relate to the centre and compelling new relations with financial actors and the financialization process. Autonomies, accountabilities, transparency, and scrutiny are being tested by local statecrafters' new financial strategies, arrangements, and instruments. This rewiring and rescaling are creating contradictions and tensions in relations between local and national government, financial actors, and local residents and taxpayers in England. Rather than the UK government's explanation of 'poor culture' and 'weak governance' in financially failing local governments,[73] local statecrafters in England are trying to manage in a dysfunctional funding system under extreme fiscal stress since 2010.

The final argument is that UK government policy and the wider extension and intensification of local statecraft's engagements with financialization risk undermining local government financial sustainability and resilience across England in the longer term. Local circumstances and systemic problems are challenging local statecraft and the knowledge, skills, and capacity of local statecrafters in England to cope. Increasing numbers of local governments are struggling to navigate this faster moving, riskier, and more challenging terrain. The contemporary situation risks undermining rather than enhancing local government's essential public service provision.

Reinvigorating the politics of local statecraft and financialization, these four contributions raise fundamental and wider questions of local political economy. What is local government for and how can it be funded and financed? Has eroded local accountability, transparency, and scrutiny of local statecraft in financialization introduced and deepened depoliticized and post-democratic local governance?

---

[73] MHCLG (2020a: 1).

Chapter 2 addresses the conceptual and theoretical issues concerning financialization and local statecraft. It assesses studies examining financialization and the state and focuses in on financialization, local government, and the local state. Key issues identified include the dominant national focus, narrow empirical range, limited attention to geographical and temporal diversity and system-wide views, and underdeveloped treatment of ramifications.

Addressing emanant (auto-)critique, local statecraft is defined and conceptualized. It is grounded within a theorization of the state which endows local government with distinctive attributes of local statehood that underpin its powers and resources as an economic and financial actor. Hitherto missing but key distinctions are drawn between financial and local statecraft, municipal and commercial worlds of finance and risk, and the processes of commercialization and financialization. The actors involved in local statecraft and their rationales are explained alongside identification of the realms examined in the book and the geographical and temporal settings of their manifestation. The strategy, methodology, design, and analytical approach for the empirical research underpinning the book closes the chapter.

The funding and financing of local government in England are addressed in Chapter 3. Local government is situated within the UK state. Its definition and powers, functions, and politics are explained. Key processes shaping its recent evolution are described, comprising centralization, new organizational models, reorganization, and disaggregation. The national system of local government funding in England is then outlined. How budgeting, expenditure, income, balance sheets, and accountability work are set out.

Informed by the new theory, the following chapters use the local statecraft realms of financial strategies and risks, external advice, borrowing and debt management, and geographies of in-area and out-of-area activities to examine and explain financialization and local statecraft in England since 2010.

Local government financial strategies amidst austerity, centralization, and risk comprise Chapter 4. The emergence and anatomy of the UK government policies of austerity, localism, and local financial self-sufficiency are explained. In response to the resulting funding gaps, the local statecraft of financial strategies, risk management, expenditure, and income generation approaches in England since 2010 are described and accounted for. The national governance and regulation of financial resilience, sustainability, and failure are then outlined. The chapter ends by outlining the differentiated landscape of financialization and local statecraft across England since 2010 and explaining local statecrafters' vanguard, intermediate, and long-tail approaches.

The roles of external advisors involved in local statecraft in the financialization process in England are addressed in Chapter 5. The origins and rise of these external actors are outlined. A widening array of advisors are integral to financialization and local statecraft in England since 2010: accountants and consultants; financial consultants; treasury management advisors (TMAs); property consultants; and professional and sectoral advisors, associations, and consultants. Their strategies and business models, activities, and implications for local statecraft in financialization are described and explained.

Chapter 6 deals with the local statecraft realm of borrowing and debt management. It sets out the national governance and regulation of local government borrowing. Evolving local statecraft strategies for borrowing and debt management in England since 2010 are documented and explained. Who is lending money to local government, why, and on what terms are then identified. Ramifications of changing approaches to borrowing are discussed.

The new and emergent geographies of in-area and out-of-area local statecraft in England are the focus of Chapter 7. The geography of national governance and regulation of local government activities is outlined. The local statecraft of existing and new in-area and out-of-area strategies and activities are set out and explained. Impacts and implications are identified.

Chapter 8 summarizes and elaborates the arguments and contributions of the book in conceptual, theoretical, empirical, and political terms, and addresses their ramifications. It explains the contributions and potential of local statecraft theory. The characteristics and explanation of local statecrafters' vanguard, intermediate, and long-tail approaches and varying engagements with financialization in England since 2010 are summarized. Finally, the chapter considers the politics of financialization and local statecraft and its future funding, financing, and governing. It closes by assessing the emergence of depoliticized and post-democratic local governance in financialization.

2

Financialization and local statecraft

2.0 Introduction

Responding to criticism of its income generation strategy, Chief Executive of Warrington Borough Council in North West England Steve Broomhead acknowledged that 'people want our heads on a stick because they think we have been gambling.'[1] The Borough had attracted attention for its high levels of leverage, borrowing £1.6 billion while holding financial reserves of £135 million, investments acquiring commercial and industrial property assets and stakes in trading companies, and lending to external borrowers including housing associations locally and nationally. Demonstrating its vanguard approach, Warrington issued the first local government bond in a decade, worth £150 million, in 2015.[2]

Concerns emerged as Together Energy ceased trading and went bankrupt amidst sectoral turmoil, exposing to losses Warrington's 50 per cent stake worth £18 million, its £20 million revolving credit facility, and £14 million guarantee to Together's wholesale energy supplier Ørsted. Established to support lending to small and medium-sized enterprises (SMEs), the Borough's 33 per cent holding in Redwood Bank halved in value to £16 million since 2017. A £151 million loan to e-commerce group THG was questioned as its share price collapsed following investor concerns about its strategy and corporate governance. In early 2022, Moody's downgraded the Borough's credit rating, noting there was a 'high amount of risk and a higher risk appetite than is typical for the sector, exposing the council to significant levels of economic, counterparty and political risk.'[3]

Mixing commercialization with financialization, Labour Councillor and Deputy Leader Cathy Mitchell explained the Borough's portfolio of investments and loans aimed to deliver £20 million net return in the financial year, helping to balance its budget and offset UK government expenditure

---

[1] Quoted in Wallis (2022: 1).
[2] Cross (2015).
[3] Cited in Rudgewick (2022).

Financialization and Local Statecraft. Andy Pike, Oxford University Press. © Andy Pike (2023).
DOI: 10.1093/oso/9780192856661.003.0002

reductions. Such income generation activities sought to contribute to local service infrastructure renewal with neighbourhood hubs combining health centres and libraries, regenerate the town centre, and support local economic growth and employment creation in business parks. Rather than gambling with public money, Broomhead argued the Borough had been 'very prudent about managing risk for a bad day'.[4] Mitigation measures included a £30 million strategic reserve that pooled rental income from its assets, monitored weekly investment portfolio performance, and required appropriate security on its loans.

Such specific instances of local government financial activities attract attention for their novelty, enabling contrasts to be drawn between traditional stereotypes of bureaucratic, staid local councils and bolder, more dynamic practices. Coverage skews attention towards high profile and innovative cases that are only minor parts of the overall landscape, slanting views of the wider picture.

Care is needed in generalizing any assessment of the runaway financialization of the local state and characterizations of gung-ho elected local politicians and officers staking local taxpayers' money in the casinos of finance capital and imperilling local public service provision. Differentiated landscapes demand a wider frame and more balanced account, prompting reflection on our explanatory concepts and theoretical frameworks.

Explaining the relations and arrangements between local councillors, officers, and financiers is a central aim of this book. A conceptual and theoretical framework and research methodology are needed to enable this task. It first interprets the intersections between financialization, local government, and the local state. Issues include the national orientation of existing studies, limited empirical coverage, underdeveloped grasp of geographical and temporal differentiation, and uneven attention to implications.

Responding to these concerns underpins the articulation of a new theory of local statecraft. Building upon critique, defining, conceptualizing, and grounding statecraft in a theorization of the state endows local government with distinctive local statehood attributes. This understanding identifies the actors doing local statecraft, their rationales, and realms, geographies, and times in and through which it is exercised. Empirical research strategy, methodology, design, data collection, and analysis complete the framework.

---

[4] Quoted in Wallis (2022: 1).

2.1 Financialization and (local) states

Amidst debate between different approaches, financialization is defined by the increasing participation and power of financial actors, relations, logics, strategies, and practices in economy, society, and polity.[5] Situating the current episode historically and geographically, the contemporary financialization process is distinctive in its extended and pervasive international reach, accelerated intensification, and scale. New institutional actors, instruments, and practices have been introduced in a marked increase in finance's integral role and exertion of increased power in the political economy.[6] Enabled and regulated by nation states, such financialization is propelled by financial actors engaged in capital accumulation, innovation, and competition.

It is important that we move beyond understandings of financialization as totalizing and aspatial, as an object or thing, or event or end state. A related break is needed from the categorization of entities as financialized or not. Financialization is best not seen as 'a departure, unique *or* recurring, from a (non-financialized) norm'.[7] This conception helps move beyond binary understandings of financialization and 'definancialisation'.[8]

Financialization comprises socially, spatially, and institutionally variegated relations and rationales in a process structured and shaped by the engagements of actors with interests.[9] Financialization is how finance and financial relations and logics become deepened and embedded, potentially reconfiguring existing actors' agency and rationales. This view sees financialization working in differentiated ways over time and space that influence how it works and its impacts, implications, and limits.[10] This work demonstrates how financialization's temporal and geographical dimensions are causal and constitutive in how it operates rather than just inert contexts. In this understanding, financialization is something to be explained *and* part of the construction of explanations. Studies emphasize that, while financialization may constitute transformation in certain settings, it can manifest in arcane, limited ways and be absent. Explaining such spatial and temporal differentiation in and through local statecraft is a central contribution of this book.

---

[5] Mader et al. (2020), Sawyer (2022).
[6] Christophers and Fine (2020), Harvey (2015).
[7] Christophers and Fine (2020: 22, original authors' emphasis).
[8] Dagdeviren and Karowski (2021: 688).
[9] Deruytter and Möller (2020), Pike et al. (2019).
[10] See, for example, Aalbers (2015), Christophers (2015a), French et al. (2011), Fields (2018), Hall (2018), Lai and Daniels (2017).

Building upon this work, the book's conception is of financialization-in-motion; fluid, uncertain, and differentiated in its spread and shaping by actors.[11] This understanding focuses on the kind, degree, and nature of the engagements of actors and institutions with the financialization process rather than just an assessment of whether it is occurring or not.

The relationships between financialization and the state are a 'less researched' and 'largely underdeveloped' but of growing interest.[12] Advancing from interpretations of finance expanding at the expense of state contraction under neoliberalism,[13] research has established how states have led and driven financialization through de- and re-regulation and facilitation of financial innovations and markets.[14] In an unprecedented and 'massive expansion' of finance's 'governmental scope',[15] nation states have turned strategically to finance to manage their public finances, support public provision, and stimulate economic growth.[16]

Nation states are pivotal in creating the conditions as well as leading in extending, deepening, and accelerating financialization in certain political economic variegations and settings.[17] Central is the emergence of a 'recursive relationship' between financialization and the state, whereby public policies have transformed financial markets and, in turn, 'reliance on financial markets can also transform political institutions in ways that promote further financialization.'[18]

Much existing work on financialization and the state has taken a national rather than local focus. Identifying national variegations of financialization,[19] studies have emphasized the distinctiveness of nation states as economic and financial actors with specific roles and interests exercised in differentiated and multi-scalar settings.[20] Financialization is explained as a 'rising paradigm of governance' and 'new form of statecraft' as national states seek to 'reinvent their relationships' with financial actors and markets.[21] A research priority is 'more systematic examinations of how the financialization of the state has engendered new forms of statecraft and systems of governance.'[22] National state objectives, incentives, autonomies, and accountabilities are mentioned

---

[11] Pike et al. (2020), Lai (2020).
[12] Mertens et al. (2020: 1), Wang (2020: 188), Davis and Walsh (2016), Hendrikse and Lagna (2018).
[13] Wang (2020).
[14] Jessop (2018).
[15] Christophers and Fine (2020: 22).
[16] Wang (2020).
[17] Brown et al. (2017), Krippner (2011), Sawyer (2022), Ward et al. (2018).
[18] Pacewicz (2013: 413).
[19] Ó Riain (2014), van Loon et al. (2019).
[20] Hendrikse and Lagna (2018), Lai and Daniels (2017).
[21] Wang (2020: 188).
[22] Wang (2020: 197).

but not fully specified and elaborated.[23] Municipal and commercial finance and their attributes and operation are underspecified. Finance-based calculation and valuation logics are assumed as ascendant and sometimes dominant.[24]

The nation state is recognized as a distinctive political entity engaging with finance and integral to an increasingly complex and differentiated 'state–finance nexus' across countries.[25] As 'state and finance are enmeshed in each other', related processes are prompting state opportunities for reinvention, altering state organization, and leveraging the 'sovereign power of the state' for 'finance via various forms of sovereign promises and guarantees'.[26] Key is explaining this state–finance nexus at different levels and in varied geographical and temporal settings.

2.2 Financialization, local government, and the local state

The subnational dimensions of financialization have received relatively less attention, despite growing finance and local state relationships.[27] Research has explained how financialization is engaging local states in differentiated ways, becoming internalized within local governments and their staff, and manifesting through financial strategies, rationales, and instruments.[28] Studies have identified the varied extension and intensification of financialization in certain settings, generating and amplifying uncertainty and risk.[29]

Financial reorganization is integral to this local state restructuring. New Public Management (NPM) and its use of standardized public administration models, financial and performance indicators, and 'market logics' underpinned change from the 1980s.[30] Key has been rendering the local state 'more legible' to external financial actors and markets.[31]

Local states mirrored national states in becoming more enmeshed with finance, seeking new public provision models, and creating 'state-backed but legally sanctioned market entities'.[32] Financialization has been extended

---

[23] Waite et al. (2013).
[24] Chiapello (2015).
[25] Wang (2020: 188).
[26] Wang (2020: 188).
[27] Wang (2020).
[28] See, for example, Christophers (2019), Hendrikse (2015), Deruytter (2022), Deruytter and Möller (2020), Lagna (2016, 2017), Weber (2010), Möller (2017), Pacewicz (2013).
[29] Engelen et al. (2014), Kass et al. (2019).
[30] Deruytter and Möller (2020: 407), Osborne and Gaebler (1992), Pinch (1995).
[31] Hendrikse and Lagna (2018: 14).
[32] Wang (2020: 192).

unevenly by local government actors within their organizations and in their relations with other institutions within wider local states. Financial logics and contradictions have been institutionalized within municipal governance in particular settings following finance interest engagement, extending financial control and discipline, and shifting its power dynamics 'into the local state'.[33]

Yet, financialization in local governance—including and reaching beyond local government into the wider local state—has been addressed patchily. Sectoral and geographical studies have addressed energy, housing, and waste management in the EU and UK.[34] NPM and local state restructuring have been precursors to financialization, changing 'the way public administrators and local policy-makers in city hall think, behave, and relate to the financial sector'.[35] How financialization relates to local government, the local state, and local governance needs further documentation and explanation.

Much subnational work has focused on city, city-regional, and metropolitan scales where the financialization process has been most evident.[36] Urban governance transformation frameworks of urban managerialism and entrepreneurialism have been influential explanations,[37] supplemented by their more recent financialized, asset price, speculative, and austerity iterations.[38] While important, their limits are being reached in explaining complex financialization experiences.[39] Conceptions constructed from certain places and times—such as 'financialized municipal entrepreneurialism' in London since 2010[40]—are helpful but need elaboration for research of other settings.

Local-level studies are less specific in defining, conceptualizing, and distinguishing local governments as economic and financial actors within specific national governance systems.[41] In different situations, local governments have varying political and officer leaderships, powers, responsibilities, resources, sizes, and geographies as well as financial aims, conditions, and strategies. Such attributes are integral to any engagements with financialization.

Few connections are made from financialization to work on the local (welfare) state as a capitalist state sustaining the conditions for capitalism's

---

[33] Peck and Whiteside (2016: 241).
[34] Deruytter and Bassens (2021), Christophers (2019).
[35] Deruytter and Möller (2020: 400).
[36] Ashton et al. (2016), Peck and Whiteside (2016).
[37] Harvey (1989).
[38] Aalbers (2015), Byrne (2016), Goldman (2011), Peck (2012).
[39] Pike et al. (2019).
[40] Beswick and Penny (2018: 162).
[41] Christophers (2019).

reproduction.[42] From the late 1980s and 1990s, these studies explained the 'restructuring of local government into local governance' through changing central–local relations, local agency, and externalization and privatization creating more distributed governing relations with a widening array of state, quasi-state, private, and civic entities involved in local decision-making and service provision.[43] These shifts were especially evident in the UK and US.[44]

Local governments have been established as objects and 'active agents' of financialization.[45] This work specifies the actors and their strategies, rationales, and practices. It moves beyond accounts of local government politicians and officers as only ever passive targets or even victims of external actors and financialization; subject to information asymmetries, relatively ignorant, and easily bamboozled with complex financial ideas by sophisticated financiers.[46]

Critical work has sought to uncover the multiple, overlapping, and evolving rationales of local government actors. Recognizing the politics of local public finance, 'professionals and politicians negotiate … within the context of varied local circumstances.'[47] Such actors are being drawn into new strategies and arrangements involving relations with existing and new actors and places within and beyond their administrative areas. New cadres of finance-savvy municipal professionals play a critical role as 'rainmaker', with what was formerly considered 'arcane expertise' now generating the 'unique power to solve intractable problems.'[48]

The financialization process is being interpreted as working as a ratchet that ensnares local governments and the wider local state. Engagement with its relations, strategies, and instruments generates risks then perceived by actors to need further financialization to manage, fostering an ongoing and potentially irreversible process. In a 'self-reinforcing' way,[49] once such financialization is engaged, it then becomes hard and costly to disengage, although not impossible. Crossing the threshold and seeing peers engaging financialization reduces the inhibition of actors to follow suit.[50] Some local governments become trapped, as their financial advisors suggest holding

---

[42] Clarke and Cochrane (1989).
[43] Pinch (1995: 966), Stoker (1989).
[44] Cochrane (1993), Duncan and Goodwin (1988), Patterson and Pinch (1995), Pinch (1995), Leitner (1990).
[45] Weber (2015: 257).
[46] Bhatti and Manley (2015).
[47] Pinch (1995: 966).
[48] Pacewicz (2013: 433).
[49] Deruytter and Möller (2020: 408).
[50] Mertens et al. (2020).

their nerve or engaging more complex products to get out of the fiscal hole, compounding initial problems and risks.[51]

External actors are recognized as 'carriers of financial rationalities and imperatives'.[52] Such intermediaries are constructing and stimulating specialized service markets.[53] Financial innovations have been made more complex and technical, fuelling demand for expert advice from within and beyond local government. Stimulating the 'changing knowledge structure of the state',[54] experts are engaging and becoming part of local government and the local state through contracting, secondment, and recruitment.[55] Whether, how, where, and when such actors are transforming local governments into 'financialized quasi-corporate bureaucracies' are empirical questions.[56]

Existing studies are relatively limited to new and high-profile examples of local governments and specific activities (e.g. borrowing and debt management), capital expenditure (e.g. infrastructure), and financial instruments (e.g. derivatives, Tax Increment Financing).[57] Most work is from a few countries (US, Italy, UK) and specific scales (cities, city-regions).[58] While the focus and geographical scope are broadening in Europe, Brazil, China, and South Africa,[59] further work is needed to strengthen, widen, and deepen knowledge of local government and financialization.

Examining the 'multiply constituted' financial contexts of financialization is critical, including the sources and costs of financing, range and expense of operations, and nature and scale of income generation activities.[60] A wider frame is needed beyond novel and small-scale cases, capturing the intersections between local governments and the financial system.

The geographies of local government financialization warrant further study: where it is and, crucially, is not occurring. Case studies are replete, but few investigations have provided wider views across particular national local government systems. Existing research reveals higher-level associations and much diversity, especially geographically and by size of local government.[61] The 'uneven geography of local circumstances' and their (dis)engagements

---

[51] Hendrikse and Sidaway (2014).
[52] Peck and Whiteside (2016: 255).
[53] Weber (2015).
[54] Wang (2020: 190).
[55] Farmer and Poulos (2019).
[56] Hendrikse and Lagna (2018: 14).
[57] Deruytter and Möller (2020), Ashton et al. (2016), Pike et al. (2019), Ward (2021), Hendrikse and Sidaway (2014), Lagna (2016), Pacewicz (2013), Singla and Luby (2020).
[58] Ashton et al. (2016), Pacewicz (2013), Weber (2015).
[59] Deruytter and Bassens (2021), Sanfelici and Halbert (2019), Wang (2020), Wu (2023), Cirolia and Robbins (2021), Migozzi (2020).
[60] Christophers (2019: 573).
[61] Mertens et al. (2020), Muldoon-Smith and Sandford (2021), Singla and Luby (2020), Pérignon and Vallée (2017).

with financialization frames the conceptual, theoretical, and empirical challenge to which this book contributes.[62]

The local politics of financialization remains critical.[63] National-level studies see financialization creating strategic opportunities for governments by providing 'access to a range of new tools and a new style of governance that allowed them to creatively cope with existing or prospective political conflicts'.[64]

Financialization is designed, negotiated, contested, managed, and regulated by multiple actors with interests and power situated in national and local governments, para-state organizations, and financial institutions. Political struggles occur between 'competing parties, ideological groups, and factions', and financialization gets used as part of a 'political project' to balance budgets, demonstrate financial competence, and prudence.[65] Recognizing how local public 'finance and budgetary behaviour are a crucial site for political struggle',[66] greater examination of local governments as complex, multifunctional, and democratically accountable political institutions with wide and multiple objectives, responsibilities, and accountabilities in financialization is overdue.

Moves towards any depoliticized or post-democratic local governance and its implications are understudied.[67] Growth of quasi-autonomous non-governmental organizations (QUANGOS) and the quango state raise issues about decision-making and local democratic control.[68] A growing concern is whether new, complex, and technical financial arrangements are beyond the knowledge and capacity of local politicians to oversee and scrutinize.[69]

The wider impacts and ramifications of any financialization for local governments and the local state are addressed unevenly in existing work. Questions have been raised over whose goals and interests are being addressed in local development, planning, and service provision.[70] Loss of local autonomy and authority relative to external financial interests has been explored.[71] Examination has been undertaken of the increased risks and speculation involved in financial innovations and growing indebtedness.[72]

---

[62] Pinch (1995: 966).
[63] Cochrane (1993). Ashton et al. (2016), Fields (2018), Mertens et al. (2020), Deruytter and Möller (2020), Lagna (2016), Peck and Whiteside (2016), Penny (2022), Pacewicz (2013).
[64] Wang (2020: 190).
[65] Wang (2020: 190).
[66] Pinch (1995: 966).
[67] Crouch (2004).
[68] Skelcher et al. (2000).
[69] Pacewicz (2013).
[70] Brill (2020), Pacewicz (2013), Ward (2022).
[71] Farmer (2014), Peck and Whiteside (2016).
[72] Davidson and Ward (2018), Raco and Souza (2018).

In the US, bankruptcy and enforced financial and service restructuring have received attention.[73]

Financially complex and long-term consequences have been documented when novel arrangements move adversely and/or unravel, for example, changing interest rates on borrowing.[74] Local governments tied into complex arrangements find it difficult, costly, and/or impossible to renegotiate or exit as local priorities and situations change.[75] Financialization introduces and/or amplifies local budgetary and fiscal stresses and dependencies and imports exposures, risks, and vulnerabilities that challenge financial sustainability and resilience.[76] Engagements with financialization generate wider implications for local service provision, accountability, well-being, and prosperity for people and places capable of furthering geographical inequalities.

Overall, work on financialization, local government, and the local state where change is most evident is critical in advancing understanding and establishing its foundations. The next step is to consolidate, reflect, and build upon these contributions. Complementing studies where financialization is evident, further work is needed where it is absent, contested, or stopped. Better understanding such differentiation over time and space, and its outcomes and implications, are central aims of this book.

2.3 Towards local statecraft

Studies of local government and local state engagements with financialization reference 'new forms of statecraft' and 'statecraft strategies'.[77] Explanations are emerging of statecraft as 'land financialisation, planning informalisation and gentrification'.[78] But the idea needs further specification, conceptualization, and theorization to address emanant critiques and reflections. Local statecraft must explain how, why, where, and when local governments are engaging financialization and their implications, and where such relations and process are being contested, stymied, and blocked.

2.3.1 What is statecraft and its critique?

Contributing to spatializing conceptions focused on the city level, statecraft was defined as the art of government and management of state affairs

---

[73] Peck and Whiteside (2016), Davidson and Ward (2018), Aldag et al. (2019).
[74] Hendrikse and Sidaway (2014).
[75] Farmer (2014).
[76] Ashton et al. (2016), Pacewicz (2013).
[77] Wang (2020: 197), Hendrikse and Lagna (2018: 8).
[78] Ward (2022: 1837).

and relations.[79] An actor-oriented and process-based geographical political economy emphasized the role of multiple actors with interests, powers,
resources, and capacities exercised in spatially and temporally differentiated
ways. Building upon its original focus upon national government, territorial
politics, and central–local government arrangements in the UK,[80] statecraft
was extended to encompass relations with multiple state, para-state, and
non-state, especially financial, actors.

Such relations were conceived as inherently geographical and historical,
reaching between and within territorial scales as well as relational networks
over time.[81] This conception sought to better capture and explain spatial and
temporal differentiation. Statecraft and its engagements with financialization moved beyond transformation frameworks to address complexity and
the mixing, mutating, and hybridizing of funding, financing and governing
relations, arrangements, and practices.[82]

Critique and reflection prompt elaboration. Local statecraft theory requires
clearer grounding in a theorization of the state as a 'complex social relation'
to better interpret its meaning and ramifications.[83] Specification of the distinctive attributes that underpin and condition the agency of actors in local
statecraft is needed alongside stronger recognition of geographical political
economy and politics.[84] Local financial statecraft must be distinguished from
broader local statecraft.[85]

While the worlds of municipal and commercial finance have been identified,[86] further elaboration is required of their actors, relations, characteristics, and working. Commercialization and 'entrepreneurialisation' of
the local state require clearer analytical distinction from financialization to
understand their substance and relations.[87] Relative neglect of risk in local
government requires remedy.[88]

To explain its differentiation over space and time, further specification
is needed of who is doing the local statecraft, why, where, and when.
Conceptions of state and finance need to be more rigorously explored to
understand the actors, agency, relations, structures, and process involved.
Responses are needed to treatments of finance as a 'process that unfolds *out
there*' by identifying existing, new, and emergent actors and practices and
connecting them back into the wider institutions and structures of which they

[79] Pike et al. (2019).
[80] Bulpitt (1983).
[81] Whiteside (2020).
[82] Pike et al. (2020).
[83] Ashton (2020: 794).
[84] Lagna (2015). McGuirk et al. (2021).
[85] Ashton (2020).
[86] Pike et al. (2019).
[87] McCann and Ward (2011: xiii).
[88] Christophers (2015a).

are part and that shape their agency.[89] While existing studies have addressed the city, city-region, and metropolitan levels,[90] the focus here is local as a way into local statecraft engagements with financialization.

2.3.2 Grounding local statecraft in a theorization of the state

Building upon a spatialized strategic-relational theorization of the state as a social relation and the agency of state personnel,[91] the state is understood as a work in progress. Its 'remit' is 'never stable'.[92] The state is constantly being (re)made by actors attempting to cohere and stabilize its structures and devise, sustain, and implement its imaginaries, strategies, and projects.[93] This understanding 'requires treating states as ensembles of organizations and sets of powerful ideas that interact with the inner working of finance in complicated ways'.[94] This geographical political-economic framing focuses on the 'mechanisms and social relations of value creation, realization, and accumulation'.[95] Statecraft provides the missing conception and theorization of the agency of actors and institutions of the state at the local scale.

In this state theorization, statecraft conceives of particular 'paths of state formation' as actors temporarily cohere and stabilize state structures and imaginaries, strategies, and projects in specific geographical and historical settings.[96] This spatial and temporal sensitivity enables statecraft to handle continuity and generality *as well as* contingency and particularity in certain places and times. Local statecraft envisages and articulates local state strategies and projects involving actors pursuing goals in differentiated geographical and temporal expressions of state power and time horizons.[97]

Differentiated paths of state formation are 'set in motion' through financialization.[98] State and finance actors become embroiled in the construction and exercise of state structures and imaginaries, strategies, and projects in certain settings. This understanding unpacks the 'conception and organization' of the state to explain how 'state ideas, state organizations, state-making processes dovetailed with the expansive mechanisms of finance'.[99] Central

---

[89] Ashton (2020: 796, original author's emphasis).
[90] Lauermann (2016), Penny (2022), Pike et al. (2019), Ward (2021).
[91] Jessop (2016).
[92] Weber (2015: 804).
[93] Brenner (2004), MacKinnon (2021), O'Neill (2004).
[94] Wang (2020: 188).
[95] Christophers (2015a: 1).
[96] Ashton (2020: 796).
[97] Ashton et al. (2016).
[98] Ashton (2020: 796).
[99] Wang (2020: 192).

questions are what geographical and temporal forms these local statecraft engagements with financialization take and their outcomes and implications.

Grounding local statecraft in this state theorization endows local governments with dimensions of statehood. Usually conceptualized for nation states and geopolitics, statehood is defined as the authority states hold to exercise sovereignty within their territories.[100] Acknowledging the territorial trap, this understanding recognizes statehood is geographically and historically particular, not solely contained within national territories, and extends beyond national borders.

Local statehood confers distinctive attributes upon local states through their variable constitutional and institutional positions within multi-level structures of government and governance. Often defined by national states, these facets include authority, power, responsibilities, resources, autonomies, accountabilities, and politics.[101] While situated and wielded within distributed local state governance, many of the powers and resources reside with local government. Local statehood is predominantly situated within specific and territorially demarcated jurisdictions *and* reaches beyond these boundaries, encompassing geographically delimited areas *alongside* wider spatial terrains over which actors exercise local statecraft.

Varying geographically and temporally in national settings, the local statehood underpinning local statecraft is determined by constitutional and legal status, (de)centralized government and governance arrangements, central–local relations, funding and financing systems, and politics. Such dimensions are complex, long-standing, and evolving; comprising a 'geo-constitution' founded upon their particular geographical and historical relations and settlements in national political economies.[102] National statehood and sovereign power and politics are integral to local statehood and statecraft, formally and informally through legal structures and regulatory frameworks as well as explicit and/or implicit government guarantees and supported borrowing.

Local statehood and its institutional arrangements wire *and* scale objectives, incentives, autonomies, and accountabilities into local government. Local statehood frames the complex and shifting institutional space for the agency of actors—the local statecrafters—by defining what is legal and illegal, what constitutes their duties and responsibilities, what powers and resources they have at their disposal, to whom they are accountable, what guarantee and support they receive from the national sovereign, and what national and local politics are at play. While varying in interpretation and practice by

---

[100] Agnew (2002).
[101] O'Neill (2004), Waite et al. (2013).
[102] Wills (2016: 43), Christophers and Fine (2020).

local statecrafters, these governing settings are critical in determining and influencing their agency.

The constitution of local governments as political organizations with different accountabilities is integral to the local statehood underpinning local statecraft. Accountabilities embed scrutiny and transparency into governance. They range from narrow and technical relations within the public sector and national government to broader democratic and political obligations to answer to local residents, taxpayers, and voters. Local governments are complex, multifunctional organizations with multiple objectives. They administer *and* govern their local areas and make political decisions about allocating resources, taxing, and spending with local and national public money.

Local statecraft involves politics internally within organizations and externally as democratically elected political leaderships in parties and groups accountable to local voters and taxpayers and national governments. Financialization complicates this geographical political economy by engaging other financial actors. Local statehood makes local government distinctive from other private or civic actors in the local state as the only entity able to exercise statecraft. It has 'distinctive capabilities, objectives and concerns that render the state essentially unlike any other actors in the financial marketplaces'.[103]

The situation is more complex and contingent for quasi-state actors in the local state endowed with differentiated attributes of statehood. These entities include arms-length bodies partly or wholly owned by or related to local or national governments in specific local service areas including education, housing, and social care. Crucial is how this 'liminal category of actors' relate to 'marketization' and 'the existence and multiplication of parastate organizations' that has 'pushed the boundaries of the states outwards and rendered the divisions between the state and the market increasingly murky'.[104]

Another critical question is whether and how the objectives, incentives, autonomies, and accountabilities of local statecraft are changing—rewiring *and* rescaling—through engagements with financialization. There is a need to explain how novel financial 'apparatuses' may 'transform' local government and the local state by 'vesting public action in extra-statal networks' as well as 'reconstructing localities as financial agents working in and through these networks'.[105] Understanding this local statecraft requires moving 'beyond questions of institutional form and arrangements' to pay more attention to

---

[103] Wang (2020: 193).
[104] Wang (2020: 192).
[105] Ashton (2020: 797).

the '"inside" of the state itself' and examine 'how financialization remaps critical functions and dynamically reconfigures city powers'.[106] Accountable actors in political and official roles exercise power through local statecraft and engage or not with financialization to varying degrees and in differing ways. Local statecraft's challenge is to explain why, when, where, and how.

2.3.3 Distinguishing financial from local statecraft

A critical interpretation is that city government financial strategies, behaviours, and arrangements represent the '"city-*fying*"' of *financial* statecraft.[107] That is, financial relations, rationales, and practices are so deeply embedded in the local state that local government is effectively governing through finance.[108] Finance is so centrally involved in local statecraft that it is impossible or meaningless to separate it out. Such financialization is manifest through local governments behaving more like finance institutions and internalizing finance, even seconding and recruiting commercial finance staff.[109]

This account connects to political science conceptions of statecraft situating the economic and financial interests of nation states in the international economic and financial system. 'Economic statecraft' is interpreted as 'economics as an instrument of politics' whereby national states utilize economic strategies and tools, including macro-economic and trade policy, to achieve political goals.[110] Similarly, 'financial statecraft' is using national financial strategies and instruments, such as capital controls and exchange and interest rates, for wider, typically foreign, policy ends.[111] This work has not addressed such economic and financial statecraft beyond the nation state and its international relations.

A sympathetic critique of *localizing* financial statecraft is that it affords an overly dominant role to finance. It risks reducing local statecraft to financial statecraft at the local level. This view narrows the frame around what local government does that is not financial statecraft or closely connected and implicated with it. Local statecraft is not *solely* focused upon nor *only* determined by financial purposes and goals for their own sake. Endowed with broader statehood attributes, local governments have wider

---

[106] Ashton (2020: 797).
[107] Ashton (2020: 796, emphasis added).
[108] Ashton (2020).
[109] Farmer and Poulos (2019), Trampusch (2019).
[110] Baldwin (1985: 4, 3).
[111] Steil and Litan (2008: 1).

than just economic and financial purposes, responsibilities, and functions. These inescapably connect with local social, environmental, political, and cultural objectives, incentives, autonomies, and accountabilities. More financially oriented local statecraft exists in certain geographical and temporal settings. But it is not necessarily a general feature and instead an expression of the agency of local statecrafters in particular situations facing certain constraints and opportunities. Other times and spaces may have less financially marked manifestations. Local statecraft involves more agency, engagements with financialization are uneven not inevitable outcomes or foregone conclusions.

Strongly financially oriented local statecraft leaves imprints and legacies. It may become embedded and locked-in through its political and officer leadership and staff, strategies, practices, and arrangements. This situation may reach a point where local statecraft is effectively governing through finance in particular times and places. But this is an empirical question to be researched rather than assumed. Distinguishing local from financial statecraft foregrounds their relations and raises the potential and politics of moving it in directions less oriented towards commercial finance and financialization.

2.3.4 Differentiating municipal and commercial finance

Strengthening local statecraft builds upon identification of municipal *and* commercial finance worlds.[112] Each has its own actors, relations, aims and objectives, accountabilities, frames of action, and geographies; their intersections are integral to local statecraft's engagements with financialization (Table 2.1). Actors and their agency are shaped by specific logics. Working within complex, multifunctional, and political institutions with multiple local objectives and resources, the 'political and career concerns' of local government staff are 'distinctive from those of economic actors'.[113] Capacity, skills, and knowledge asymmetries are endemic as local statecrafters engage the commercial finance world.[114]

The agency of local state and finance actors (re)produce and adapt municipal and commercial finance worlds over time and space. Their relations cannot readily be generalized: accommodations exist alongside legal conflicts. The hallmarks of financialization in financial innovation—historically termed 'creative finance', 'creative accounting', 'financial ingenuity', and

---

[112] Pike et al. (2019).
[113] Wang (2020: 190).
[114] Kass et al. (2019).

Table 2.1 Municipal and commercial worlds of finance

Dimension	Municipal	Commercial
Actors	National and local governments and agencies Politicians, officials	Financial institutions Executives, specialists
Social relations	With publics as residents, voters, and taxpayers	With finance actors as investors and/or intermediaries
Objectives	Public goods provision Economic, social, and environmental welfare Social and spatial equity and distribution Value for money (economy, efficiency, and effectiveness)	Financial returns on investment
Accountabilities	Formal and legal to national and local governments, voters, and taxpayers External investors and lenders	Formal and legal to investors, lenders, and/or owners
Frames of action	Slow, stable, bureaucratic Longer-term and intergenerational outlook Low future discount rate, higher present value of future cash flows Risk-averse Incremental innovation	Fast, unstable, agile Shorter-term outlook High future discount rate, lower present value of future cash flows Risk-seeking Incremental and radical innovation
Geographies	Territorialized, immobile, geographically bounded	De-territorialized, mobile, geographically unbounded

'financial engineering'—are long-standing and evident in relation to funding and financing in *both* worlds.[115]

Broadly, funding is where the money comes from. This includes national government grants, local taxes, charges and fees, and commercial incomes. Financing comprises the financial actors, arrangements, and instruments that provide the finance. Financing is mainly borrowing and leases, as external investors cannot take equity (shares) in the local state. Funding provides the revenue streams that repay the financing.

Recognizing the different worlds of finance underpins greater attention to the conception and management of risk by local statecrafters. While long-standing in commercial finance, local municipal finance's exposure to 'wider socio-political, non-commercial and service-related risks' is recent.[116] Due to its high levels of public accountability and formalization, local government

---

[115] Tickell (1998: 865), Parkinson (1986: 27), Singla and Luby (2020: 1).
[116] Knight (1921), Hood and Young (2005: 565).

is characterized as relatively risk-averse, conservative, and incremental and limited in any innovation.[117] Contrasting commercial finance actors, local municipal finance directors address multiple goals, lack incentives for individual or organizational risk-taking, face public scrutiny of their behaviour and decisions, and operate in bureaucratized settings which 'reward certainty over chance'.[118]

In the US, tightened financial constraints have increased risk-taking, innovation, and entrepreneurial orientation by local government staff.[119] Financialization has made risk and its distribution and transfer more important and widespread issues for local statecrafters.[120] Local governments now confront the issue that 'not embracing financial innovation would actually constitute an irresponsible handling of taxpayers money'.[121]

Countering the 'councillors at the casino' narrative, local statecraft emphasizes the conception, creation, and distribution of risks and their measurement, management, and mitigation. Local statecraft incorporates an understanding of risk types being generated and distributed by a range of actors in particular historical-geographical contexts.[122] It broadens the frame by moving beyond only considering external financial actors and the international financial system. Differentiation exists in local statecrafter rationales and gravitation towards specific parts of the 'risk spectrum'.[123] Generating risks *within* the state,[124] new financial instruments can be formulated and pushed by 'professionals working within municipal bureaucracies'.[125]

Given the purposes and responsibilities resulting from their statehood, local statecrafters face risks with multiple origins and relations: macroeconomic policy; the governance and funding system; local service demand growth; geo-economic and geopolitical shifts; and emergencies. Such risks intertwine those originating from external financial actors and the financial system including credit rating changes, interest rate shifts, and banking crises.

How actors more systematically diagnose, measure, manage, and mitigate the downsides and upsides of risks are integral to local statecraft. Risk management models from commercial finance need adaptation for municipal settings.[126] Local government is traditionally a cautious,

---

[117] Bozeman and Kingsley (1998), Hood and Young (2005).
[118] Kass et al. (2019: 1042).
[119] Singla et al. (2018).
[120] Christophers (2015b).
[121] Deruytter and Möller (2020: 406).
[122] Christophers (2015b).
[123] Kass et al. (2019: 1035).
[124] Ashton (2020).
[125] Pacewicz (2013: 414).
[126] Hood and Young (2005).

risk-averse, and slow-moving part of the public sector now facing a more pro-risk, faster moving, and financialized world.

2.3.5 Distinguishing commercialization from financialization

Differentiating the worlds of finance in which local statecrafters work enables the distinction of commercialization from financialization. Each has been loosely handled in some existing accounts. Commercialization is local government operating in more commercially oriented and market-facing ways geared towards providing more cost-efficient services and/or raising revenue.[127] This conception includes local statecrafter adoption of commercial principles and practices in existing local government activities as well as activities explicitly designed to generate income. Sometimes blurred in its relationship with financialization, 'entrepreneurialisation' is a related term used to describe the introduction of 'new forms of *entrepreneurial* statecraft' and 'innovative ways to generate finance', skewing policy towards the interests and profitability of 'investors, developers and speculators'.[128]

Commercialization and entrepreneurialization have distinctive relations, processes, and arrangements. Neither are synonymous with financialization but are related. Commercialization and entrepreneurialization inhabit the worlds of municipal and commercial finance but do not inherently *require* financialization. Local governments can be commercial and entrepreneurial but not necessarily engaging financialization. Municipal finance strategies and activities can still be innovative and involve risk, including invest-to-save initiatives, capitalizing revenue costs, and lending to other local governments. Trading companies selling services to public, private, and civic sectors *without* the involvement of external financial actors, novel financial arrangements, or the international financial system are commercial and entrepreneurial but not automatically nor only embroiled in financialization. Such commercialization or entrepreneurialization may involve financialization but it is not a *necessary* element. It is less plausible to see financialization without commercialization and/or entrepreneurialization given the related and complementary logics involved. Local statecraft engaging external financial actors and the international financial system embodies commercial and entrepreneurial thinking and approaches.

---

[127] Leitner (1990), Fenwick and Johnston (2020).
[128] Raco and Souza (2018: 145, original authors' emphasis).

Identifying and distinguishing such processes is integral in understanding and explaining the how, why, where, and when of financialization and local statecraft in particular settings. This task is challenging to address empirically, however, given the overlapping of commercialization and financialization in practice.

2.3.6 Who is doing local statecraft and why?

Strengthening local statecraft requires greater specification of the actors, agency, and rationales involved. This elaboration addresses the critique of 'a somewhat formal approach to intergovernmental relations *between* institutions and a Whitehall-meets-City Hall account of financialization'.[129] If 'policy elites' have 'reconstituted statehood and reengineered statecraft to meet their political needs' in a 'finance-mediated fashion',[130] then greater specification of these actors and their logics and relations are needed. Distinguishing municipal and commercial finance and elaborating the rationales of actors avoids narrow and superficial characterizations of the state and finance.

Responding to the critique that statecraft is used as a catch-all category for the agency of state actors must identify these actors and their roles, rationales, resources, capacities, and relations. These are the local statecrafters doing the local statecraft. Their agency is expressed and manifest in the day-to-day administration, business, and organizational and professional politics of local government and the local state.[131] Local statecrafters are the actors engaging if at all with any 'financialisers'.[132]

This actor-oriented approach to local statecraft is critical given local statehood diversity within national systems. Different types of local government, funding and financing systems, political leaderships, local economic conditions, and other factors determine and shape actor rationales, powers, resources, capacities, and relations in particular temporal and geographical conjunctures. Such elements are the structuring and shaping context rather than inert 'environmental variables'.[133] While there may be 'palpable enthusiasm for financial markets and innovation' amongst some local government actors in some places and times,[134] this is differentiated rather than

---

[129] Ashton (2020: 797, original author's emphasis).
[130] Wang (2020: 190).
[131] Clarke and Cochrane (1989).
[132] Christophers (2019: 572).
[133] Turley et al. (2015: 402).
[134] Deruytter and Möller (2020: 400).

generalized. Claims of 'gradual colonization', 'internalization', and 'normalization' of 'financial market logics in local state administrations' require documentation, substantiation, and explanation.[135]

Local statecrafters have to relate to actors in other state (e.g. national government politicians, civil servants), quasi-state (e.g. non-departmental public bodies), private (e.g. external advisors, financial institutions), civic (e.g. community sector organizations), and public/political (e.g. campaigns, protest groups) organizations. Moving beyond the 'bounded spaces of local government'[136], such multi-actor and multi-level relationships intersect and require appropriate and analytical research strategies.

2.3.7 Where and when are actors doing local statecraft?

Addressing this question responds to the critique that statecraft happens everywhere and all the time, and is underspecified and vague. Existing accounts are said to lack sufficient spatial and temporal specificity.[137] Financialization and local government are inescapably geographical and historical.[138] Key is identifying local statecraft's functional areas, geographical settings, and temporality.

Underpinned by local statehood attributes, the idea of realms is defined as domains of activity, responsibility, or interest with territorial and relational geographies.[139] These realms are where local statecraft is manifest and where local statecrafters exercise varying degrees of authority, power, and resources derived from their local statehood. Given the focus upon local government's engagements with financialization, several related statecraft realms are identified: financial strategies; external advice; borrowing and debt management; and in-area and out-of-area strategies and activities. Other realms of local statecraft are for future work.

Developing conjunctural theorizing, explanations are constructed for the spatial-temporal instances of local statecraft in their 'structuring contexts' as a means of going beyond transformation frameworks better to account for the complexity of particular situations.[140] Local statecraft is used to theorize the relations, activities, and process through which local governments

[135] Chiapello (2015: 15), Deruytter and Möller (2020: 400).
[136] Hendrikse and Sidaway (2014: 195).
[137] Ashton (2020, Whiteside (2020).
[138] Lagna (2016).
[139] Borja and Castells (1997).
[140] Peck (2017: 10), Christophers (2019), Hall and Massey (2010).

are engaging financialization and, crucially, where, when, and why they are not.

The challenge is distilling the general conceptual components and their theoretical connections to explain local statecraft conjunctures. No attempt is made to identify specific kinds of local statecraft in a more typological approach.[141] Doing this would encounter the same limitations of archetypes and transformation frameworks statecraft has sought to overcome.

This conjunctural approach does not mean that local statecraft is entirely heterogenous and different in each-and-every place and time. Instead, conjunctural theorizing allows for common features, resemblances, and continuities alongside differentiating characteristics, discontinuities, and changes. How these are configured in specific times and spaces is an empirical question. This book examines local government in England from 2010 to challenge the 'councillors at the casino' narrative of badly governed, weak players losing at the financialization game.

2.4 Researching financialization and local statecraft

Key to explaining local statecraft's varying engagements with the relations and process of financialization is excavating the layering and (re)combining of a political-economic and institutional landscape marked by geographical and historical differentiation.[142] A multi-actor and multi-level approach situates the agency of local statecrafters within their particular government and governance setting nationally and internationally. Analysing change in the 'specific political and social circumstances policymakers were embedded in',[143] this frame encompasses state, quasi-state, private, and civic actors working at and between spatial scales and networks. The approach links and relates macro, meso, and micro levels; zooming in and out and back again to trace, understand, and explain the relations, process, and arrangements involved.

Capturing local statecraft within and beyond local government areas, a relational approach interprets the geographies of this conjunctural framework. Recognizing territorial scales *and* relational networks, the focus is on inside *and* outside the Town Hall to understand the relations within *and* between the different local government types, national government, and external financial actors in England from 2010.

---

[141] cf. Beswick and Penny (2018), Kutz (2017).
[142] Peck and Whiteside (2016).
[143] Wang (2020: 190).

Complementing and reaching beyond existing case studies, the approach takes a landscape view. Remedying partial and unbalanced accounts, this perspective outlines and explains the overall dynamics, situates changes in context, and provides a fuller aspect across the local government system in a specific national case. It avoids citing case studies 'purely in illustration of wider trends' and simply aligning 'individual local experiences' with 'generalised tendencies'.[144] Instead of only addressing the higher-profile instances of financialization, it documents and explains where and what kind of local statecraft engagements with financialization are *and* are not happening.[145] This wider geographical frame enables comparison between local government types and local statecrafters acting in different spatial and temporal situations across England.

The temporal dimensions of this approach recognize the timing of financialization is important. Contemporary developments are situated in their historical context,[146] recognizing the legacies that pattern and shape current and future paths. Periodization identifies and explains meaningful episodes of financialization and local statecraft.

Understanding financialization-in-motion over space and time underpins recognition of its geographical and temporal dimensions, manifest in the paths that actors create, follow, and/or are forced down.[147] Attention is focused on the 'making, unfolding, negotiation and contestation' of financial innovations and deals.[148] Arrangements are often the unstable and contingent outcomes of struggles, accommodations, and contradictions between actors negotiating financial pressures and opportunities.[149]

Interests and behaviours are not viewed in light of the structural positions of actors, given the difficulties of generalizing about 'collective dispositions' and the incentives and accountabilities actors face in particular conjunctures.[150] The paths actors are entwined with are not only linear, regular, and/or one-way; they can be non-linear, irregular, and reversible.

2.4.1 Why local government in England from 2010?

Local government in England is long-established, complex, and highly centralized. It is diverse, with over 300 local governments of five types

[144] Christophers (2019: 572).
[145] Kass et al. (2019).
[146] Whiteside (2020).
[147] Engelen and Konings (2010).
[148] Hendrikse and Sidaway (2014: 196).
[149] Engelen and Konings (2010).
[150] Kass et al. (2019: 1042).

responsible for 800 functions, accounting for around £100 billion and 10 per cent of total UK government spending and employing 1.4 million people in 2021–22.[151] From 2010, the UK government pursued austerity to reduce the national deficit following the 2008 crash, increase local government's financial self-sufficiency, and reduce its dependence upon transfers from the centre. This period involves contradictions between the UK government's centralization, conservatism, and risk-averse administrative culture *and* simultaneous promotion of commercialization, innovation, and risk-taking by local statecrafters to reduce expenditure and generate new income sources to close funding gaps. Local government in England has been integral to responses to the pandemic and economic recovery since 2020.

The UK state is a leader and bellwether of local public sector restructuring internationally, including privatization, contracting-out, and strategic partnerships.[152] Local government in England is a long-standing test bed for experiments and innovations in commercialization, financialization, NPM, and public service delivery models.[153] Such ideas have been pursued in differentiated ways by local statecrafters across England. Relatively few high-profile cases have garnered disproportionate attention and generated controversy.

England is in the UK's liberal market-oriented and financialized political economy and variegation of capitalism.[154] It has a large and advanced financial and business services sector concentrated in the City of London that targets the UK public sector and local government as a service and product market.

Existing work has treated local governments in England in somewhat homogenous ways. This view misses the differing situations and agency of different local government types and their political leaderships and politics, powers, functions, resources, sizes, and locations across England that matter fundamentally to their local statecraft and any engagements with financialization. This diverse landscape is further complicated by the broadening and increasing institutional complexity and density of the wider local state in England.[155] England and the UK are also marked by long-standing and high levels of geographical inequalities, rising local service demands, and increasingly differentiated political geographies since the 2016 EU referendum and Brexit.[156]

---

[151] DLUHC (2021a), ONS (2020).
[152] Whitfield (2010).
[153] Patterson and Pinch (1995), Pinch (1995).
[154] Peck and Theodore (2007), Davis and Walsh (2016), Sawyer (2022).
[155] Cochrane (2015).
[156] Martin et al. (2021), Jennings and Stoker (2019).

The spatial and temporal specificity of the case study is integral to conjunctural theorizing. The research discloses a 'more-than-England since 2010' story because it acknowledges its historical and geographical political economy and variegation of capitalism in making its conceptual and theoretical claims of local statecraft and financialization. As a 'critical case',[157] it is not being objectified and generalized. Instead, this particular conjuncture is used to situate, challenge, and develop the conceptualization and theorization of local statecraft.

2.4.2 Research design, data collection, and analysis

Organized around four local statecraft realms, the empirical research used mixed methods in four connected stages. Review of secondary qualitative data documented the context and issues. Sources comprised: (i) national government departments for finance (HM Treasury (HMT)) and local government; (ii) Chartered Institute of Public Finance and Accountancy (CIPFA); (iii) national scrutiny bodies; (iv) sector organizations; (v) think tanks; and (vi) economic, financial, public policy, and sector trade press. Unpublished data were also collected.

Stage two examined the financial strategies and arrangements of local governments across England and their engagements (if any) with financialization. It focused on the five types of local governments: London boroughs, metropolitan districts, counties, districts, and unitaries.[158] Given their specific nature, it excluded the Isles of Scilly, City of London, Greater London Authority, combined and mayoral combined authorities, police and crime commissioners, and authorities for fire and rescue, waste, and national parks.

This stage used financial data on local governments from the Department and National Audit Office (NAO),[159] covering the austerity decade 2010–19 and preceding the pandemic impacts from 2020.[160] In providing a landscape-wide view of local statecraft engagements with financialization, the research encounters indicator, data, and analysis issues. Much existing work documenting financialization focuses upon firms and commercial finance.[161] Most municipal finance work examines strategies and instruments

---

[157] Flyvbjerg (2006: 226).
[158] DLUHC (2021a). The total number of local governments is being reduced through reorganization.
[159] DLUHC (2021b), National Audit Office (2021a).
[160] NAO (2021b). The data and code are available in an open access GitHub repository: http://github.com/CaitHRobinson/councillorsatthecasino.
[161] See, for example, Sawyer (2022).

in the US.[162] Studies in England have addressed specific public finance activities, including inter-local government borrowing, and external engagements with commercial finance such as LOBO loans and Money Market Funds (MMF).[163]

The local government funding system in England is complex. Local governments' changing relationships with a widening local state of public, private, civic, and hybrid bodies imparts further intricacy. Distinguishing commercialization from financialization and where they are connected and overlapping is difficult to discern in the aggregate data without detailed case study analysis. The lack of clear measures of financialization means only imperfect indicators are available. The selection here is not exhaustive and is used to begin outlining the landscape with necessary caveats. There is scope for much further work undertaking critical financial analysis using financial data through which to explore contested practices, power relations and spaces as well as engaging municipal and commercial finance disciplines.[164]

Indicators selected comprise the following. A standard, tried-and-tested form of treasury management activity places cash deposits in MMF provided by external financial institutions. It reflects local governments' cash reserves and offers high liquidity and low risk. Levels of deposits illustrate the willingness of local statecrafters to engage with external financial actors and the financialization process, albeit in a low-risk and standardized way.

Interest and investment income is derived from earned interest from bank deposits and assets. This indicator demonstrates commercialization in showing how active and successful the local government is as an investor (in-area and out-of-area) and in generating income from these investments. It does not necessarily reveal financialization, since, beyond bank deposits, such commercial activities may not involve external commercial finance actors or innovative instruments. Such markers of financialization may be evident in only some cases.

Gross external borrowing reveals the willingness of local statecrafters to take on debt. Given that lending to local governments is dominated by HMT's Public Works Loan Board (PWLB), this is not a clear indicator of engagement with external commercial finance lenders or new loan instruments hence evidence of financialization. While high borrowing levels relative to resources demonstrate a higher risk appetite, only in specific cases are they definitive examples of financialization such as LOBO loans and interest rate swaps.

---

[162] See, for example, Singla and Luby (2020).
[163] See, for example, Dagdeviren and Karwowski (2021), Mertens et al. (2020), Muldoon-Smith and Sandford (2021).
[164] Kass (2020), Andrew and Cahill (2017), Ferry and Murphy (2018).

Surpluses on external trading accounts demonstrate cash accumulation resulting from local government trading activities selling goods and services to external customers. It indicates commercialization to generate revenues and, minus costs, income. Such trading activities do not always or necessarily involve external financial actors and/or innovations, therefore they cannot only be categorized as evidence of the process of financialization. Specific examples exist but cannot be discerned from this aggregate data. Surplus levels demonstrate success in commercial trading activities and a willingness to retain rather than deploy the surpluses generated.

These four indicators were calculated per capita to control for different local government sizes measured by population. Data were analysed by local government type, political control, and geography to explore how different powers, resources, and politics shape local statecraft and varying engagements with financialization.

Stage three comprised in-depth interviews between 2019 and 2021 with over fifty key actors from the municipal and commercial finance worlds. Research subjects included: civil servants in the UK government and national scrutiny organizations; executives in national professional organizations and sector associations; councillors and finance leads, and Chief Financial Officers (CFOs) in different local government types and locations; officers in local government treasurer societies; executives in financial institutions; external advisors; academics; researchers in think tanks; journalists; and campaigners. Interviews were recorded and transcribed, mostly using online channels due to pandemic restrictions. Informed consent, anonymized use, and the cross-checking of data accuracy were agreed with participants. Additional participation and notetaking were used at various local government finance events.

The final stage constructed ten case summaries for each local government type in different locations across England. Balancing reach and depth, these were neither single-case in-depth studies nor superficial overviews. They were designed as meso-level investigations of local government types with varying engagements with the financialization process and behaviours identified in stage two. These case summaries illuminated how more general relations, strategies, instruments, and practices were being pursued by specific local statecrafters in times and places. Where access was authorized, primary interviews in stage three focused on these local governments. The case summaries collated information from publicly available sources from each local government's website and the sector press including corporate visions and strategies, annual statements of accounts, and audit reports.

The analysis of data from the four stages identified and followed the actors, relations, and process at work in the differentiated landscape. It involved piecing together the overall picture and zooming in and out and back again to investigate the multiple actors and levels to understand, document, and explain local statecraft's varying engagements with financialization in England since 2010. Acknowledging financialization's historical and temporal dimensions,[165] analysis matched detailed engagement with actors, relations, and process through their 'workings on the ground' with simultaneous attention to 'structural positions, systemic rationalities, and recurrent patterns'.[166]

---

[165] Christophers and Fine (2020).
[166] Peck and Whiteside (2016: 262).

3
Funding and financing local government in England

3.0 Introduction

Local government in England is a relatively recent creation, beginning in urban municipal service provision and democratic accountability in the early 1800s.[1] Lacking constitutional or legislative protection, the local government system evolved through largely incremental change, punctuated by moments of radical reorganization.[2]

England is a historically and internationally resonant laboratory for experiments and changes in local government organization, funding, and innovation.[3] The creative accounting of intra-public sector borrowing, lending, and sale-and-leaseback deals characterized the 1980s. Commercialization, the Hammersmith and Fulham swaps affair, and local taxation reforms—including the infamous poll tax—marked the 1990s. Trading activities, exotic borrowing instruments, and the Icelandic Banks collapse defined the 2000s. Local financial self-sufficiency through expenditure reductions and income generation emerged from 2010.

Situating the characteristics of local government in England within the context of the UK is integral to understanding local statecraft and locating where interpretations of this particular geographical and temporal episode are coming from. It is a creature of the national government and Parliament, operating in a highly centralized and evolving system of central–local relations. The geographical and temporal situation of this local government setting is crucial to theorizing and explaining local statecraft's engagements with the relations and process of financialization.

Distinctive processes structure and shape local government in England, with implications for its funding and financing. Centralization concentrates powers and resources at the national level. Repeated modernization efforts

---

[1] Parr (2020).
[2] Jennings (1947), Robson (1931).
[3] Copus et al. (2017).

Financialization and Local Statecraft. Andy Pike, Oxford University Press. © Andy Pike (2023).
DOI: 10.1093/oso/9780192856661.003.0003

involve experiments with new organizational models. Continued pressure for fewer, larger local government units underpins ongoing reorganization. Disaggregation increases the number of organizations constituting the local state working with local government.

The local government funding system in England is complex, fragmented, and highly centralized. Incremental changes layer upon each other over time. Byzantine arrangements accumulate, structuring and shaping local statecraft and other financial actor agency.

3.1 Local government in England in the UK state

The UK is a unitary state. It is governed through its national Parliament, the principal source of authority located in Westminster in the national capital city London. The UK has a distinctive political economy for local government. As a constitutional monarchy, it has no written constitution nor formal constitutional position for local government that establishes its powers.[4] Based upon convention, custom, and practice, the UK government legislates through the national Parliament to create the statutory framework, defining what local government is required and permitted to do and how its resources are determined. National government retains the sole right to authorize and change what is intra vires (within its powers) and legal for local government and, conversely, ultra vires (beyond its powers) and illegal.

The national Parliament is sovereign over local government in England. Local governments are 'the creatures, the creations, of parliamentary statute' and their 'boundaries, duties, powers, memberships and modes of operation are laid down by Acts of Parliament … they can be abolished by Parliament and … restructured and reorganised at Parliament's will'.[5] This status means local government is subordinate within the UK state, governed through the low politics of local service provision and policy delivery distinct from the high politics of central government's national policy responsibilities.[6]

Local government in England differs from other national systems. In comparably sized countries including France, Germany, and Italy, a right to local self-government is enshrined and protected in written constitutions.[7] Local government is endowed with general and wide-ranging competencies and rights and, through its democratic election, seen as the 'organic

[4] Robson (1931).
[5] Wilson and Game (2011: 33).
[6] Bulpitt (1983).
[7] Boggero (2017).

self-expression of the people'.[8] While varying in functions, powers, and resources in different national settings, self-government principles confer upon local governments specific autonomies protected from national interference and unilateral change. Constitutional safeguards exist for the local government system and individual local governments. In contrast, local government in England operates as only 'semi-autonomous' from national government.[9]

The UK evolved into more of a pluri-national state from the late 1990s.[10] Devolution and constitutional change established legislatures and executives in Northern Ireland, Scotland, and Wales. Local government is a devolved responsibility for these devolved governments, while in England it remains governed through the UK Parliament. Administration and management of local government in England are by elected government ministers, their appointed special advisers, and officials (civil servants) in UK central government departments based in Whitehall in London. Accountability between national and local government is a complex system with multiple channels and levels. Most important are the finance (HMT) and local government departments.

As the largest part of the UK's economy and population, governing England has been historically problematic for the national state. Since 1945, local government has been subject to continual change by the UK government. The search for an effective governance tier between national and local levels is marked by endemic, ongoing churn, and reorganization. Pendulum swings are evident between local, regional, and subregional arrangements.[11]

Even following the late 1990s devolution, the UK remains amongst the most highly centralized states internationally.[12] Local autonomy is lower than comparable countries in Europe, decreasing between 1990 and 2014 (Figure 3.1).

The UK's centralized governance is pronounced in England.[13] Reflecting the geographical concentration of political-economic power, it was claimed in the 1990s that this 'super-centralism' means 'local government is directed from London in a semi-colonial fashion.'[14] While evolving, centralization limits local government's 'fiscal space' for taxing and spending,[15] constraining its revenue raising capacity, and fostering dependency upon the UK

---

[8] Wilson and Game (2011: 32).
[9] Wilson and Game (2011: 33).
[10] Keating (2001).
[11] Pike et al. (2016).
[12] Hooghe et al. (2016).
[13] Copus et al. (2017).
[14] Seitz (1998: 274).
[15] Ostry et al. (2010: 3).

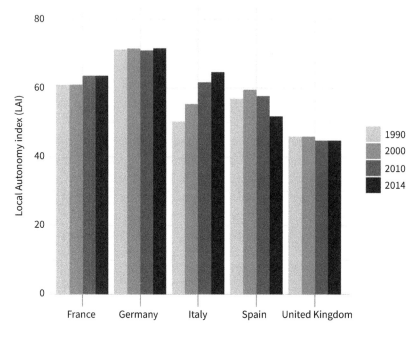

Figure 3.1   Local autonomy index by selected country, 1990–2014
Source: Ladner et al. (2021).

government for funding. Centralization exerts a profound and enduring influence upon local statecraft and its engagements with financialization.

Highly centralized governance through Parliament and Whitehall's location in London reinforced the UK's unbalanced geographical political economy, contributing to its long-standing and persistent spatial inequalities.[16] Local governments across England are marginalized due to their relational and physical distance from centralized decision-making power in the national capital.

3.2 Defining local government and its powers and functions

Addressing England in the UK, the terms 'local authority', 'local council', 'local government', and 'local state' are often used interchangeably. Terminology needs clarification of specific meanings. A local authority is an

---

[16] Martin et al. (2021).

institution legally authorized by the national government to act and undertake specific responsibilities within its territorial jurisdiction. This definition also includes combined authorities, Greater London Authority, and fire and rescue, national parks, policing, and waste authorities.[17]

The local council is the local authority's legal embodiment. It is the democratic body of representatives (councillors) elected by residents from the local area. As the full council, it decides the authority's strategy, policies, budgets, and activities within its nationally determined powers and responsibilities. Depending upon its specific arrangements, the majority political group or coalition forms the council leadership, elects a leader, and governs the use of the local authority's powers and resources. The leadership sets the priorities and is accountable democratically to local residents in their areas as voters, taxpayers, and service users. Local politicians lead a staff of appointed officers occupying legally defined and other roles, recruited to provide expert advice to political leaderships and undertake functional tasks. These politicians and officers are the local statecrafters.

Local government comprises the local authority *and* local council. Local governments *govern* rather than just administer their local areas. The local state is the widening array of bodies—public, quasi-public, private, and civic—with relationships with local government. In this local governance, local government is 'just one part of a complex organisational mosaic'.[18]

Local government is used in this book because it captures the distinctive nature of this government form at the local scale as a democratic institution with multifunctional powers, responsibilities, and resources subject to public oversight, scrutiny, and accountability. Incorporating the local statehood that characterizes local government as an economic and financial entity, this term underpins the conception of local statecraft and agency of local statecrafters in financialization to explain the case of England from 2010.

The local government system in England is 'diverse' and its geography is an historically evolved patchwork: 'it's quite hard to talk about the whole sector when there's 350 of them in different sorts of size and scale'.[19] It comprises five local government types: London boroughs; metropolitan districts; counties; districts; and unitaries. Each has specific powers, functions, resources, and geographies (Figure 3.2). Treating local government as a single homogenous entity misses these fundamental aspects that profoundly shape funding and financing strategies, capacities, and activities. These differences are integral to

[17] National Audit Office (2019a).
[18] Wilson and Game (2011: 151).
[19] Copus (2017: 8). Associate director, professional association (2020).

explaining the differentiated landscape of local statecraft and financialization across England.

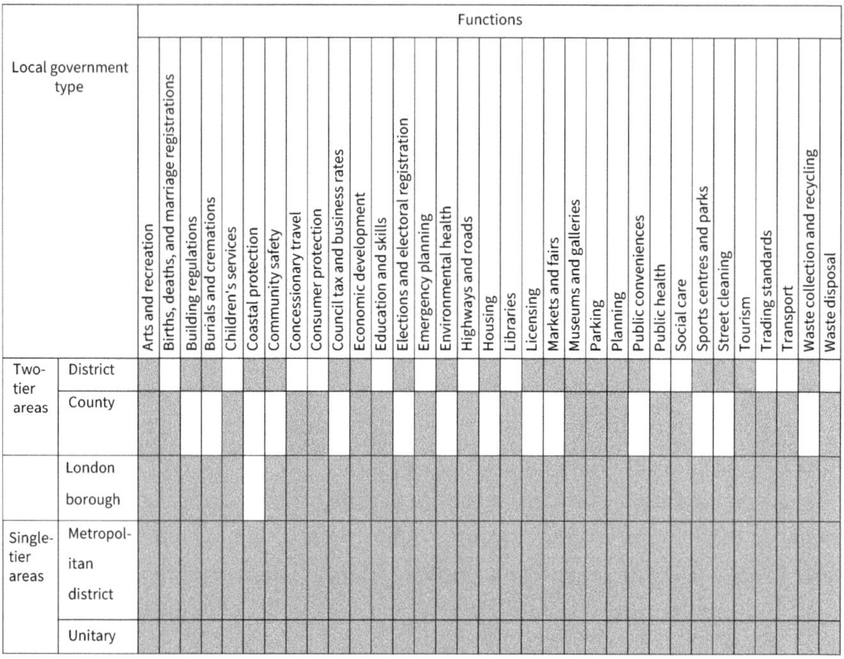

Local government type		Functions
		Arts and recreation · Births, deaths, and marriage registrations · Building regulations · Burials and cremations · Children's services · Coastal protection · Community safety · Concessionary travel · Consumer protection · Council tax and business rates · Economic development · Education and skills · Elections and electoral registration · Emergency planning · Environmental health · Highways and roads · Housing · Libraries · Licensing · Markets and fairs · Museums and galleries · Parking · Planning · Public conveniences · Public health · Social care · Sports centres and parks · Street cleaning · Tourism · Trading standards · Transport · Waste collection and recycling · Waste disposal
Two-tier areas	District	
	County	
Single-tier areas	London borough	
	Metropolitan district	
	Unitary	

Figure 3.2 Distribution of functions by local government type, 2019

Source: Adapted from Institute for Government (2021: 1).

There were 331 local governments in England in 2021.[20] The single-tier authorities comprise thirty-two London boroughs. The City of London has specific functions and is considered *sui generis*. The thirty-six metropolitan districts cover urban areas. The fifty-eight unitaries make up the rest. Isles of Scilly is the only other *sui generis* authority. The remaining two-tier arrangements comprise the twenty-four counties and 181 Districts (Table 3.1 and Figure 3.3). The lowest tier of 10,000 parish and town councils are smaller scale and uneven across England.[21]

Local governments are multifunctional organizations responsible for their local areas across economic, social, environmental, cultural, and political dimensions. Authorized by the UK Parliament through legislation, their statutory powers are threefold: compulsory and detailed (e.g. 'right to buy' for public housing tenants); permissive giving local governments autonomy to

[20] DLUHC (2021a).
[21] DLUHC (2021a).

Table 3.1 Local government types in England, 2021

Type	Number	Percentage of total
County councils	24	7
District councils	181	55
London boroughs	32	10
Metropolitan boroughs	36	11
Unitary authorities	58	17
Total	331	100

Note: Excluding *sui generis* authorities City of London
Corporation and Isles of Scilly (unitary).
Source: Department of Levelling Up, Housing and Communities
(2021a).

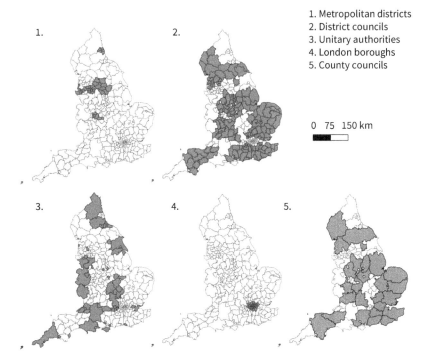

1. Metropolitan districts
2. District councils
3. Unitary authorities
4. London boroughs
5. County councils

0   75   150 km

Figure 3.3 Local governments by type, England, 2021
Note: Boundaries are based on the most recent 2021 Local Authority District (LAD)
boundaries.
Source: Ordnance Survey (2021). OS OpenData was freely downloaded under the Open
Government Licence.

decide for themselves (e.g. discretionary services); and, mixed (e.g. planning
and commissioning powers).

Local government functions are multiple and overlapping: direct service
provider (e.g. in-house delivery of local public services); owner (e.g. land,

buildings, infrastructure, companies); regulator and monitor (e.g. business registration and certification, trading standards); facilitator (e.g. lead investor in regeneration schemes); and service commissioner (e.g. outsourced service delivery from private and/or civic third parties).[22]

Local government services comprise those governed by statute and legally mandatory (e.g. adult social care). Others are discretionary meaning local statecrafters must decide to budget for them (e.g. community and leisure centres). Lacking legal requirement for their provision, these services are rationalized or withdrawn during fiscal stress.

Important service dimensions comprise: universality (e.g. street cleaning); demand-led (e.g. advice and information); eligibility or assessed need (e.g. council housing); and legislative (e.g. education)[23]. In practice, service types overlap. Adult and child social care are demand-led and based on eligibility and/or assessed need.

Local politicians are councillors directly elected for four-year terms from local constituencies (wards) comprising their local areas. Each are elected to represent the local residents' interests. They provide local knowledge and legitimacy to local government's right to levy local taxes and take decisions in locally accountable ways.[24] Outside the sixteen local governments that directly elect mayors, council leaders are indirectly elected from within the governing political group with the largest number of councillors or from coalition members.

Concerns exist that councillors' importance, voice, and oversight have been eroded in the move from committee-based to executive decision-making structures. Reorganization, especially unitarization, has reduced total councillor numbers and raised representation questions. Women and ethnic minority councillors are lacking,[25] with many councils remaining male-dominated and slow to improve gender representation.[26]

Elected politicians play a fundamental role because local government governs rather than just administers and delivers services in its local area, albeit within a national system. This local statehood dimension is integral to its local statecraft, distinguishing local statecrafters' agency from other economic and financial actors.

Local government Statutory Officers comprise the Head of Paid Service (Chief Executive), Section 151 Officer (CFO) named after the relevant section

---

[22] Wilson and Game (2011).
[23] Wilson and Game (2011).
[24] Wilson and Game (2011).
[25] Clark and Middleton (2022).
[26] Fawcett Society (2019).

in the 1972 Local Government Act, and Monitoring Officer (MO). These officers are nominally objective, neutral, and professionally qualified experts. They are responsible to the full council rather than any political leader or governing party. While recruited not elected, they must operate in a political environment, generating tensions between technocratic neutrality, rationality, and (de-)politicization.[27]

Officer roles are governed by multiple accountabilities: legal statute; professional codes; employment contracts; full council; and political leaderships. Especially for finance, the roles have highly standardized descriptions, procedures, and practices.[28] The finance or treasurer's department with a Chief Officer and their 'dominant penny-pinching role' in controlling resource allocation to spending departments has evolved.[29] A corporate shift towards CFOs is evident, requiring additional managerial skills and experience.[30] The influence and power of finance professionals has grown since the 1980s, reflecting political leaderships' increased reliance on technical fixes in fiscal stress.[31]

In addition to statutory officers, other senior staff include service department roles, including directors of education, or cross-cutting responsibilities, such as human resources. The remaining employees are typically divided into administrative, technical and clerical 'white collar' staff (e.g. finance) and manual, variously skilled, and 'blue collar' staff (e.g. housing maintenance).

3.3 Local politics

As a democratic institution that governs places in the local government system in England, politics is critical to understanding local statecraft in financialization. Reflecting the adage that 'all politics is local',[32] local politics are a distinct, but subordinated, 'microcosmos' of national politics in England.[33] As a 'Cinderella' of politics,[34] local elections receive less public interest and engagement. Average turnouts ranged between 30 per cent and 45 per cent since 1980, only matching national levels when coinciding with Parliamentary general elections.[35]

---

[27] Clarke and Cochrane (1989).
[28] Newton and Karan (1985).
[29] Clarke and Cochrane (1989: 44).
[30] Wilson and Game (2011).
[31] Clark and Cochrane (1989).
[32] O'Neill (1995).
[33] Wilson and Game (2011: 8).
[34] Clark and Middleton (2022: 84).
[35] Sandford (2020a).

'Varieties' of local politics are long-standing,[36] resulting from the interaction of historical and current national and local political agendas and concerns. Diversity has been reinforced by geographically differentiated patterns of local party organization, capacity, and competition. Variegation is increased by the continued existence and recent growth of locally oriented non-partisan independents, residents' associations, hyper-local and often single-issue political groupings, and mayoralty arrangements.[37]

Reflecting long-run 'party politicisation' from the nineteenth century,[38] local politics has become dominated by the main national political parties of right and left, Conservative and Labour. The first-past-the-post electoral system cemented their local presence.[39] Total numbers of councillors of the main parties wax and wane over time, reflecting local views on the party in power nationally. While the Liberal Democrats are a national party, by 2021 they had fewer councillors than during their peak support in the late 1990s and early 2000s.[40]

Smaller parties reflect specific interest groups. They have a long history, including the Greens, UKIP (UK Independence Party), Brexit Party, British National Party, Christian People's Alliance, English Democrats, Justice Party, and Monster Raving Loony Party. Non-party independents remain important, especially in closely contested areas and those changing political control. They reflect local interests, sometimes splintering from national party groups. Each adds to local political diversity, although their representation and voice is highly uneven across England.

There is 'great variety of practice'[41] within local government in England, and the political geography is differentiated across local governments. Conservatives have controlled the highest number of councils since the mid-2000s, followed by Labour, No Overall Control (NOC), Liberal Democrats, and Independent/Other.[42] Local politics is one of several factors shaping local statecraft's engagements with financialization. How councillors act as local statecrafters cannot, however, simply be assumed from their political party membership.

The high visibility of local service provision, direct connection with people's everyday lives, and legally required payment of local taxes forges strong and enduring relations between local populations and their local government and its funding. New financial practices and the 'councillors at the casino'

---

[36] Jones (1975: 17).
[37] Clark and Middleton (2022).
[38] Wilson and Game (2011: 317).
[39] Clark and Middleton (2022).
[40] Pilling and Cracknell (2021).
[41] Wilson and Game (2011: 309).
[42] Pilling and Cracknell (2021).

narrative of local governments taking a public services gamble with local taxpayers' money raise new issues, concerns, and tensions.

3.4 Centralization, new organizational models, reorganization, and disaggregation

Several overlapping and reinforcing processes have structured and shaped local government and its funding in England. Spreading in geographically and temporally differentiated ways, each are integral to local statecraft and its engagements with the relations and process of financialization. Centralization, first, increased national government control of local government. Shifting from municipal provision in larger cities in the nineteenth century, public services were centralized at the national level. Informed by post-1945 spatial Keynesianism,[43] integrated national systems were created to deliver fairness, minimum standards, scale economies, and efficiencies across the country.[44]

Successive national Conservative and Labour governments further centralized essential local services including education, health, housing, and infrastructure.[45] This high level of centralization generated an 'inherent tension' in central–local relations between local governments as local democratic institutions and 'arms of government' delivering local public services on 'behalf of the centre'.[46]

Local governments in England operate in one of the most highly centralized systems internationally. Centralization has continued with the local attribution of tax revenues falling from over 11 per cent to under 5 per cent between 1975 and 2017 (Table 3.2). Compared to other countries, local government's organization into over 300 relatively large units enabled national government's centralized control.

Centralization generated distinct effects and implications for the funding of local government and the wider local state. Up to 2010, centralization was interpreted as having 'diminished, but not eliminated, discretion' allowing powers in specific areas 'subject to greater national discretion, oversight and control'.[47] Local autonomy increased incrementally, specifically with the Local Government Act 2000's general well-being power, before the 2010 changes.

---

[43] Wills (2016).
[44] Travers and Esposito (2003).
[45] Campbell-Smith (2008), Copus et al. (2017), Wilson and Game (2011).
[46] Wilson and Game (2011: 38).
[47] Wilson and Game (2011: 21).

Table 3.2 Attribution of tax revenues to subsectors of general government as percentage of total tax revenue, selected unitary countries, 1975 and 2017

	Supranational		Central government		State or regional government		Local government		Social security funds	
	1975	2017	1975	2017	1975	2017	1975	2017	1975	2017
France	0.7	0.4	51.2	34.2	–	–	7.6	13.3	40.6	52.1
Italy	–	0.6	53.2	53.6	–	–	0.9	15.5	45.9	30.3
Japan	–	–	45.5	37.4	–	–	25.6	22.7	29.0	39.9
Korea	–	–	89.0	57.0	–	–	10.1	17.3	0.9	25.7
UK	1.0	0.5	70.5	75.5	–	–	11.1	4.9	17.5	19.2

Note: The total tax revenue has been reduced by the amount of any capital transfer that represents uncollected taxes.
Source: OECD (2020).

Centralization limited local statecraft's engagements with financialization since the 1990s. Pivotal was the UK House of Lords' ruling that the London Borough of Hammersmith and Fulham's pioneering use of credit default swaps was ultra vires: beyond the powers of the local authority and illegal.[48] The UK government used such experiences as 'cautionary tales',[49] underpinning the conservatism, distrust, and risk-aversion of its governing code for local governments.[50] These views persisted despite such episodes affecting relatively few local governments and generating limited longer-term financial ramifications.[51]

The legal precedent dramatically cooled financial institution interest in working with local governments to grow this market in England. This position lasted several decades before political-economic shifts unevenly changed local statecrafters and financial actors' perspectives towards a 'pro-finance, innovation bent', and they began renewing their relations and engagements.[52]

Propelled by the market-led political economy of the 1980s and later importation of NPM from the US,[53] second, local government has been subject to changing organizational models. As a creature of Parliament and national government in a highly centralized system, the centre has sought continued organizational modernization of local government. UK government distrust of local government competency and capacity

---

[48] Campbell-Smith (2008).
[49] Sandford (2017: 3).
[50] Bulpitt (1983).
[51] Sandford (2017).
[52] Fuller (2016: 91).
[53] Osborne and Gaebler (1992).

reproduced and deepened this governing code. National civil servants' 'mixture of ignorance and superiority' is interpreted as intertwined with British class snobbery and an entrenched, nationally centralized 'Whitehall knows best' mindset.[54] Such views have been formed and reinforced by national perceptions of weak local governance, corruption, and illegality.[55]

Reflecting local government's subordinate constitutional position, national government has typically deemed the status quo unacceptable and change necessary. New organizational models have embodied the UK government's ambition for more visible and accountable political leadership, streamlined and quicker decision-making, improved effectiveness and efficiency, and enhanced scrutiny and accountability.[56] Reforms from the 2000s attracted criticism, however, as undemocratic in abolishing councillor-led committee structures, returning to the cronyism and patronage of the Victorian era, reducing opportunities for public involvement and scrutiny, and encouraging privatization.[57]

Integral to new leadership and organizational models are reorganizations of local public services provision. This local NPM involved the promotion of commercial and private sector ideas of consumer choice in competitive public service markets, performance efficiency, outcomes, and quality. From the 1980s, the New Right sought to modernize what were portrayed as inefficient, costly, and inflexible local monopolies dominated by unionized labour, the political-economic project sought to roll back the local state, reduce overall public spending, shift to 'enabling not providing' through compulsory market-testing, and meet annually to let contracts to private firms.[58] A countermovement of municipal socialism concentrated in larger, Labour-run, and urban local governments aimed to rebalance central–local relations, stimulate local economies, and meet local community needs with directly employed local labour.[59]

The 1980s market-testing model evolved in the 1990s under New Labour towards the 'contracting authority' required to demonstrate 'best value' for public money rather than only lowest cost.[60] Iterations since the 2000s were around the 'commissioning authority' guided by proactive, market challenging and making principles, and direct provision.[61]

---

[54] Leach et al. (2017: 65).
[55] See, for example, Communities and Local Government Committee (2009).
[56] Newton and Karan (1985), Wilson and Game (2011).
[57] Latham (2017).
[58] Ridley (1988: 1), Newton and Karan (1985), Patterson and Pinch (1995).
[59] Cochrane (1993).
[60] Wilson and Game (2011: 25–26).
[61] Wilson and Game (2011: 25–26).

The 2003 Local Government Act enabled local governments to establish trading companies and generate revenues by selling discretionary services related to their functions to external customers. Stimulating commercialization, local statecrafters could now establish business ventures to 'trade for a profit', 'go, tentatively at first, into business', embrace an 'entrepreneurial ethos', and gain expertise.[62]

Widening the local state, reorganization encouraged innovation and more diverse local service provision models beyond only local government and stimulated growing involvement of private, public, hybrid, and civic/voluntary sector organizations.[63]

New organizational models have had profound implications for local statecraft in funding and financing. Some interpret them as a necessary precondition for financialization through providing and normalizing transparent systems and indicators that are legible to external commercial finance actors.[64] UK government modernization agendas emphasized the local political leadership's responsibility to ensure accountable, transparent, and effective financial decision-making. Demonstrating local statehood, local statecrafters have continuously to prove their efficient public money management and local public services provision in market settings. It has become increasingly important that they show they can operate in more entrepreneurial and commercially oriented ways.

Reorganization, third, has been central to UK governments' local government modernization agendas. Key rationales are removing the complexities and costs of two-tier systems and consolidating local government into fewer, larger units with increased potential for scale economies, efficiencies, and cost savings in national policy and service delivery.[65]

Critics question the economic rationales for changes over local accountability and democracy, the local centralization generated by increased size and distance from local populations, the lack of meaningful fit of new areas with local attachments and identities, the reduction in the number of councillors, and continued dominance of national political parties.[66]

Following major reorganization in the early 1970s, national government pursued an ad hoc approach, creating a patchwork governance geography, mainly through introducing unitary or single-tier structures—unitarization—at the county level.[67] Reorganization has occurred in phases linked to national legislation (Table 3.3). Since 2010, reorganizations have

[62] Carr (2012: 10, 16, 17; 2015).
[63] CIPFA (2019).
[64] Deruytter and Möller (2020).
[65] Sandford (2021a).
[66] Copus et al. (2017), Copus (2017), Leach et al. (2017).
[67] Copus (2017).

Table 3.3 Local government reorganizations in England, 1963–

Act	Changes
London Government Act 1963	Established Greater London Council (GLC) and 32 London boroughs
Local Government Act 1972	Reduced 45 counties to 39 Replaced 1086 urban and rural districts with 296 district councils Abolished 79 county borough councils Created six metropolitan county councils Replaced 1,212 councils with 378
Local Government Act 1985	Abolished six metropolitan county councils and the GLC
Local Government Act 1992	Results in: 34 county councils; 36 metropolitan borough councils; 238 districts; 46 unitary councils
2009 reorganization under the provisions of the 1992 Act New unitaries since 2009	Reduced 44 councils to 9 across 7 English county areas Bournemouth, Christchurch and Poole: reduces 3 councils to 1 (2019)
Merged districts post-2009	Dorset: reduces 7 councils to 1 (2019) Buckinghamshire: reduces 5 councils to 1 (2020) West Northamptonshire: reduces 4 councils to 1 (includes the county) (2020)
	North Northamptonshire: reduces 5 councils to 1 (includes the county) (2020) Somerset West and Taunton: reduces 2 councils to 1 (2019) East Suffolk: reduces 2 councils to 1 (2019) West Suffolk: reduces 2 councils to 1 (2019) Cumbria: reduces 6 councils to 2 (2021) North Yorkshire: reduces 8 councils to 1 (2021) Somerset: reduces 4 councils to 1 (2021) Essex, Gloucestershire, Hampshire, Hertfordshire, Lancashire, Leicestershire, Lincolnshire, Nottinghamshire, Oxfordshire, Surrey, Warwickshire: Ongoing (2021–)

Source: Adapted from Copus (2017) and Sandford (2020a, 2021a).

been part of the decentralization of powers and resources and grouping of single-tier areas into combined authorities. The main reasons have been government policy or local initiative rather than local economy, geography, or identity.[68]

Reducing the number of local governments has been the UK government's central aim: from 540 principal councils in 1994, 434 in 2009, and 331 in 2021.[69] Average population size increased above Continental European levels, raising questions about political representation and legitimacy.[70]

[68] Sandford (2020a).
[69] Copus (2017), Wilson and Game (2011).
[70] Sandford (2021a).

Funding and financing are integral to reorganization. Efficiencies are expected from integrating decision-making into streamlined organizations covering larger areas and populations and reducing councillor numbers.[71] Reorganization opens up new opportunities for local statecraft including borrowing against larger asset and tax bases at favourable interest rates and terms, articulating stronger economic growth prospects, and connecting disadvantaged with advantaged places in functional economic areas.

Last, since the 1970s, the local state in England has grown through dis-aggregation. The UK government established special purpose bodies with powers and resources at arm's-length or wholly outside local government aiming to improve the formulation of policy, decision-making, resource use, and delivery of functions and/or services.

Reflecting NPM ideas, quangos increased and 'quangoization' extended.[72] Their centrally and nationally appointed, rather than locally elected, leadership and management have been dubbed the 'quangocracy' and the 'quango state'.[73] Raising questions about where accountability and decision-making power reside, it represents a particularly English and local form of post-democratic governance.[74]

Quangos were interpreted as furthering the UK government's central control and deliberate introduction of alternative institutions to bypass or marginalize local government and local democratic accountability. Demonstrating their role, national government categorizes quangos as non-departmental public bodies (NDPBs). Their introduction overlaps centralization when the new bodies have national rather than local objectives, funding, and accountabilities. Disaggregation imparted a particular character to local state growth and extension in England. The range of organizations and their powers, resources, and geographies has expanded since the 1980s, especially in education, health, housing, skills, and transport.[75]

New bodies established by the UK government have been joined by increasing numbers of entities created by local statecrafters. Local government has established companies, joint ventures, public–private partnerships (PPPs), arm's-length, and wholly owned public and private companies. Relations with this widening array of organizations making up the local state have become increasingly complex and important to local statecraft.

---

[71] Sandford (2021a).
[72] Skelcher et al. (2000).
[73] Wilson and Game (2011: 19), Skelcher et al. (2000).
[74] Crouch (2004).
[75] McCarthy (2018).

Fragmentation and varying geographies have, however, created problems of coordination and joint working in certain places.

This expanding local state is integral to local statecraft. Certain bodies were established, controlled, and funded by UK government departments. New funding channels were deliberately established outside of local government control and influence. Other bodies are business- or private sector–led and claimed to be more agile, efficient, and flexible.[76] They are purportedly more business-friendly than bureaucratic, rigid, and slow local government and able to attract and secure private sector engagement and investment.

Institutional innovations in the wider local state are one way the door has been opened to financial and other external actors and their importation of commercial finance into their organizations and local government. Growing numbers of local state organizations have introduced competitors to local government for national government funding and financing from external financial institutions.

3.5 Funding and financing local government

Funding and financing arrangements determine the scope and nature of local statecraft and any financialization, structuring and shaping local state-crafters' autonomies, resources, and accountabilities. The long-standing and highly centralized system in England and its historically incremental, layered evolution means its 'enduring feature' is its 'complexity'.[77]

From the 1940s, three main 'meta-narratives' broadly characterize changes in local government in England: 'the sovereign council'; 'new public management' (NPM); and 'network governance'.[78] Each has distinctive features across a range of dimensions, including funding and financing (Table 3.4).

While undergoing mostly incremental change, the local government funding system has been punctuated by episodes of more radical shifts. Annual and ad hoc fixes are recurrent for acknowledged as well as emergent, politically salient dysfunctions at certain times. Persistent issues include the (mis)matching of resources with responsibilities, centralization and tighter controls, circumscribed autonomy and increased national minister and civil servant involvement, and debate over what is raised and spent locally and centrally.[79]

---

[76] Carr (2015).
[77] CIPFA (2019: iii).
[78] Copus et al. (2017: 47).
[79] Copus et al. (2017).

Table 3.4 Local government policy narratives in England, 1940s–

Dimensions	The sovereign council	Policy narratives	
		New public management	Network governance
Timing Political economy	Mid-1940s to early 1980s Local welfare state	Late 1970s and 1980s– 'Rolling back' and reforming the local state Private sector managerialism Controlling and limiting local government expenditure	1990s– Shift from local government to local governance involving public, private, and civic sectors
Guiding principles	Universalism Public service Citizen service users	Economic rationalism Market-based reform Value for money, quality, and choice Service customers	Networks and partnerships Pragmatism and post-ideological 'what works' Exchanging resources, negotiating shared purposes Trust
Central–local relations	Degree of local autonomy within centralized national system	Nationally controlled and regulated market-based reform within centralized system	Negotiated within centrally orchestrated national system
Politics	Locally sovereign Democratically legitimate	National command and control Local subordinate	Indirect and imperfect steering of networks Post-political and post-democratic 'governing without government'
Accountability	Democratically accountable to local voters and taxpayers	National government via performance indicators, inspection, and league tables Unclear, blurred accountability amongst multiple public, private, and civic actors	For outcomes within self-organizing networks Unclear, blurred accountability amongst multiple public, private, and civic actors

Organizational and service provision models	Locally sovereign providing services to citizens Direct, in-house service provision	Commissioners, coordinators Purchaser–provider relations Indirect, outsourced service provision	Local government as one actor amongst many in the local state Enabler, broker Diversified, hybrid in-house, outsourced, and mixed
Funding and financing	Centralized Local innovations to circumvent national restrictions	Centralized Spending assessments and controls Local innovations to cope with national controls Vanguard experimentation until Hammersmith and Fulham swaps affair	Centralized with later elements of localization Local innovations differentiated by local government
Critique (sub narratives)	Bureaucratic ('Bureaucracy gone mad', 'Political correctness gone mad') Ineffective, inefficient Incompetent ('Dangerously incompetent', 'Chronically failing') Monolithic Isolationist and unresponsive ('only democratically accountable at local election time') Corrupt ('Rotten borough') Change and innovation averse ('Stick-in-the-mud')	'Hollowing out' and privatizing the local state ('Selling off the family silver') Presumption of private sector efficiency ('private good, public bad') Fragmentation of service provision Internal rather than external organizational focus Increased complexity and system gaming Growth of quangos and 'quangocracy' Loss of local democratic accountability ('democratic deficit')	Loss of local government control, assets, and revenue streams Utopian ideal of 'governing without government' and trust Neglect of embedded power and institutionalized relationships Lack of accountability of self-organizing networks and democratic deficit Limited empirical evidence

Source: Copus et al. (2017), Newton and Karan (1985), Unlock Democracy (2021), and Wilson and Game (2011).

Integral to its local statehood and statecraft, local government funding is politicized nationally and locally because of its proximity and accountability to people as local voters, local public services users, and residents living in places and paying local taxes.[80] Local statecrafters have legal responsibilities for their financial affairs and a principal accountability to their local electorates.[81]

3.5.1 The national system of local government funding

The centralized system of UK government funding for local government persists for several reasons. Local government is required to provide services of 'importance to the nation as a whole' of a similar range and level 'at broadly the same cost to local taxpayers across the country'.[82] Providing subsidies to local taxpayers and contributions to service provision costs and capital expenditure, UK government funding underpins its influence over local government expenditure and implementation of national policies. The nationally integrated system enables resource redistribution between areas with different economic and social conditions across England. Given local government's size, the UK government controls its total expenditure and borrowing as part of overall national public finance management.

The UK finance minister the Chancellor of the Exchequer provides the political lead for national economic policy and public expenditure through annual budgets and spending reviews. HMT sets the level of Total Managed Expenditure (TME). Public expenditure is then controlled through two totals. For planned items, Departmental Expenditure Limits (DEL) cover resource or revenue expenditure on public services, grants, administration, and investment or capital spending.[83] Items less amenable to multi-year planning comprise Annual Managed Expenditure (AME), including welfare payments and interest on borrowing shaped by economic cycles. Local government also funds revenue and capital expenditure from local sources, mainly local property taxes. This item is Local Authority Self-Financed Expenditure (LASFE) and is included in HMT's AME calculation.

Operationalizing the centralized system, HMT sets a control total that is the 'overall public spending envelope [national government] decides should be spent by local government.'[84] This total is then adjusted by any specific

---

[80] Wilson and Game (2011).
[81] Sandford (2020b).
[82] CIPFA (2019: 5).
[83] Office of Budget Responsibility (2021).
[84] CIPFA (2019: 24).

grants added to or subtracted from core funding to provide an aggregate start-up funding assessment. Following consultation on a provisional version, the UK government then agrees the typically annual finance settlement for local government. Demonstrating its sovereignty, this settlement must then be approved by Parliament.

3.5.2 Budgeting and the balanced budget

Within the national settlement, each local government's political leadership must propose an annual budget and secure support of a majority in its full council. A specified process is followed based on the identification of a budgeting requirement. This procedure involves calculation of estimated expenditure to discharge its functions less various income sources. The budget requirement is then divided by the residential property tax base, comprising the number and type of properties in its area, to provide the required council tax (CT) charge.[85]

Estimated expenditure must include all costs the local government incurs. This comprises the revenue budgets for service delivery, borrowing to pay for capital investment, and contributions to other local service providers including paying levies to fire and rescue authorities.

Demonstrating the required prudent stewardship of public funds and risk management, the budget must make provisions for liabilities incurred with unknown amounts and timing, including pending court cases and associated award costs, and contingencies to cope with unforeseen events, including higher than budgeted inflation.[86]

Rather than a mundane and routine local government finance activity, budget setting is central to local statecraft as a 'financial representation of the council's policies'.[87] Demonstrating the local statehood underpinning local politicians and officers' statecraft within a highly centralized national system in England, the budget expresses their answers to questions of what and how much to spend and how to pay for it. As a democratically accountable public institution, for local government budget decisions including 'whether to subsidise a particular service, by how much and in what way, or whether to try to maximise profit—raise fundamental political questions'.[88] Incorporating technical financial issues, local statecraft is underpinned by local statehood,

---

[85] Sandford (2020b).
[86] CIPFA (2019).
[87] CIPFA (2019: 50).
[88] Wilson and Game (2011: 218).

inherently political, and inhabits a distinctive position interrelating national and local municipal finance.

Contrasting the private sector, councillors and officers cannot have personal investments or equity in their local governments. They are 'freed from personal financial risk when being entrepreneurial (although there is always political risk)'.[89]

In theory, budgeting is integrated with overall strategic planning. Through internal financial control, the budget is monitored, scrutinized, and overseen by the relevant finance or policy committee and the full council. Major financial decisions including agreeing the annual budget, setting the CT, and introducing any precept require majority approval.

The legislative framework requires local governments to set a balanced budget with forecast expenditure matched with income. Importantly, reduced income translates into reduced expenditure. It is 'illegal for an authority to budget for a deficit'.[90] This 'balancing act' has long-standing public finance management roots.[91] Such institutionalization of the limits on local government budgeting and statecraft are integral to the UK government's financial control in central–local relations.[92]

Local government is legally required to report 'if the budget fails to balance'.[93] Section 114 of the Local Government Act 1988 requires the accounting officer to inform the full council 'if there is, or is likely to be, unlawful expenditure or an unbalanced budget'.[94] If a Section 114 report is issued, the local government cannot incur any new expenditure commitments and the full council is required to meet to consider the report, although there are no legal requirements on what actions must be taken.[95] Such reports are usually only 'issued in the gravest of circumstances and when all other options have been exhausted'.[96]

3.5.3 Expenditure

A key distinction is between revenue and capital. The revenue budget is spent on running local public services. It includes staff wages and pensions, property, transport operational costs, and paying goods and services suppliers.

---

[89] Singla et al. (2018: 773–774).
[90] CIPFA (2019: 63).
[91] Bartley Hildreth (1996: 320).
[92] Sbragia (1996).
[93] CIPFA (2019: 67).
[94] CIPFA (2019: 140).
[95] Sandford (2020c).
[96] CIPFA (2019: 67).

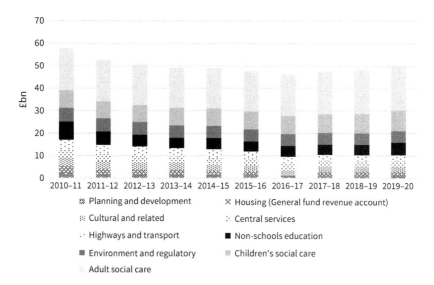

Figure 3.4 Revenue expenditure by service, 2010–11 to 2019–20

Note: Net of sales, fees, and charges. Real terms in 2019–20 prices.
Source: National Audit Office (2021a).

Many revenue expenditure items are commitments relating to statutory and contractual obligations.[97] These include previous policy decisions, salary increments, pay awards, and inflation. Revenue budgets also comprise items related to financing in the capital budget, including interest costs on borrowing. Reflecting its multiple functions and responsibilities, local government expenditures are numerous. Across local governments, total revenue expenditure in 2019–20 was around £100 billion.[98] Service expenditure since 2010 was increasingly dominated by adult and children's social care (Figure 3.4).

The capital budget is expenditure on investment in capital goods: 'physical assets that have a useful life of more than one year'.[99] This includes buildings, infrastructure, and vehicles. Reflecting the highly centralized system and only with the UK Secretary of State's permission, the capital budget also covers substantial one-off expenditures including equal pay claims and statutory redundancy costs. Capital expenditure is financed through internal (including revenues, reserves, and capital receipts) and external sources (including borrowing).

---

[97] CIPFA (2019).
[98] MHCLG (2020b).
[99] CIPFA (2019: 30).

Integral to its local statecraft, capital expenditure is a 'key part of an authority's overarching corporate strategy'.[100] It expresses the local statecrafters' strategic and longer-term ambitions for their area by providing investment for its local economic and social infrastructure. Capital expenditure has remained around £25 billion annually since 2010.[101] It is focused on housing services and highways and transport, although trading services have grown since 2015–16 following commercialization (Figure 3.5). Customer-first local public service provision models from the 2000s focused capital expenditure on improving service accessibility and quality and reducing costs.[102]

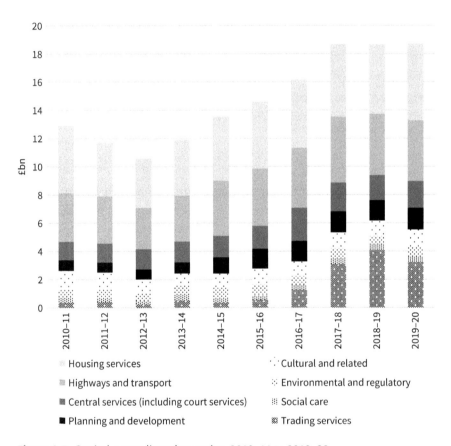

Figure 3.5 Capital expenditure by service, 2010–11 to 2019–20

Note: Real terms in 2019–20 prices.
Source: National Audit Office (2021a).

[100] CIPFA (2019: 30).
[101] MHCLG (2020b).
[102] Wilson and Game (2011).

Reflecting the UK government's centralized view of local government as low politics and shifts from the sovereign council to networked governance (Table 3.4), relations between revenue and capital expenditure have changed since the 1960s. The UK government historically exerted increasing control over local capital expenditure, introducing limits and leaving a legacy of underinvestment. The revenue to capital expenditure ratio was less than 2:1 in the 1960s, 3:1 in the 1970s, 5:1 in the 1980s, 8:1 in the 1990s, and reached 12:1 in the 2000s.[103] Mechanisms used included controls on overall capital expenditure levels, credit approvals for borrowing, and limits on capital receipts use from asset sales.

Since the early 2000s, the UK government reduced direct control of local capital expenditure and increased local autonomies and responsibilities. The capital budget is now governed by CIPFA's Prudential Code for Capital Finance (the Prudential Code). This framework was designed to ensure such plans are 'prudent, affordable and sustainable without the need for external control'.[104]

3.5.4 Income

Reflecting its multiple functions and the system's complex evolution, income is from a range of sources. Since 2010, UK government grants have been dramatically reduced, local taxes on residential property (CT) and commercial property (national non-domestic rates (NNDR) or business rates) increased, while commercial and selected other income (including fees and charges) remained relatively small scale and grew only modestly despite commercialization (Figure 3.6).

UK government grant reductions increased local statecrafter reliance upon local property taxes and other revenue sources, especially commercial and investment activities. This dependence created a gearing effect on budgeting. Whereby even 1 per cent budget increases would need unauthorized and politically challenging 4–5 per cent increases in CT.[105]

UK government grants are long-standing, underpinning centralized objectives and transfers to local governments in England. Grant allocation mechanisms include automatic, formula driven, discretionary, and competitive bid–based. Like determinations of overall expenditure and integral to local statecraft, for the UK government: 'grant distribution formulae are not

---

[103] Wilson and Game (2011).
[104] CIPFA (2019: 37).
[105] Wilson and Game (2011).

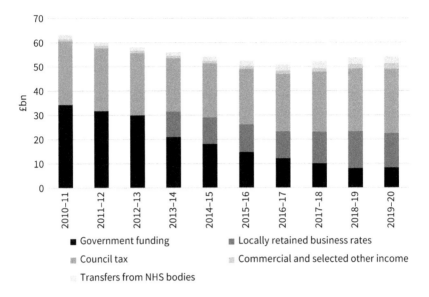

Figure 3.6 Selected main revenue income sources, 2010–11 to 2019–20

Note: Real terms in 2019–20 prices.
Source: National Audit Office (2021a).

value-neutral mathematical equations, but strings of weighted factors and indicators, almost every one of which has political, and usually party political, implications.'[106]

Different grant types embody UK government aims, including revenue to cover running costs and capital to support investment. The revenue support grant (RSG) was the main formula grant, affording local government some autonomy in its use. RSG was allocated by a model informed by local indicators including population and deprivation.[107] It aimed to compensate local governments with demographic, social, and economic characteristics that required higher levels of services and local property tax bases which limited revenues.

Other grants are ring-fenced, reflecting UK government priorities and circumscribing local discretion. These grants require expenditure in predetermined service areas, including education and housing. Such grants mean local government 'acts essentially as a local post office, passing on central government funding to recipients, as instructed from Whitehall.'[108] Some grants are compensation for service provision in the wider public interest,

---

[106] Wilson and Game (2011: 220).
[107] CIPFA (2019).
[108] Wilson and Game (2011: 215).

reducing financial claims upon local taxpayers. Varying geographically in their allocation, these include asylum-seeker support, mental health services, and rural bus subsidies.

The UK government retains powers to give grants to local governments for any purpose.[109] These Section 31 grants, under the Local Government Act 2003, are used to ensure local governments are not disadvantaged by funding system changes or to address priority or emergency shortfalls, including adult social care and pandemic response.

Local government receives grants from other sources. These are often allocated by the widening array of bodies in the local state, adding to income source complexity. They include various economic development and regeneration agencies and, prior to Brexit, European institutions.

Additional grants and contributions are received from third parties within and beyond the local state mostly for specific projects. These include NDPBs. Leaseholders pay local governments as the lessor. Charitable and philanthropic organizations provide grants. Public and/or private developers make contributions to community costs (Section 106 Agreements) and/or pay localized taxes (e.g. Community Infrastructure Levy (CIL)) related to planning permission and obligations.

Local property taxes are a source of income after grants. As CT since 1993, residential property tax is 'collected from residents within a council's area based on the value of the property they live in'.[110] The CT level is set annually by the billing authority as the 'final residual outcome' once the other elements of expenditure and income are known.[111] This local tax has been subject to UK government controls to limit increases, moving from often politically motivated discretionary and selective to mandatory and universal budget and rate-capping. While such 'crude and universal' controls were abolished in 1999, the UK Secretary of State retains powers to introduce limits.[112]

Accounting for almost a third of total annual income, CT revenues are dependent on the structure and value of local properties and local taxpayers in a centrally controlled system. Further, the tax is based upon 'drive-by' or 'second-gear' valuations from 1991, so-called to characterize the approximate property assessments undertaken by local estate agents.[113] Property values and potential tax revenues have since increased, often in nominal and real

[109] Sandford (2020b).
[110] CIPFA (2019: 9).
[111] Wilson and Game (2011: 224).
[112] CIPFA (2019: 16).
[113] Wilson and Game (2011: 223).

terms, differentially across England. While potentially increasing local tax revenues following any revaluation, raising CT bills for residents has made this politically difficult for successive UK governments and been deferred.

The second local property tax is on commercial properties introduced in 1990. The national non-domestic rate—or uniform business rate—is based on the rateable value of the premises occupied. This value is calculated by how much the premises would cost to rent out. The national Valuation Office Agency undertakes five-yearly valuations. Reflecting the centralized system, the bill is calculated by local government through applying the 'rate multiplier'—set by the UK government as a rate in the pound—to the rateable value and subtracting any assistance including transitional relief between valuations.[114]

Replacing more localized arrangements, this England-wide system redistributes revenues between areas. Higher business rate revenue local governments pay a tariff into a national pot which covers top-ups to those with relatively lower business rates.[115] This transfer provided a 'safety net mechanism' between areas with more and less valuable and buoyant commercial property markets and local economies, and insulated them against reductions in business rate income from business cycle downturns or economic shocks.[116]

Accounting for almost a fifth of total income, business rates are an important funding source. When introduced, the national system was interpreted as breaking the direct linkage between local taxpayers and local government.[117] The close relationship of business rates with local economic and commercial property market conditions and the size and value of commercial property tax bases made them a focus for change since 2010. Valuations have been more regular than for residential properties, most recently in 2017. As a local tax on business, it is similarly politically sensitive at local and national levels.

The remaining income sources constitute smaller proportions of the total. Local government has powers to set fees and charges for local services including parking. Some rates are nationally controlled, others offer local autonomy. Changes are evident from historic national requirements not to exceed service provision costs. Some local statecrafters 'choose to set charges for some services by reference to what the market will bear, rather than the cost of provision, in order to hold down the council tax or pay for the development

---

[114] CIPFA (2019: 17).
[115] Sandford (2020b).
[116] CIPFA (2019: 23).
[117] Wilson and Game (2011: 220).

of other services'.[118] Politics are often decisive in local government positions, often producing similar outcomes for different reasons. Conservative-led councils desire low levels to demonstrate small state principles, while Labour-led councils seek to protect vulnerable residents from increased charges.

As UK government grants were reduced and local property taxes remained subject to national control, local statecrafters have been forced to generate revenues from other sources. Introduced and gathering pace from the 1990s, commercialization promoted income generation activities by selling services, establishing trading companies, and more actively managing balance sheets to raise revenues from their assets.[119]

Given the nature of commercial trading activities, local governments were required to decide how much surpluses (positive net revenues minus costs) and deficits (negative net revenues minus costs) were allowed, and how surpluses would be used and deficits recovered.[120] The concept and language signal an important difference between municipal and commercial finance: 'The word "surplus" is used instead of "profit" in not-for-profit organisations such as councils.'[121]

Linked to budgeting, commercialization, and more active financial management, treasury management activities have faced income generation pressures. In municipal finance, treasury management administers the organization's cash flows, including transactions with banks, money, and capital markets, in pursuit of 'optimum performance' and management of associated risks.[122] Historically focused on managing cash to meet day-to-day running costs and borrowing, treasury management has had to become more strategic and focused on generating returns. Often engaging commercial finance actors, this new approach includes switching cash deposits between banks to earn more favourable interest rates and refinancing debt.

Another growing income source is local government borrowing. Borrowing and debt management have become an increasingly central realm in local statecraft and financial strategies, especially for the capital budget and its associated revenue costs. The Prudential Code focused local statecrafters on outcomes rather than inputs to encourage 'responsibility by forcing a council to consider value for money, its future revenue streams, and council tax implications at the time of borrowing, in a way that Credit Approvals [from the national government Minister] did not'.[123] Local governments cannot legally borrow to cover annual revenue expenditure. Borrowing is

---

[118] CIPFA (2019: 54).
[119] Carr (2015).
[120] CIPFA (2019).
[121] CIPFA (2019: 75).
[122] CIPFA (2019: 82).
[123] Wilson and Game (2011: 210).

only allowed for periods over one year for capital expenditure.[124] Borrowing to invest in assets to generate returns has grown in importance.

3.5.5 Balance sheets

Expressing its historical financial decisions and condition, local government balance sheets are integral to local statecraft's financial management and budgeting. The top half reports assets and liabilities (including provisions) with other parties. Contrary to commercial finance, where assets are equal to liabilities plus equity, local governments 'do not have equity'.[125] As a distinctive feature of local statehood, external financial actors can invest *with* but not *in* local government to acquire ownership shares. The bottom half of the balance sheet reports reserves which are equal to its net worth and categorized as useable and unusable. Crucially, 'for the balance sheet to balance, the sum of the reserves must equal the council's total assets less liabilities.'[126]

Assets are entities that can be valued, generate future benefits, and are owned by the local government.[127] With the rise of public asset management approaches since the 2000s, the identification and more active management of assets have increased. Given their historical roles and locally embedded responsibilities, local governments are often relatively asset-rich but cash-poor. They hold assets—including land and property—that are valued. They sit on balance sheets with potential to generate future benefits, including revenue streams, as well as liabilities or future obligations, including claims against these assets. Such balances have been critical in shaping local state-crafters' strategies for dealing with incumbent assets. Capital receipts are the proceeds from asset sales and one-off income sources. Such revenues are shaped by economic conditions and asset valuations, varying geographically and temporally across England. Use of proceeds is nationally controlled.

Liabilities are future obligations, including claims against assets and legal requirements for payment from their owners.[128] They include known claims such as contributions to the Local Government Pension Scheme and provisions for liabilities of uncertain timing or amount such as equal pay claims.

Balances for local government are effectively reserves. Determined nationally, reserves are either useable for expenditure or unusable. The purpose,

---

[124] Sandford (2020b).
[125] CIPFA (2019: 56).
[126] CIPFA (2019: 56).
[127] CIPFA (2019).
[128] CIPFA (2019).

usage, and basis of transactions for every reserve must be identified.[129] Reflecting longer-term financial sustainability, reserves can only be used once and require replenishment.

Reserves are of three main kinds. Working balances manage cash flow, avoid temporary borrowing, and cover service department and business/trading unit finances. Contingency reserves are for unexpected events or emergencies, including disaster responses alongside the financial assistance from the national Bellwin Scheme. Earmarked reserves are identified to accumulate funds for known or predicted requirements, including capital projects. Other reserves relate to legislative requirements and accounting standards, including pensions, revaluations, and financial instruments.

Managing balances and reserves—the local government's accumulated financial resources—is integral to budgeting. This area includes the management of cash and cash flows. Following CFO advice, the full council has a statutory duty to decide what is deemed an 'appropriate' level of general reserves according to their local financial circumstances.[130] Shaped by multiple factors over time, there is 'no theoretically right level' or 'generally applicable minimum level'.[131]

Reflecting the centralized system and constrained scope for local statecraft, under 'the promotion of local autonomy' in the Local Government Act 2003, the local council has the 'financial freedom' to set their reserves level.[132] However, this legislation also gives the UK Secretary of State power to intervene and set a local government's reserves levels if it is deemed not to be acting 'prudently, disregards the advice of its CFO and is heading for serious financial difficulty'.[133] Demonstrating local statecraft's distinctive nature, the CFO has a 'fiduciary duty to local taxpayers, and must be satisfied that the decisions taken on balances and reserves represent proper stewardship of public funds'.[134]

3.5.6 Accountability

Matching the funding system, arrangements for the accountability of public funding between national and local government in England are 'complex'.[135] The system involves multiple organizations with different roles at different

---

[129] CIPFA (2019).
[130] CIPFA (2019: 56).
[131] CIPFA (2019: 56, 60).
[132] CIPFA (2019: 60).
[133] CIPFA (2019: 60).
[134] CIPFA (2019: 56).
[135] National Audit Office (2019a: 4).

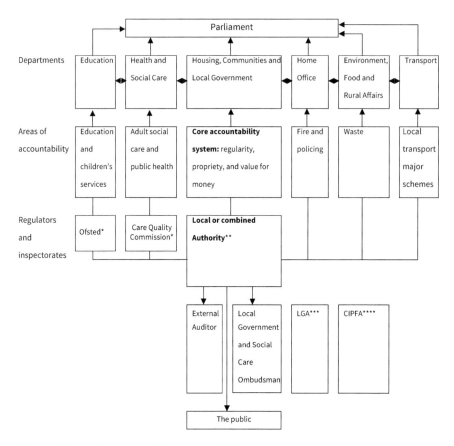

Figure 3.7 Local accountability system, 2020

Notes: *The roles of the regulators and inspectorates differ in scope.
**Ultimate accountability lies with the full council, elected mayor, or governing body.
***The Local Government Association (LGA) provides peer challenge and support to local governments, but they are not accountable to the LGA.
****CIPFA produces statutory codes, professional accreditation, training, and mentoring for public finance professionals.
Source: Adapted from National Audit Office (2019a, 2019b).

levels and numerous accountabilities (Figure 3.7). Central is the department's relationship to Parliament in its responsibility for funding through its own accountability system. This includes the monitoring framework and financial reporting covering relevant organizations in the wider local state.[136]

Within local governments, the political leader and group are ultimately accountable through the full council and, as locally elected councillors, to local residents, taxpayers, and voters. Decisions are monitored, overseen, and scrutinized by finance and audit committees, chaired by members of the

---

[136] Sandford (2020b).

political leadership, and including opposition councillors. Public disclosure requirements enable member and public oversight and scrutiny.

The CFO is the officer 'responsible for the legal and financially prudent administration of the council's affairs.'[137] Historically termed the treasurer, the CFO must be a professionally trained and qualified public finance accountant. While relatively well-paid, the CFO is an employee and 'servant' of the council with a fiduciary responsibility to local taxpayers.[138]

The CFO is subject to multiple accountabilities. In addition to the accountability system between national and local government, there are specific legal frameworks governing powers, regulations, and accounting directions.[139] CIPFA is the standard setter for England, Northern Ireland, and Wales. While the International Accounting Standards Board (IASB) rules were designed for private sector use as the International Financial Reporting Standards (IFRS), the United Kingdom (UK) government adopted them in 2007 for the public sector as 'best practice' and to enable international comparison.[140] The rules have been adapted for local government use in the annually updated CIPFA Code of Practice on Local Authority Accounting in the UK.

A further layer of accountability is provided by the legally required annual internal and external audits of local government finances[141]. Internal audit requires councillors to maintain financial control systems overseen by the council's audit committee. Formerly undertaken by the Audit Commission's units until its abolition in 2012 and the liberalization and opening up of a local audit market by the UK government, external auditors are appointed to provide opinions on reports and accounts and value for money.

3.6 Conclusions

Fundamentally determining the distinctive local statehood underpinning local statecraft, subordinate constitutional status and highly centralized control by the UK government define local government in England. Local government has, however, evolved through the overlapping 'meta-narratives' from the 'sovereign council' through NPM to 'networked governance.'[142] Key processes have configured local government and widened the

---

[137] Wilson and Game (2011: 105).
[138] Wilson and Game (2011).
[139] CIPFA (2019).
[140] CIPFA (2019: 68).
[141] Sandford (2019).
[142] Copus et al. (2017).

local state: centralization; new organizational models; reorganization; and disaggregation.

Different local government types with varying powers, resources, capacities, locations, and politics across England constitute an inherently diverse system. Funding and financing are complex, fragmented, and highly centralized for budgeting, expenditure, income, and balance sheets. A highly technical and convoluted system has evolved, shaped by close interrelations between national government actors and local statecrafters.

The geographical and historical political economy of local government and the local state fundamentally structures and shapes local statehood and local statecraft in its engagements with financialization. Reflecting UK government management of central–local relations, funding and financing experiments and innovations punctuate local government's history as local statecrafters sought to exert their autonomies.[143]

---

[143] Sbragia (1996).

4

Local government financial strategies amidst austerity, centralization, and risk

4.0 Introduction

Following the 2008 crash, the newly elected Conservative and Liberal Democrat coalition government pursued austerity from 2010. Senior ministers convened to decide expenditure reductions. Former Conservative leader of Bradford City Council, then UK Secretary of State, Eric Pickles volunteered the highest level of cutbacks for local government. Signalling his modus operandi and echoing 1980s rhetoric, rationales were articulated of 'unsustainable growth, unsustainable public finance', 'big government', 'waste', financial mismanagement, and the need for greater local transparency and public scrutiny.[1] Reproducing historically entrenched low politics, the highly centralized system and distrust of local government by UK government ministers and civil servants meant such reductions were deemed appropriate and implementable.

Illuminating local government financial strategies and activities provides the setting for financialization and local statecraft in England since 2010. This conjuncture is marked by austerity, localism, local financial self-sufficiency, and funding gaps. Local statecrafters' financial strategies moved towards more active and strategic risk management, challenging the depictions of 'councillors at the casino' as a partial explanation.

Looking beyond the high-profile and novel activities, local statecrafters formulated new expenditure and income generation strategies. Financial resilience, sustainability, and financial failure governance have become critical. The missing overview of financialization and local statecraft across England since 2010 outlines a differentiated landscape of vanguard, intermediate, and long-tail approaches amongst local governments.

[1] Quoted in Crewe (2016: 9).

Financialization and Local Statecraft. Andy Pike, Oxford University Press. © Andy Pike (2023).
DOI: 10.1093/oso/9780192856661.003.0004

4.1 Austerity, localism and local financial self-sufficiency, and funding gaps since 2010

The period since 2010 is distinctive in local government and its funding in England. Originating in the collapse of financial innovations in mortgage lending in the US that triggered a banking sector liquidity crunch, the global financial crisis of 2008 generated an economic shock and recession unprecedented since the 1930s.

As a liberal market and highly financialized political economy, the UK was especially impacted.[2] Hit by a sharp economic contraction, the UK government responded with increased borrowing, and stabilization and recapitalization of the banking system through short-term loans, guarantees, state-backed insurance, and partial and wholesale nationalizations.[3] The crash occurred during Gordon Brown's Labour government, and a general election followed in 2010.

4.1.1 Austerity

The coalition government's diagnosis of the UK's predicament blamed the Labour government's high-tax, high-debt, and high-spending strategy rather than the global financial crisis. Then Conservative Chancellor George Osborne argued Labour had left the country 'living beyond its means', risking a Greek-style debt default and collapse in economic confidence, concluding 'unless we deal with our debts there will be no growth'.[4] This interpretation underpinned fiscal consolidation as the national economic policy priority.[5] Narrating Labour wastefulness and imminent fiscal crisis, Osborne introduced an Emergency Budget and Spending Review in 2010. It aimed to reduce the deficit and rebalance the public finances through reduced expenditure (80 per cent) more than increased taxes (20 per cent).

This strategy introduced a 'prolonged period of austerity' from 2010.[6] Using the Department's preferred spending power measure,[7] the NAO calculated a 26 per cent reduction between 2010–11 and 2020–21, levelling off from 2016–17 (Figure 4.1). This scale of reduction was unprecedented

---

[2] Davis and Walsh (2016).
[3] HM Treasury (2012).
[4] Osborne (2010: 1).
[5] Blyth (2013).
[6] CIPFA (2019: 6).
[7] 'Spending power' is based on grants, business rates revenue, and capacity to raise council tax, and excludes transfers from the National Health Service (NHS) and retained business rates growth (National Audit Office 2021a).

and higher than those sought in previous national public sector efficiency initiatives.

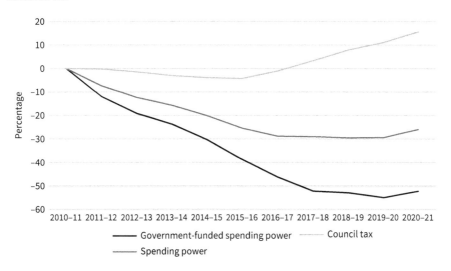

Figure 4.1 Spending power and its components, 2010–11 to 2020–21

Note: Indexed to 2010–11 = 0%. Real terms in 2019–20 prices.
Source: National Audit Office (2021a).

Expenditure reductions varied by local government type and location across England. Reduced spending hit hardest those most dependent upon UK government grants for deprivation-related services, especially larger northern cities with high social need.[8] Local governments with less grant dependence, more prosperous economies, vibrant housing markets, and stronger local tax bases were less adversely affected, especially some counties and districts in southern England.

4.1.2 Localism and local financial self-sufficiency

Alongside deficit reduction, the coalition drew upon Conservative critique of Labour's centralism, regionalism, and financial profligacy.[9] Their localism sought to return power to individuals and communities from national government. It was framed as a radical reorganization of central–local government relations and statecraft.

Underpinned by a vision of diverse service provision, greater competition, and enhanced efficiencies, this localism proposed decentralization to

---

[8] Gray and Barford (2018), National Audit Office (2021a).
[9] Conservative Party (2010).

specific levels for different functions: individuals (e.g. personalized budgets); frontline professionals (e.g. general practitioner commissioning); local groups (e.g. Right to Challenge); communities (e.g. free schools); and local governments (e.g. public health).[10] It encouraged further local government disaggregation and local state expansion.

The 2011 Localism Act's centrepiece was a new general power of competence. Reframing the basis of local statehood, it gave local governments additional 'legal capacity to do anything an individual can do that is not specifically prohibited' and 'more freedom' to work in partnership and innovate to provide lower cost local services meeting local people's needs.[11]

Integral to this localism was local government financial 'self-sufficiency'.[12] The aim was getting local governments 'standing on their own two feet' by replacing UK government grants as the principal funding source with local revenue-raising, especially from business rates, and ensuring the changes were fiscally neutral.[13] Then Liberal Democrat Deputy Prime Minister Nick Clegg sought to remove the 'endless tug of war about resources between central and local government' and make local government 'raise more of their own funds'.[14]

Central was 'phasing out the main grant from Whitehall' to local government—the RSG—and moving to 100 per cent redistribution of business rates so that 'local government as a whole would become financially self-sufficient'.[15] The rationale was 'we're taking all this money away from you but we're giving you more freedoms to be able to raise more revenue yourselves.'[16]

Increasing local government responsibility for stimulating local economic growth was seen as embodying localism and integral to fiscal localization and replacing UK government transfers.[17] Breaking the principle of funding following duties, the new system tied local government's funding more directly to the condition and development of its local economy and tax base.[18]

Abolishing RSG fundamentally changed local government and its funding. RSG was a national transfer to local governments to provide common public service standards at broadly the same costs to local taxpayers across

---

[10] HM Government (2011).
[11] Communities and Local Government (2011a: 4).
[12] Civil servant 1, finance department (2021). See also Communities and Local Government (2017).
[13] Civil servant 1, local government department (2021). HM Treasury (2015: 1).
[14] Clegg (2014: 1).
[15] HM Treasury (2015: 1), CIPFA (2019: 48).
[16] Sector journalist (2021).
[17] CIPFA (2019).
[18] Sandford (2016a).

the country. Changing to local financial self-sufficiency enabled greater local political discretion to differentiate local public services and their costs.[19]

Alongside fiscal localization, the number of funding streams were reduced from ninety to ten.[20] Multi-year financial settlements were introduced to provide greater certainty and enable longer-term financial planning.[21] Reproducing central control, this innovation was only offered to local governments providing efficiency plans. Demonstrating desire for greater certainty, 97 per cent of local governments signed up.[22] As fiscal stresses and uncertainty mounted from 2010, the UK government reverted to annual settlements.

Reflecting national government's engrained governing code for local statecraft, the coalition's localism was accompanied by liberalization and continued centralization. UK Secretary of State Pickles sought no further local government reorganization but aimed to ensure its transparency and accountability. Encouraging public scrutiny by 'armchair auditors',[23] a new code required local governments annually to report standardized indicators, including all expenditures over £500.

Comprehensive Performance Assessment, the Audit Commission, and Standards Board were abolished. The local audit market was reorganized and self-regulation encouraged to maintain and promote conduct standards. Existing UK government powers were retained, including over capitalization and capital receipts use. Revisions of statutory guidance and codes of practice were introduced, including treasury management following the 2008 Icelandic Banks' collapse.

The local state patchwork of subnational governance in England was reconfigured with new institutions and funding arrangements. Regional Government Offices, Regional Development Agencies, and Regional Chambers were abolished.[24] Linked to unitarization and streamlining local government into fewer, larger units, combined authorities of local government groupings were introduced, some with mayoralties. Controlled by the UK government, deal-making introduced tailored packages of devolved powers and resources negotiated between national and local governments.[25] Thirty-nine new Local Enterprise Partnerships were established at broadly functional economic

[19] CIPFA (2019).
[20] Wilson and Game (2011: 220).
[21] CIPFA (2019).
[22] CIPFA (2019).
[23] Communities and Local Government (2011b: 1).
[24] Pike et al. (2018).
[25] O'Brien and Pike (2019).

area scales.[26] Housing associations and companies grew,[27] alongside the creation of nationally-controlled academy schools.[28]

This localism and local financial self-sufficiency reconfigured elements of local statehood and afforded limited licence to explore new forms of local statecraft for those sufficiently ambitious, capable, and willing to take greater risks. Amid austerity and greater self-regulation, localism began the process of changing objectives, incentives, autonomies, and accountabilities for local statecrafters, although their statecraft was geographically and temporally differentiated.

4.1.3 Funding gaps

Austerity and local self-sufficiency opened up funding gaps between local government expenditure and income. CIPFA noted the UK government assumes local government 'can set a balanced budget, i.e. one where the budgeted expenditure is fully financed' but with 'reducing grant and rising pressures, there will be a funding gap requiring savings strategies.'[29]

Compounding UK government funding reductions, statutory service demand was increasing. Total population was growing and ageing, increasing those aged 65 or over needing adult social care. Children requiring social care was rising too due to growing homelessness and welfare reforms.[30]

Funding gaps became acute as more local governments were forced into overspends on their budgets from 2010.[31] Gaps manifest differently across local government types and locations with northern and metropolitan boroughs with high levels of social need acutely affected.[32] Districts without social care responsibilities in more prosperous southern economies and property markets were less impacted.

As austerity intensified, funding gaps stoked growing concerns about local governments' legal responsibility to balance budgets annually. Some local statecrafters noted how 'all councils are facing difficult financial times.'[33] Others described local government 'on the brink', facing the 'jaws of doom' and 'perfect storm' of rising expenditure and falling income.[34] By 2019,

---

[26] Pike et al. (2015).
[27] Morphet and Clifford (2017).
[28] Eyles et al. (2017).
[29] CIPFA (2019: 67).
[30] National Audit Office (2018a).
[31] National Audit Office (2021a).
[32] Gray and Barford (2018).
[33] Cumbria County Council (2020: 9).
[34] Whiteman (2021: 1), Bore (2013: 1), Carr (2015: 7).

CIPFA noted the 'complex and concerning picture for local government' following continued expenditure reductions and no expected return to previous funding levels.[35] Funding gaps were becoming chronic even prior to the pandemic from 2020.

Unprecedented expenditure reductions by the UK government created a decade of austerity for local government in England from 2010. Localism and local financial self-sufficiency reshaped central–local government relations, reduced capacity, increased inequality between governments, and exacerbated territorial injustice.[36] Local statecraft was afforded degrees of constrained autonomy, with 'encouragement to be more innovative, more commercial' and entrepreneurial while increasingly pressured by expenditure reductions and funding gaps.[37] The centralized system and its institutional and cultural bases remained intact.[38]

4.2 Financial strategies

The overwhelming 'need to address financial austerity' meant local statecrafters have 'sought to balance budgets in innovative ways', generating an 'increase in commercial activity and business transformation'.[39] Financial strategies, instruments, and practices of local statecraft broadened and differentiated from 2010.

As local statehood underpinning local statecraft, democratically elected political leadership and decision-making determine local government vision and aims with financial strategies formulated in support. Fiscal stress meant budgeting and financial planning have 'never been more important' in balancing budgets and transforming organization and service provision for longer-term survival.[40] Yet, it is more challenging as the 'margins for error are reduced' and 'consequences of failure' are 'magnified if it results in the inability to provide statutory services'.[41] Moreover, local service provision changes have rendered financial decision-making more sensitive, higher profile, and subject to local public scrutiny and contestation.[42]

An uneven shift towards more proactive and strategic financial planning is evident. Finance has become a more 'corporate activity', replacing

---

[35] CIPFA (2019: 7, 26).
[36] Gray and Barford (2018).
[37] Civil servant 2, local government department (2021).
[38] Copus et al. (2017), Latham (2017: 8).
[39] CIPFA (2019: iii).
[40] CIPFA (2019: 46).
[41] CIPFA (2019: 46).
[42] Penny (2019).

the 'tussle' and 'trade-offs' in budget-setting between 'competing Directors' for resources.[43] CFOs are mostly on senior management teams. Some have wider 'Director of Resources' roles, squeezing capacity for strategic financial planning.[44]

In austerity and uncertainty, local statecrafters need to 'look further ahead than ever before,'[45] encouraging longer-term forecasting, sensitivity-testing, and scenario planning. Such capacities are uneven across local governments, stimulating external advice procurement amidst staff reductions.

The CFO's role has become more challenging. Intensifying their statutory responsibility to safeguard public money, fiscal stress loaded greater pressure upon financial strategy to ensure viability. As strains have built up, the difficulty, importance, and visibility of the CFO's responsibilities for the robustness and resilience of local government finances have heightened,[46] especially in relation to any financialization by ensuring 'innovative financial approaches comply with regulatory requirements.'[47] Such changes tested CFOs that were 'just naturally cautious in local government … reflective of their upbringing in that world,'[48] challenging their traditional role in 'calming councillors down and stopping them doing daft things.'[49]

Contrasting European and US interpretations of CFO ascendance as financialization,[50] there is mixed evidence of shifts from municipal bean counters to strategic financiers. Limited but high-profile examples of wheeler-dealer councillors, Chief Executives, and CFOs exist, often with finance and/or property backgrounds, in leading local governments. Such local statecrafters sought to build teams of more 'solution focused' and 'liquid thinkers', different from the 'old way of [local] government … [that] says, oh no, you can't do that … 50 reasons, particularly on the legal side, why you … have never done this.'[51]

Approaches from the 1980s and 1990s were adapted to deal with the depth and rate of cuts and different geographical and temporal setting.[52] From 2010, financial strategies changed the balances between service spend, appropriations to/from reserves, other spending, and alternative income generation (Figure 4.2).

[43] Sector finance advisor (2021).
[44] National Audit Office (2019a).
[45] CIPFA (2019: 50).
[46] Sandford (2020c).
[47] CIPFA (2019: 137).
[48] Partner, Top 6 accountancy firm (2020).
[49] Liberal Democrat Councillor, Deputy Leader, and Cabinet Member for Finance, County Council (2021).
[50] Deruytter and Möller (2020), Farmer and Poulos (2019).
[51] CFO, Unitary council (2021).
[52] Pinch (1995).

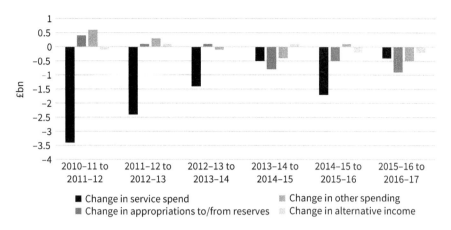

Figure 4.2 Methods used to address year-on-year income reductions, 2010–11 to 2016–17

Note: Real terms in 2016–17 prices.
Source: Adapted from National Audit Office (2018a: 22).

Providing a more nuanced account of austerity, broad periods of financial strategies are evident. Spanning 2010–13, efficiencies and savings marked early-stage austerity. CFOs acknowledged more efficient and productive ways of working, targeting relatively straightforward gains. Some local statecrafters emphasized the opportunities to undertake more substantive and innovative changes than hitherto. Discretionary services had expenditure reduced. The rate of spending reduction was higher than for income, enabling reserve build-up in response to uncertainty and potential future cuts, and offsetting other spending area growth.[53] Local tax increases were constrained in the centralized system. Increasing fees and charges offered limited contributions. Local growth-oriented strategies and investments aligned with the UK government's fiscal localization and financial self-sufficiency agendas were beginning, specifically amongst leading local governments.

Rationalization and service transformation characterized the second 2014–17 period. As austerity deepened, local statecraft was forced beyond 'salami slicing' into more root-and-branch review.[54] Local governments were depicted as being on a 'burning platform' where the 'status quo' was the 'riskiest option'.[55] Obvious efficiencies and savings had already been exhausted.[56] Service spending accounted for under half of required savings with other alternative spending reduced, contributions to reserves cut, or reserves

---

[53] National Audit Office (2018a).
[54] Deputy Chief Executive and CFO, District Council (2021).
[55] Chief Executive, think tank (2021).
[56] Hastings et al. (2015).

drawn down.[57] Given their local political visibility and sensitivity to councillors 'retaining services in diluted form tended to be preferred over service
deletions.'[58]

Integrated organization-wide strategies and transformations were sought.
Initiatives included service targeting, aligning capital and revenue towards
invest-to-save projects, and increasing collaboration with local state agencies. Service demand reduction was pursued through preventative activities, encouraging citizens to take greater responsibility for 'delivering their
own wellbeing', and using digital technologies to promote online and lower
cost 'self-service' by residents.[59] Income generation strategies were growing, especially amongst the leading local statecrafters, including building up
trading surpluses from commercial activities and earning external interest.[60]
Post-crisis low interest rates challenged treasury management, encouraging
borrowing but problematizing depositing cash.

Continued reductions marked the third 2017–20 period. Local governments grappled with accumulated risks and uncertainties following nearly
a decade of austerity. Demand-led pressures on statutory services increased.
Local statecrafters were forced into one-off budgetary fixes, including asset
disposal, utilizing capital receipts, and reserve use. Income generation and
commercial activity were extending beyond the leaders. Some struggling
local statecrafters retrenched towards a legally mandatory 'core' provision
of local services, changing local governments from a 'mini-welfare state into
a local economic growth agency'.[61] Financial resilience and sustainability
concerns were increasing.[62]

The period since 2020 has been dominated by Brexit, the pandemic, inflation, rising interest rates, and the Ukraine conflict. Local governments faced
additional cost pressures on expenditures and income reductions given their
pandemic response roles and maintenance of existing service delivery.[63]
The 'whammy of COVID' intensified existing inequalities as the austerity
decade left local governments with a weakened 'underpinning' to support
vulnerable groups.[64] While differentiated locally, the pandemic effectively
'crystallized or exacerbated stuff that may have been floating underneath' in
how expenditure and income were structured.[65]

[57] National Audit Office (2018a).
[58] Hastings et al. (2015: 612).
[59] Hastings et al. (2015: 612).
[60] National Audit Office (2018a).
[61] Tony Travers (London School of Economics) quoted in Crewe (2016: 9).
[62] National Audit Office (2018a).
[63] National Audit Office (2021b).
[64] Labour Councillor and Cabinet Member for Finance, London Borough (2021).
[65] Civil servant 1, local government department (2021).

Seeking to provide the 'right level of support' and ensure the sector could 'handle the pressures',[66] the UK government provided unplanned financial contingency arrangements. These comprised non-ring-fenced funding, compensation schemes underwriting some income losses (e.g. sales, fees, and charges), longer-term support covering shortfalls in CT and business rates collection, and an 'exceptional financial support safety net' for those facing 'unmanageable pressures'.[67] National government has not covered losses from commercial investments, despite having encouraged such activities for local financial self-sufficiency. Local statecrafters entered 'survival mode' with more struggling to balance budgets, increasing S114 report incidence.[68]

Structured and shaped by local statehood in England, local statecrafters are trapped in annual budget balancing and struggling to formulate medium or long-term strategic financial plans. Prolonged, multiple uncertainties and disruptions intertwined as financial system changes were further delayed including annual financial settlements and business rates and Fair Funding reviews. Dysfunctions have been intensified and reinforced as a result. Risk and its conception and management have grown substantively in their importance to local statecraft's engagements with the relations and process of financialization.

4.3 Risk

The uncertain and volatile economic situation and world of commercial finance together with municipal finance austerity since 2010 forced local statecrafters in England into more active recognition and management of risk. Changes in the public sector insurance market, NPM's growth, and innovative financial instruments increased risk management since the early 1990s.[69] By 2019, CIPFA identified it as a 'key area' for local statecrafters because it is 'essential' local government is 'fully aware of the risks that it may be taking and the possible consequences'.[70]

Local governments in England historically relied upon insurance, especially the '"comfort blanket" that protected them from the commercial realities of the market place' provided by the local government owned Municipal Mutual Insurance.[71] This business was acquired by the Zurich

---

[66] Civil servant 1, finance department (2021).
[67] National Audit Office (2021b: 9).
[68] Local government financial consultant 4 (2021).
[69] Hood and Young (2005).
[70] CIPFA (2019: 88).
[71] Hood and Young (2005: 568).

Insurance Company and rebranded Zurich Municipal Insurance in the early 1990s. The new owners introduced a more commercial approach, encouraged risk management initiatives, and forced local governments to bear an increased proportion of the cost of risk.

Local statecrafters' risk aversion, need for budgetary stability, limited ability to introduce substitute taxes, and general conservatism prompted further change.[72] But, shaped by the Hammersmith and Fulham swaps ruling stymying financialization, local governments in England were unwilling to experiment with 'alternative risk transfer innovations' in 1990s commercial finance (e.g. weather bonds, derivatives, and hedging).[73]

Into the 2000s, specific risks were described for particular initiatives but the 'overall quantum of risks facing council treasury management had never been identified'.[74] Corporate management typically reviewed the corporate risk register monthly 'then it would go back in the drawer until next month'.[75]

Local statecraft has been pushed into more comprehensive and strategic risk management in financial planning to consider the increasing scale of risks and their nature, likelihood, potential impacts, implications, and mitigation. Challenging the 'councillors at the casino' narrative, such approaches are distinguished from a gamble 'when you do something, and if it goes wrong, you lose everything' to a calculated and measured risk with appropriate indicators providing the potential to take 'corrective action'.[76] Although CIPFA acknowledge 'uncertainty', there remains no distinction of risk as measurable uncertainty from uncertainty as unmeasurable.[77]

Local statehood comprises statutory requirements for annual reviews of internal financial control systems and CIPFA/SOLACE (Society of Local Authority Chief Executives) guidance on good governance include risk management.[78] The NAO's Code of Audit Practice requires local governments to identify and manage operational and financial risks. Treasury policy and practice statements require risk management coverage. Local governments now publish risk management strategies.

Local statehood now requires local statecrafters to state their risk appetite. This is determined by 'current', 'tolerable', and 'optimal' risk positions and scales from 'opposed' to 'eager'.[79] Critical are upsides, downsides, and asking

---

[72] Hood and Yound (2005).
[73] Hood and Young (2005: 568).
[74] CIPFA (2019: 91).
[75] Sector finance advisor (2021).
[76] Labour Councillor and Cabinet Member for Finance, London Borough (2021).
[77] CIPFA (2019: iii), Knight (1921).
[78] CIPFA (2019: 61).
[79] Government Finance Function (2021: 5, 19).

Table 4.1 Risk types for local governments

Risk Type	Description
Contingency management	Emergencies including environmental, infrastructural, and public health disasters
Credit and counterparty	Transaction counterparty default before settlement
Exchange rate	Decrease in value of investment or transaction due to changes in relative value of currencies involved
Fraud, error, and corruption	Impacts arising from fraudulent, erroneous and/or corrupt practices (e.g. deception, manipulation, and/or theft)
Interest rate	Change in interest rates leading to increased costs due to increases or losses on deposits and investments when interest rates decrease
Legal and regulatory	Impacts of changing legal and regulatory frameworks
Liquidity	Inability to meet financial obligations from current financial resources
Market	Changes in markets to which the local government is exposed
Political	Change in political control, strategy, and direction following local and/or national elections
Price	Changes in prices decreasing values of investments or transactions
Refinancing	Insufficient finance or lenders unavailable at appropriate terms when borrowing required

Source: CIPFA (2019).

'what is the opportunity cost of insulating myself against various risks? What kind of risk should I be insuring myself against?'[80]

Numerous risk types exist in local government's complex and wide-ranging financial affairs (Table 4.1). A key risk for local statecraft is governance. Contrasting existing accounts of financialization risks generated only by *external* financial actors, this risk is embedded *within* the state and governance system and produced by changing national government politics and policies. Governance risk is generated and amplified in the highly centralized system in England. Tied to the electoral cycle, initiatives are often 'delayed and modified'.[81] HMT's economic and public finance strategy determine the parameters of local statehood for local statecraft.

---

[80] Civil servant 1, local government department (2021).
[81] CIPFA (2019: 7).

The UK government traditionally sought to minimize annual variations in local government income. But changes from 2010 introduced greater risk. External auditors identified 'financial pressure' as the most significant risk facing local governments in England, while 'commercial investments and ventures' ranked fourth.[82] Dependence upon UK government grants was replaced with local commercial property taxes, introducing risks from variations in local tax bases, business cycles, reliefs, and appeals.

Differentiated risk appetites are evident, structuring and shaping local statecrafter engagements with financialization. Strong legal and fiduciary safeguards exist in the local statehood framing local government's public money management. CFOs must advise the full council on risks which are 'set in the context of the authority's risk register and medium-term plans and should not focus exclusively on short-term considerations'.[83]

Demonstrating the financializing ratchet, new and additional risks that require further management have been introduced. CIPFA notes 'some risks can be managed by using specific financial instruments' such as derivatives 'but [are] not always trouble-free' and 'are complex and introduce new and less obvious risks'.[84] Some instruments used historically including exotic forms of borrowing, factoring, and leasing. Some local statecrafters have deployed the Localism Act to support their use of financial instruments, including derivatives (e.g. futures, options, and swaps), income strips, and sale-and-leaseback deals. Engaging such financial innovations, local state-crafters have commissioned external advisors to provide 'appropriate legal and professional advice prior to deciding on whether they are an appropriate risk management tool'.[85]

4.4 Expenditure strategies

Local statecrafters' expenditure strategies were determined by the particular scale and type of their resource reductions. Flexibility in varying expenditures is restricted by legal service provision responsibilities and grants for specified purposes. Evolving through the austerity periods from 2010, strategies focused on: efficiency savings; service provision reorganization; non-statutory service rationalization and withdrawal; capital; and reserves.[86]

---

[82] National Audit Office (2019a: 19).
[83] CIPFA (2019: 63).
[84] CIPFA (2019: 93).
[85] CIPFA (2019: 93).
[86] CIPFA (2019), Gray and Barford (2018), Hastings et al. (2015).

4.4.1 Efficiency savings

Drawing upon private sector techniques and NPM, local statecrafters experimented with changing from incremental to zero-based budgeting (ZBB) to identify savings. ZBB involves justifying budget items annually rather than starting with the previous year's budget. CIPFA sees that ZBB 'adds value to the budget process' because it encourages assessment of 'different ways of achieving those objectives'.[87] In numerous local governments, standardized savings identification processes were formulated, sometimes with public participation.

Representing costs of over £20 billion throughout the decade,[88] efficiency savings were sought from the local government workforce. Staff numbers were reduced largely by voluntary redundancies and leaving vacancies unfilled. Overall, local government employment was reduced from 1.34 million to 1.02 million (full-time equivalents) between 2012 and 2020, especially temporary, part-time, and women employees.[89] Some smaller districts even outsourced their entire staff.[90] Loss of experienced senior staff weakened local statecraft capacity to address austerity.[91] Remaining employees were subject to wage constraints including freezes on pay, promotions, and increments. Although such strategies were shaped by relatively high levels of national collective bargaining coverage and trade union density.[92]

Worth around £55 billion in 2018,[93] goods and services procurement were a further efficiency savings target. Strategies reflected political leaderships' views on organizational structure and direct/in-house, outsourced, and/or insourced provision. Activities included renegotiated contracts with existing providers and pooled purchasing to reduce costs including for local residents (e.g. energy).

4.4.2 Service provision reorganization

Service provision strategies were differentiated. Depictions of one-way privatization, outsourcing, and the irreversible hollowing out of local government are partial.[94] Privatization and outsourcing are only two of multiple strategies

---

[87] CIPFA (2019: 52).
[88] Local Government Association (2021a).
[89] Local Government Association (2021a).
[90] CFO, District Council (2020).
[91] Hastings et al. (2015).
[92] ONS (2020b).
[93] Local Government Association (2018).
[94] cf. Latham (2017).

pursued by local statecrafters across England since 2010. Local statecraft involves hollowing out *and* filling in a mixed economy of alliances, joint ventures, and partnerships as well as continued direct provision and in-sourcing of formerly outsourced functions.

Strategic, multifunction, and long-term partnerships between local governments and companies—such as Amey, Capita, and Kier—were established during 2010–13 austerity to contribute to efficiency savings and transformation projects. Such arrangements raised concerns about value for money and limited competition as local public services markets became oligopolistic and dominated by a few large, often internationalized, companies.[95] Reflecting international re-municipalization,[96] from the mid-2010s local statecrafters brought many contracts back in-house through non-renewal or termination to regain the assets and revenue streams, increase financial control, reduce costs, and improve performance.[97]

As austerity intensified, local governments were pushed towards more root-and-branch organizational changes to deliver larger-scale and longer-lasting savings. Such local statecraft was informed by new organizational models seeking transformational change including: the Co-operative Council based upon community collaboration (e.g. Lambeth, Oldham, and Rochdale); Barnet's EasyCouncil low tax, transactional format inspired by low-cost airline easyJet; and Northamptonshire County Council's Next Generation Council of a small-commissioning core and federated, multisector delivery vehicles.

Reflecting NPM, internal reorganizations devolved decision-making and budgeting to service managers using service level agreements.[98] Responsibility was delegated to review service provision models, manage expenditure reductions, and generate income.

Shared service arrangements between mostly neighbouring local governments were another reorganization strategy. The Local Government Association (LGA) identified 626 such partnerships across England in 2021 and estimated £1.34 billion of 'cumulative efficiency savings'.[99] Integrating back-office activities, including routine financial processes and transactional services, generated scale economies to reduce costs. Some smaller districts shared CFOs and other senior officers.

---

[95] Latham (2017), Whitfield (2020).
[96] Pearson et al. (2021).
[97] APSE (2019).
[98] CIPFA (2019).
[99] Local Government Association (2021b: 1).

In later austerity, local statecrafters began to re-separate out the strategic financial activities and discontinue and reorganize some shared service arrangements. The aim was to better support financial planning capacity as it grew in importance and regain control over costs especially when planned savings failed to materialize.

4.4.3 Non-statutory service rationalization and withdrawal

Fundamental change involved reducing or ending non-statutory service provision. This strategy focused on services with high fixed costs and ongoing revenue outlays including libraries and swimming pools. As local manifestations of austerity, such statecraft was politically contentious and often resisted by communities.[100]

The Localism Act enabled Community Right to Challenge and asset transfer, opening up questions of who owns and manages local assets and provides services. Community management and ownership often occurred in more prosperous areas by residents with greater social and other capital.[101] Given the political visibility and difficulty of reducing expenditure, some local statecrafters used participatory budgeting ideas to involve local residents in decision-making processes.[102]

4.4.4 Capital

In addition to revenue expenditure strategies, local statecrafters had to address their capital budgets in response to austerity. Larger-scale and longer-term investments in capital goods and their associated financing, especially borrowing, were targeted for potential savings.

Following the 2003 Prudential Code, the UK government, CIPFA, and sector associations encouraged a more strategic and active approach to capital expenditure and borrowing. Formalizing the strategizing of local statecraft, the 2017 code update required local governments to produce a capital strategy and programme. It aligned with the UK government's financial local self-sufficiency agenda, reinforcing the emphasis on 'self-financing investment'.[103] Rather than a project-by-project approach, local governments

---

[100] Penny (2019).
[101] Co-op and Locality (2020).
[102] Communities and Local Government (2011c).
[103] Wilson and Game (2011: 210).

were advised to consider their capital programme strategically to identify priority investments contributing to their multiple aims and functions.

Expenditure strategies included internal rather than external borrowing by the local government lending to itself, avoiding transaction and borrowing costs. Local statecrafters sought to manage their overall debt portfolio with the aim of reducing costs from transactions, fees, and interest rates for debt service. Demonstrating their interrelations, the revenue squeeze limited borrowing for capital investment by reducing revenues available to service interest payments and repay debt.

Seeking to reduce capital expenditure, existing commitments to capital projects and programmes were reviewed. This activity enabled reductions in borrowing demand as local governments utilized internal balances or reserves and/or delayed borrowing.[104]

Local statecrafters in England changed how they financed capital expenditure over the decade from 2010. Borrowing and use of capital receipts increased. Revenue account resources, other grants, Housing Revenue Accounts, and major repairs reserves remained stable. Grants from UK government departments declined.

New capital expenditure increasingly focused on invest-to-save initiatives. These comprised capital projects that addressed multiple local objectives and reduced longer term and ongoing revenue costs. Building a new or refurbishing an older leisure centre, for example, meant investing to create or increase the value of an asset, enhance local service provision, earn additional revenue, stimulate local economic activity through procurement, and generate local training and employment opportunities. Such approaches were often underpinned by anchor institution and community wealth building ideas aiming to localize public investment and purchasing power multipliers.[105]

Local statecrafters increasingly connected revenue and capital expenditure strategies to address funding gaps. In later austerity, the UK government afforded flexibility to use capital receipts, generated by the sale of capital assets including buildings and land, to fund expenditure 'designed to generate ongoing revenue savings' and transform service delivery to reduce demand and costs.[106] Examples included staff sharing, joint procurement, public sector land management, and alternative service delivery models.

Capitalization is when expenditure is treated in the accounts as capital, allowing its costs to be met over multiple years, rather than revenue, whose costs must be met in-year in balanced budgets. Local statecrafters have

---

[104] CIPFA (2019).
[105] CLES (2021).
[106] CIPFA (2019: 30).

Table 4.2 Capitalization directions by local government, 2020–21 and 2021–22

Local government	Capitalization directions agreed for 2020–21 (£m)	In-principle support agreed in respect of 2021–22 (£m)
Croydon	70	50
Luton	35	14
Nottingham	20	15
Wirral	9	10.7
Eastbourne	6.8	6
Peterborough	4.8	20
Bexley	3.87	5.125
Authorities that have requested support for 2021–22 only		
Copeland	–	1.5
Slough	–	15.2
Authorities that have requested support for 2020–21 only		
Redcar and Cleveland	3.68	–
Total	153.15	137.525

Source: Adapted from Department for Levelling Up, Housing and Communities (2021c).

increasingly sought such financial flexibilities from the Department to manage their expenditure over longer time periods. Capitalizations increased across local governments in England, especially from 2020–21 (Table 4.2). Demonstrating continued central control over local statecraft despite localism, capitalization requires explicit UK Secretary of State permission.

4.4.5 Reserves

Reserves are a further connection between revenue and capital budgets. Fiscal stress impacted upon local statecrafter determinations of prudent levels of reserves appropriate for managing risks.[107] Then UK Secretary of State Eric Pickles exhorted local government in 2010 to stop 'turning town hall vaults into Fort Knox' by building up reserves and use the 'over £10bn in their piggy banks' to manage funding system changes.[108] CIPFA cautioned that 'reserves can only be used once' as one-off, short-term responses to fiscal pressures and resources for dealing with major contingencies and emergencies.[109]

As austerity wore on, local statecrafters in England were using reserves at a faster rate, increasing as a proportion of their spending power from over

[107] CIPFA (2019).
[108] Quoted in Curtis (2010: 1).
[109] CIPFA (2019: 63).

20 per cent to nearly 50 per cent between 2010–11 and 2019–20, and threatening their financial resilience and sustainability.[110] Levels and rates of use were differentiated by local government type, financial situation, and accumulated reserve levels, political control, and location.

Reflecting an integral characteristic of local statecraft, expenditure strategies varied by local government type, financial condition, and geography. Situated within two-tier systems where the upper-tier County has responsibility for large service expenditure budget items facing rising demand pressures, districts benefitted significantly from retained business rates revenues and national New Homes Bonus grants especially in more prosperous local economies and housing markets.[111] Such situations enabled reserves increases some then used for income generation through investments seeking higher returns than cash deposited in banks. Districts generally had high levels of reserves, registered the largest aggregate increases, and increased their reserves levels.[112] Districts with lower levels and reduced reserves had higher levels of deprivation and weaker local economies and tax bases.

4.5 Income generation strategies

As expenditure was reduced, income generation strategies became increasingly critical for local statecrafters addressing funding gaps. While commercialization emerged amongst the leaders from the 1980s,[113] the UK government's local financial self-sufficiency agenda actively encouraged local entrepreneurialism to generate income and reduce dependence upon transfers from the centre. Working within the centralized system, local statecrafters pursued multiple strategies differing in their focus upon municipal and commercial finance and engagements with the relations and process of financialization.

4.5.1 Grants and contributions

As their level and type were being reorganized and reduced, local governments sought to maximize income from UK government grants. This long-standing local statecraft involved demonstrating eligibility for

---

[110] National Audit Office (2021a).
[111] Local government financial consultant 2 (2020).
[112] Local government finance consultant 2 (2020).
[113] Carr (2012).

continued grants, managing transition from grants being reduced, reformed, or phased out, and accessing new grant funding.[114] Maximizing grants and contributions were also pursued through S106 developer contributions and the CIL. This strategy related to wider local political and development strategies, especially planning employment and housing. Multiple grant funding streams—nationally allocated, ring-fenced and disbursed through competitive bidding—afforded less high-profile opportunities for local statecraft within the municipal finance system.

4.5.2 Local taxes

The UK government's emphasis upon locally generated revenues placed greater financial weight upon local taxation strategies. Local autonomy was limited in the highly centralized national system, constraining increases, and controlling innovations in the local residential (CT) and commercial (business rates) property taxes.

Local government calls for a wider range of local tax instruments in localism went unheeded by the UK government concerned about losing control of locally managed tax revenues. Local statecrafters explored US local government powers to levy taxes on numerous activities including airport departures, hotel accommodation, and sales.[115] But HMT only authorized one new tax: the Workplace Parking Levy for Nottingham City Council, agreed in a devolution deal to fund local transport infrastructure.

Within national constraints, strategies sought to maximize local tax revenue. Geographical differences are evident in local property markets and the CT base across England (Table 4.3). CT is a visible and 'sensitive local tax' with levels set by local political leaderships, following a defined procedure, and articulating their priorities.[116] Demonstrating their commitments to low taxes, numerous Conservative-led councils froze CT.

Those seeking CT increases encountered national limits despite localism and funding gaps. The UK government made increases above 5 per cent subject to a local referendum. None were held given the uncertain outcomes and costs.[117] Incentivizing low-tax positions, UK government grants were made for CT freezes. Rigidity in local statecraft's fiscal space pushed national government into short-term fixes, however. As demand for statutory

[114] Sandford (2020b).
[115] Strickland (2016).
[116] CFO, County Council (2021).
[117] Sandford (2021b).

Table 4.3 Local tax revenue-raising capacity per person by region, 2015–16

Region	Business rates		Council tax		Total	
	Total (£)	Mean = 100	Total (£)	Mean = 100	Total (£)	Mean = 100
London	798	182	448	105	1,246	144
South East	402	92	474	111	875	101
East of England	378	86	447	105	825	96
South West	363	83	455	107	818	95
North West	387	89	391	92	778	90
Yorkshire and the Humber	370	85	385	90	755	87
West Midlands	356	81	395	93	751	87
North East	329	75	382	90	712	82
East Midlands	318	73	394	93	712	82
England	438	100	426	100	863	100

Source: Adapted from Amin-Smith et al. (2018: 26).

services intensified funding gaps, UK government authorization was given for a time-limited 2 per cent precept on CT hypothecated to fund social care.

CT strategy intersects with planning locally in land allocation for residential housing development and future revenue generation. Local statecrafters sought to increase the proportion of higher-value (band D) housing. While the UK government incentivized housing growth, this proved difficult in high-demand areas facing local anti-development opposition and in places with weak demand.

Increasing CT revenues was further hampered by national restrictions on domestic property revaluations. Depending on local residential property markets, revaluations would have increased CT rates and boosted tax revenues in some areas, encountering political opposition and local discontent. A final element of CT strategy was maximizing collection rates and minimizing reliefs while protecting vulnerable local people.

More central to the UK government's local financial self-sufficiency agenda was local commercial property tax. Like CT, local economic structure and the tax base varies across England.[118] Such geographical differences stimulated concerns about fiscal localization given the different revenue implications for places.[119]

---

[118] Amin-Smith et al. (2018).
[119] Greenhalgh et al. (2016).

In early austerity from 2010, local government collected business rates for national government. The revenues were returned to local governments through a nationally determined formula. National pooling enabled redistribution between surplus and deficit areas with stronger and weaker tax bases and higher and lower revenues.

From 2013, the UK government introduced partial localization. Under the Business Rates Retention Scheme (BRRS), local government retained a 'local share' of 50 per cent of revenue raised and passed the remaining 50 per cent 'central share' to national government.[120] A 'tariff' or 'top-up' element was applied to local government's 'local share' to redistribute revenues, smooth out local differences in business rate revenue generation, and provide greater revenue predictability. Local governments could retain up to 50 per cent of any additional business rate revenue generated above a nationally determined baseline in 2013–20.

This fiscal localization aimed to incentivize local governments to generate additional tax revenues by prioritizing local economic growth, encouraging business expansion, attracting new businesses, and expanding their local commercial property tax base.[121] Conversely, it also afforded local statecrafters the power to reduce their business rates locally as a 'localism discount'.[122] Although reliefs and exemptions were used under acute fiscal pressure, none reduced the tax.

From 2016, 100 per cent and 75 per cent retention were piloted in selected single tier areas. Local governments formed pools with a single tariff and top-up level and decided distribution between members, foregoing selected national grants.[123] The UK government authorized local precepts in devolution deals. As geographically targeted supplements on existing business rates, they were typically hypothecated for specific purposes especially local infrastructure.

Business rates localization strongly incentivized local statecrafters' income generation strategies. Increasing the commercial property tax base became a priority for economic development and planning. Prioritizing employment land creation was critical to enable the attraction and growth of existing and new businesses. Strategies sought larger floorspace developments generating higher business rate revenues. This rewiring of incentives tilted local statecraft towards securing larger scale businesses including out-of-town retailers and

---

[120] Sandford (2020b).
[121] Sandford (2020b).
[122] CIPFA (2019: 23).
[123] Sandford (2020b).

logistics operations with substantial footprints. Simultaneous mitigation was needed for negative impacts displacing consumer demand from central high street retail and using up employment land by businesses with relatively low employment.

Business rates localization stimulated local statecrafter innovations and engagements with financialization. Negotiated arrangements emerged in central–local deals, especially in larger metropolitan areas, including changes to tax revenue distributions between national and local government such as 'earn back' and 'gain share' models.[124] Borrowing against future business rates income for up-front infrastructure investment was authorized by the UK government as part of New Development Deals. Melding municipal and commercial finance and embedding new risks in core revenue streams, local government financial fortunes were more closely tied to their local economies. Additional revenues needed to service and repay borrowing became dependent upon local commercial property market dynamics.

Rendering this fiscal localization partial, the UK government maintained control over the valuation central to the rateable values of property. Revaluation was delayed from 2015 to 2017. This postponement reflected national politics and the UK government's desire to provide certainty to ratepayers, debates about online retail and high street decline, and concerns that falling commercial property values would reduce local tax revenues and break the revenue-neutral principle for revaluations.[125]

Like CT strategies, for business rates local statecrafters sought to maximize collection and minimize reliefs where local conditions allowed. Introducing further risk and uncertainty, the UK government introduced an appeals system in 2017 leading to increased revenue collection and administrative costs volatility. Local governments varied business rates eligibility as part of addressing high street retail decline. Business rates holidays were used in the 2020 pandemic response.

Making business rates central to local funding increased reliance upon a volatile tax revenue tied to local business cycles and its administration. It magnified differences in tax bases and revenue streams between local economies with different economic structures, conditions, and trajectories. Such partial fiscal localization risked unpicking redistribution. Problems were acute for local governments with higher social need and grant dependence, and weaker economies with limited revenue generation opportunities.

[124] O'Brien and Pike (2019).
[125] CIPFA (2019).

4.5.3 Sales, fees, and charges

Income generation strategies involved sales, fees, and charges reviews. Changes in balances and levels were deliberated, although the overall range remained relatively stable from 2010.[126] Increasing charges was constrained by UK government restrictions and local conditions. Some local politicians were reluctant to be portrayed as squeezing local residents during austerity. Others felt compelled to cover rising provision costs. Specific areas have benefitted from local assets including infrastructure such as airports and internationally important visitor attractions with large footfalls. Other local statecrafters were committed to free parking for high street revitalization. In the 2020 pandemic, however, revenues were described as having 'fallen off a cliff' with reductions of 50–60 per cent.[127]

4.5.4 Commercialization

Many leading local governments have been actively involved in commercialization to generate income since the 1980s, but austerity forced others into action. Numerous local statecrafters remained sceptical, however, and considered it was not the job of local government to use its 'muscle', 'cheap borrowing' and 'ability to hide its overheads'—local statehood attributes—to compete with local or other businesses.[128] All categories of commercial and selected other income increased from 2010 (Figure 4.3). More active treasury management and engagements with external financial actors and the financialization process increased interest and investment income.

Commercialization strategies became more widespread. Some local statecrafters recognized grey areas between avoiding all activities deemed commercial and those that related closely to core local government responsibilities and aims 'in developing and delivering the council plan' and doing something other than only 'making a profit'.[129] Organizational and financial strategy included corporate council group structures to manage growing arrangements and relations internally and externally with organizations in an expanding local state. Activities included joint ventures, partnerships, and subsidiaries. Expanding relations with other organizations made strategic

---

[126] National Audit Office (2021a).
[127] Associate Director, professional association (2020).
[128] Liberal Democrat Councillor, Deputy Leader, and Cabinet Member for Finance, County Council (2021).
[129] Liberal Democrat Councillor, Deputy Leader, and Cabinet Member for Finance, County Council (2021).

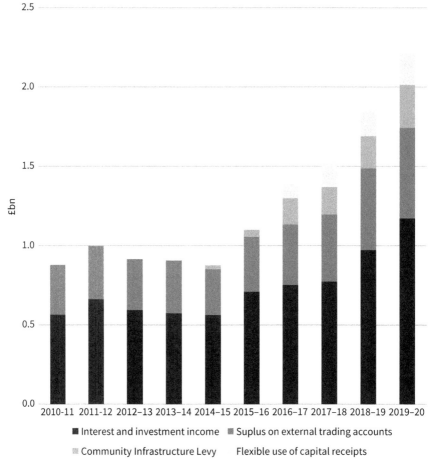

Figure 4.3 Commercial and selected other income, 2010–11 to 2019–20

Note: Real terms in 2019–20 prices. Community Infrastructure Levy in 2011–12 of –£525,733 not included.
Source: National Audit Office (2021a).

financial management and planning more complex, especially with pooled budgets and funding streams.[130]

Commercialization of existing activities and services sought to increase their actual and potential revenue generation. This strategy included revamping existing and underperforming trading entities through changing management, reorganization, rebranding, and/or relaunching. Maintaining ownership and control over such entities and their revenue generation was integral for numerous local governments to stimulate local economic activities, job and training opportunities, and local multipliers.

---

[130] CIPFA (2019).

New commercial entities were established from existing activities. Akin to commercial spin-offs and related to in- or outsourcing services, local state-crafters assessed current activities for their commercial potential, evaluating demand from public, private, and civic sectors. Growing from 300 to over 800 in 2009–19, this corporatization was public entrepreneurship associated with larger local governments with high levels of grant and debt dependence.[131]

If deemed non- or insufficiently commercially viable, activities were retained in-house, outsourced, or discontinued. Much early austerity out-sourcing to reduce costs changed to later insourcing due to increased costs, perceived loss of control, and poor external provider service.[132] Reflecting international re-municipalization,[133] strategic change was evident towards holding and owning assets 'rather than pay for their use through annual revenue payments to a private sector partner'.[134]

Commercialization strategies have also created wholly new entities. Extending the corporate council group, new organizations have been estab-lished by local statecrafters to address local needs and sell services more widely. Examples include housing and energy companies.[135]

Demonstrating local statecraft innovation in municipal finance, some local governments began behaving like financial institutions to address wider local objectives. In more active treasury management strategies, cash surpluses were used to provide loans to local governments, other related third parties, and local businesses. Echoing local governments offering loans and mort-gages in the 1960s and 1970s, local financial institutions were established offering financial services for residents, for example Essex County Coun-cil's Banking on Essex partnership with Abbey to address financial exclusion and high-cost short-term credit.[136] Low interest rates on cash deposits in banks and fiduciary duties prompted CFOs to find alternative uses to generate income.

4.5.5 Assets and investments

In more integrated financial strategy, balance sheet management of assets and liabilities has become 'more proactive'.[137] Informed by new public wealth ideas and UK government policy, 'strategic asset management planning' is

---

[131] Andrews et al. (2019).
[132] APSE (2019).
[133] Pearson et al. (2021).
[134] Wilson and Game (2011: 210), CIPFA (2019).
[135] CIPFA (2019).
[136] Larsen (2009).
[137] Associate Director, professional association (2020).

key for local statecrafters in 'generating real savings and delivering assets where they are needed, to enable effective front-line service delivery'.[138] Local statecrafters have been compelled to make their balance sheets 'work harder' to generate income.[139]

UK government initiatives led this agenda. The One Public Estate partnership between the Office of Government Property and the LGA promotes and enables locally coordinated and integrated public sector asset management. CFOs focused on better managing existing assets and acquiring new assets with revenue streams to offset fiscal stress. Rather than only outsourcing and privatization, local statecraft strategies involved sell, hold, and buy approaches.

Existing assets were identified and valued. Asset types were categorized: operational—in use and providing services; commercial—income generating; non-operational—not currently in use and providing services and considered as underutilized and/or surplus; and strategic—relating to overall and long-term aims.[140]

Asset valuation was critical in securing high sale prices to meet value for money criteria and provide collateral to borrow against.[141] More regular revaluation was undertaken, five-yearly minimum or more frequently. Risk was acknowledged when asset values fall because revaluation loss or impairment need accounting for in the revaluation reserve. Asset-based strategies made depreciation an issue because 'in using an asset to provide services, its value is consumed.'[142]

Assets were disposed of when not considered core to longer-term plans or cash was required. Sales generated capital receipts, prescribed by the UK government in their use. The level and timing of disposals needed 'to take into account changes in the property market and adjust estimates and assumptions for reserves accordingly.'[143]

Greater recognition of asset ownership and management led local statecraft to hold and develop existing assets.[144] A mixed economy of different models emerged: publicly owned (solely or jointly); Local Asset-Backed Vehicles (LABVs); land commissions and property boards; community-owned and/or mutuals; pension and insurance funds; public–private and strategic partnerships; public–private shareholder companies; public sector

[138] Detter and Fölster (2017), CIPFA (2019: 37, 65).
[139] Executive Director, property company (2021).
[140] Pike et al. (2019).
[141] Halbert and Attuyer (2016).
[142] CIPFA (2019: 73).
[143] CIPFA (2019: 61).
[144] Cumbers (2012).

commercial landlord; and private sector (including wholesale and leasehold ownership and strategic partnerships).[145]

Complementing invest-to-save initiatives, local statecrafters pursued invest-to-earn strategies. These included local governments lending to local commercial entities for wider regeneration purposes. Liverpool City Council loaned £250 million to Everton Football Club for its new stadium.[146] Rather than external and commercial financialization, this local statecraft was an example of municipal financial innovation. The loan was underpinned by the local statehood attribute of lower-cost borrowing from the PWLB backed by the UK sovereign guarantee connected to the local statecrafters' capital expenditure strategy. In a changing 'regulatory space', such strategies involved taking a 'gamble' on investments, emphasizing the importance of understanding the assets and liabilities involved.[147]

Other strategies involved relatively asset-rich and cash-poor local governments using their land holdings to 'de-risk' sites for development by contributing or gifting assets.[148] This 'delivery-based, pro-development planning' was used to attract private investors and developers into residential, specifically housing, and commercial property schemes.[149] Local governments then benefited financially through increases to local tax revenues and planning gains.

New commercialization strategies involved asset acquisition with revenue streams to generate income.[150] Investments included commercial property such as factories, industrial estates, and offices. Strategies increasingly involved out-of-area asset acquisition. Alongside such local statecraft innovations, the UK government tightened guidance on investment strategies and introduced security, liquidity and yield tests.

4.6 Financial resilience, sustainability, and the national governance of financial failure

Local government financial resilience and sustainability became UK government and sector concerns as fiscal stress accumulated from 2010.[151] Reflecting their local statecraft, local governments addressed funding gaps with varying degrees of success. The agency, outcomes, and implications of

---

[145] Pike et al. (2019).
[146] Wilson (2018).
[147] Professor of Accounting, UK university (2021).
[148] Raco and Souza (2018: 145).
[149] Raco and Souza (2018: 145).
[150] CIPFA (2019: 33).
[151] Sandford (2020c).

their financial strategies are structured and shaped by systemic constraints and geographical situations. Local statecrafters experience mediated versions of national fiscal pressures, exposing those less able to manage them.

The Department has been forced into recognition and responses to sector-wide financial issues.[152] In early austerity, the NAO addressed local government finances, prompted by sustainability and resilience concerns. It reported the Department's weak oversight meant it was 'poorly placed to understand the scale of financial pressures' and 'whether … [they] … are close to failing financially' or 'are diverting financial pressures onto their services'.[153] As austerity deepened, financial stress impacts grew in importance and visibility.

Devices to identify and manage increasingly problematic financial situations were sought. The Department's sustainability tool models proportions of inflexible spend on social care and debt servicing, and reserves levels. Financial resilience was equated with lower shares of inflexible spend and higher levels of reserves. The tool is used to model policy scenario impacts on financial risk, track spending review assumptions' robustness, and inform assessment of risk levels and potential for financial failure.[154] CIPFA developed a financial resilience index as a diagnostic device to identify good practice and factors related with financial risk and failure.[155]

Amidst increased national monitoring of financial pressures, specific local government's difficulties became public. External auditors published public interest reports, noting concerns on income generation strategies including commercial property investment and commercialization ventures. These included the City of York, London Borough of Croydon, Northamptonshire County Council, and Nottingham City Council.

Rumours claim the Department has a list of at-risk local governments facing financial difficulty. Suggesting UK government concerns about the negative impacts of austerity and policy since 2010, this record has not been made public. In 2018, then departmental Permanent Secretary Melanie Dawes denied any local governments had reached 'the level of risk that Northamptonshire presented'—the County experiencing high profile financial difficulties at the time—but acknowledged no 'categorical assurance' could be given that others would not issue S114 notices of their inability

---

[152] Sandford (2020c).
[153] National Audit Office (2014: 33–34).
[154] Sandford (2020c).
[155] CIPFA (2018).

to set a balanced budget.[156] The UK Public Accounts Committee called for the Department to define financial sustainability and its underpinning assurance model. As the pandemic hit in 2020, a leaked Cabinet Office document warned 'one in 20 councils' were 'already at high risk of financial failure'.[157]

Failing local statecraft and finances broke into the open with several local governments issuing S114 reports. These formal notices are required when the full council has been unable to set or maintain the legally required balanced budget. Issuance is a last resort and irreversible step by CFOs to meet legal and professional obligations. They are only published 'when regular discussions have failed' and, in CIPFA's view, when CFO advice has been ignored, not acted upon sufficiently, or responded to in high level emergency meetings to rectify the situation.[158] Amongst CFOs, S114 reports are seen as the nuclear option and career suicide following the breakdown of trust with the local political leadership.

S114 reports were last issued by the London Boroughs of Hackney and Hillingdon in 2000.[159] Each was portrayed by the UK government and the sector press as cases of local incompetence, corruption, mismanagement, and/or political intransigence. S114 reports have increased since 2010, including Northamptonshire County Council, Croydon Borough Council, and Slough Borough Council.[160] These unbalanced budgets were manifest in different local government types, situations, and locations. Their increasing incidence suggested systemic elements to the causes rather than the Department and CIPFA's narrative of unique and localized outbreaks of rogue or weak statecraft by specific local governments.

In 2018, CIPFA suggested the 'majority' of local governments were in a 'stable financial position' and 'not showing signs of financial failure in spite of managing severe budget cuts'.[161] It acknowledged, however, that 'there is a tail, of 10–15 per cent of councils, where there are some signs of potential risk to their financial stability'—around thirty-three to fifty local governments—and sought to engage and support their CFOs.[162]

Unplanned, in-year, and increasing rates of reserve use signalled local statecrafters' financial difficulties.[163] Alongside Northamptonshire, other counties

---

[156] Cited in Sandford (2020c).
[157] Cited in George (2020: 1).
[158] Sandford (2020c: 8).
[159] Sandford (2020c).
[160] Housing, Communities, and Local Government Committee (2021).
[161] CIPFA (2018: 1).
[162] CIPFA (2018: 1).
[163] Sandford (2020c).

registered large reductions in usable reserves including Lancashire, Norfolk, and Somerset.[164] Surrey and Worcester commissioned external CIPFA reviews to examine their funding gaps and responses to rising service demands and run-down reserves.[165] Financial issues emerged at other types of local government too, including Metropolitan boroughs (e.g. Leeds City Council) and districts (e.g. Thanet). Unitaries demonstrating the impacts of fiscal stress included Torbay Council. Amongst London boroughs, Croydon and Slough issued S114 notices in 2020. By the 2020 pandemic, the Department commissioned CIPFA to review eight local governments in receipt of exceptional financial support: Bexley; Copeland; Eastbourne; Luton, Peterborough; Redcar & Cleveland; Slough; and Wirral councils.

Financial sustainability concerns question whether the UK government's local financial self-sufficiency agenda and funding system since 2010 are fit for purpose.[166] Unlike other countries such as the US,[167] 'there is no procedure in law for a UK local authority to go bankrupt, and none has ever done so' and 'when local authorities have encountered financial difficulties in the past, normal practice has been for the Government not to provide any financial support or "bailout".[168] This status rests on the local statehood attribute of the *implicit* guarantee of national government as the UK sovereign. A safeguard that is not *explicit* and codified to avoid moral hazard. In the discourse of local financial self-sufficiency and competence, UK government ministers have communicated varying approaches to support and 'no bail outs for commercial investments.'[169] The UK government has, however, formally intervened and overridden elected local governments for time-limited periods when confidence and trust in their local statecraft and financial management has collapsed.

Historically, UK government support has not been forthcoming, either in response to individual cases such as the Hammersmith and Fulham swaps affair or sector-wide issues affecting local governments such as the 2008 Icelandic banks episode. The only exception was the £30 million loan to *Comhairle nan Eilean Siar* (Western Isles Council) in the Outer Hebrides, Scotland, following its £24 million loss related to borrowing and on-lending from the collapsed Bank of Credit and Commerce International (BCCI) in 1991.[170]

---

[164] Davies (2018).
[165] Sandford (2020c).
[166] Housing, Communities and Local Government Committee (2021).
[167] Davidson and Ward (2018).
[168] Sandford (2020c: 8, 20).
[169] Jameson (2020: 1).
[170] Sandford (2020c).

4.7 The differentiated landscape of financialization and local statecraft

Local statecrafters in England have engaged the relations and process of financialization in varying ways and degrees since 2010. Different local government types and their powers, resources, sizes, political and officer leaderships, politics, and locations structure and shape this picture. Outlining this complex and diverse landscape extends existing work. Some identify two leagues of local governments, one with the capacity and context to be led beyond austerity and into economic recovery and the other with constrained capacity, limited growth opportunities, and unassailable service demand increases.[171] Others see a 'patchwork pattern' and spatial variation through differential austerity impacts and financial responses across England.[172]

A differentiated landscape exists in England since 2010 marked by local statecraft involving three approaches: vanguard; intermediate; and long tail. Reflecting their inherent diversity, the complexity of their financial strategies, and varying engagements with financialization, local statecrafters are pursuing these approaches in specific activities. Some of the same local governments are undertaking vanguard actions with high levels of gross external borrowing *and* interest and investment income. But they are not always the same as the local governments leading investments in MMF and the generation of surpluses on external trading accounts. Local statecraft encompasses different approaches and arrangements in specific activities. Beginning to outline this differentiated landscape in England since 2010 opens the door for future research to explore in more detail the relationships between local statecrafters' approaches and their geographies and changes over time.

Investments in MMF illustrate the predominance of intermediate approaches and few long-tail behaviours with no involvement except amongst counties (Figure 4.4). Vanguard approaches exist amongst a small number of districts and London boroughs at higher levels than the leaders amongst counties, metropolitan districts, and unitaries. The breakdown by political control reveals Labour and Liberal Democrat leadership of vanguard activities, followed by NOC and Conservatives (Figure 4.5). The geography is

---

[171] Hastings et al. (2015).
[172] Gray and Barford (2018: 550), Dagdeviren and Karwowski (2021).

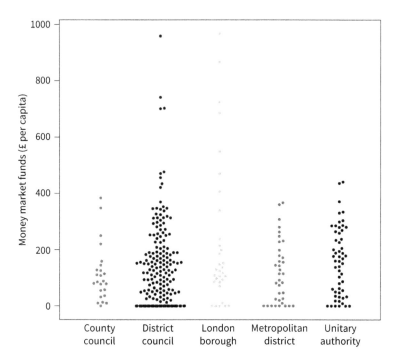

Figure 4.4 Local government investments in money market funds by local government type, 2019–20

Note: This analysis is based on out-turn data reported to the Department by local governments which have not been externally audited. The data for each local authority district (LAD) are from different time periods and years, varying according to the release of different indicators. As a result, the proportions of different types of LAD vary across years as new councils are dissolved or created and direct comparisons between different time periods should be made with this in mind. Population is based on 2018 data, therefore only 325 comparable areas from across England are included for which population data is available. The data and code are available in an open access GitHub repository: http://github.com/CaitHRobinson/councillorsatthecasino.
Source: MHCLG (2021).

differentiated, with the highest levels amongst London boroughs and southern counties, intermediate approaches spread unevenly across England, and the long tail making up the rest (Figure 4.6).

Demonstrating commercialization but not always financialization, interest and investment income reveals few following vanguard approaches with high levels amongst several unitaries, a district, and metropolitan district (Figure 4.7). Intermediate behaviours are bunched at much lower levels across all local government types and most are adopting long-tail approaches. NOC and Labour constitute political control of vanguard local

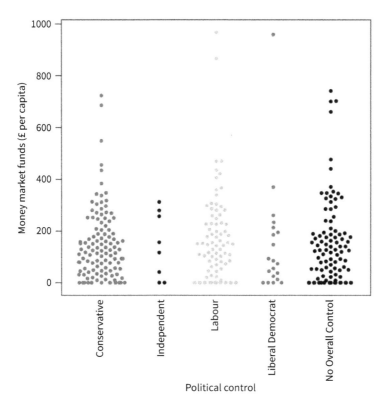

Figure 4.5 Local government investments in money market funds by political control, 2019–20

Note: Political control data for 2019 from Open Council Data
http://opencouncildata.co.uk/history.php.
Source: MHCLG (2021).

statecrafters and they are located in the outer South East and North West. Intermediate and long-tail approaches are spread across the rest of England (Figure 4.8).

Revealing commercialization but not necessarily financialization, sur-pluses on external trading accounts are led by vanguard approaches in districts with several unitaries and a London borough. Districts and uni-taries dominate those following intermediate approaches with most local governments exhibiting long-tail behaviours. Conservative control leads the vanguard, followed by Liberal Democrat and NOC amongst the intermediates. Vanguard activities are located in the outer South East, while the rest of England is a patchwork at much lower levels.

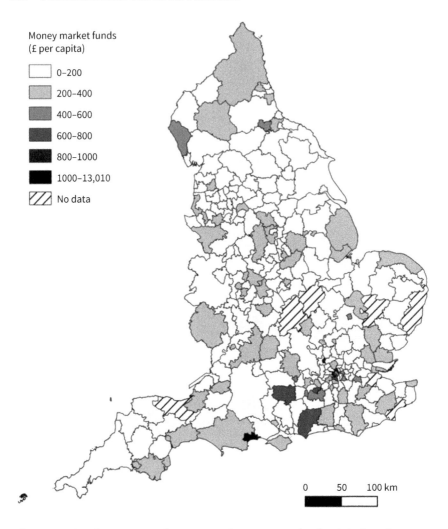

Figure 4.6 Local government investments in money market funds by location, 2019–20

Source: MHCLG (2021).

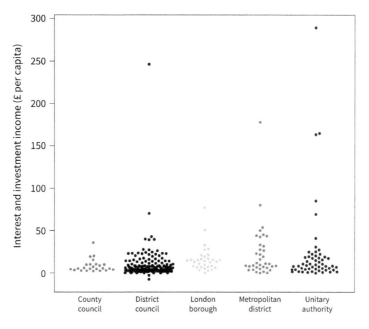

Figure 4.7 Local government interest and investment income by local government type, 2019–20

Source: MHCLG (2021).

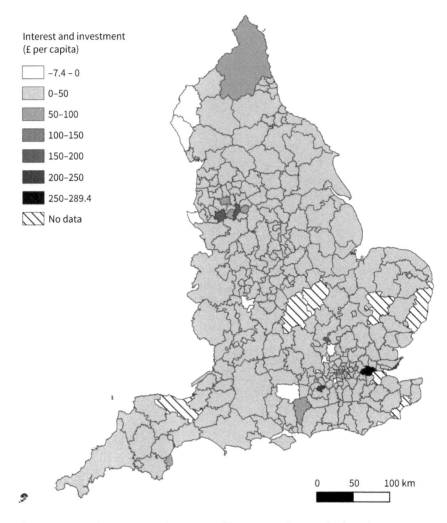

Figure 4.8 Local government interest and investment income by location, 2019–20
Source: MHCLG (2021).

4.8 Conclusions

Within the highly centralized governance and funding system in England, local statecrafters have had to navigate UK government policy shifts to austerity, localism, and local financial self-sufficiency alongside centralized management, top-down control, and risk aversion. The local outcomes and ramifications reflect their statecraft in coping with systemic problems in particular situations. This interpretation challenges the narrative of local governments as poorly governed and rookie players in a financialized casino, gambling with local taxpayers' money and public services.

Local statecraft provides an understanding and explanation of financial strategies in this setting. Differentiation is evident across local government types, financial conditions, politics, and locations in England since 2010. Cases support the 'competing narratives' of 'adaptation, survival and resilience' through creative and innovative entrepreneurialism,[173] 'residualisation and marginalisation' through service rationalization and targeting the most vulnerable[174], and 'responsibilisation' encouraging reduced service demand through individualized preventative measures.[175] While helpful in summarizing change in certain cases, such narratives miss some of the differentiation across local governments in England since 2010.

The missing understanding of the strategies of different local government types within the governance system, their contexts, and the understudied risks is remedied. A differentiated landscape of local statecraft engagements with financialization exists in England since 2010, characterized by vanguard, intermediate, and long-tail approaches. The next task is to investigate the local statecraft realms—external advice, borrowing and debt management, and in-area and out-of-area strategies—in order to construct an explanation of this landscape and its outcomes and implications.

---

[173] John (2014: 687).
[174] Kennett et al. (2015: 622).
[175] Hastings et al. (2015: 601).

5
Advising financialization?

External actors in local statecraft

5.0 Introduction

Newly formed in 2019, Bournemouth, Christchurch and Poole Council in southern England appointed international business services firm KPMG in a contract worth over £18 million to design and implement the 'fundamental transformation … required to fully realise the opportunities' of local government reorganization and reduce the complexity, duplication, and costs of its operating model.[1] Local statecrafters' engagement of such external actors has increased since 2010 to help navigate their changing situations amidst austerity, centralization, and risk.

Addressing such intermediaries as potential 'carriers', enablers, or even 'drivers', of financialization,[2] the local statehood realm of external advice warrants further examination. Critics consider these actors' involvement the ascendancy of a technocratic, post-democratic 'shadow state', siphoning off public resources beyond scrutiny and accountability.[3] The following analysis reveals the roles and activities of a widening array of external actors, providing specialist advice to local statecrafters and shaping their varied approaches and engagements with financialization.

Fiscal pressures in England since 2010 compelled local statecrafters to increase their relations with a broadening range of existing and new external actors. They include those providing legally required services (e.g. auditors), consultancy (e.g. economic), specialist advice (e.g. tax), and professional association (e.g. CIPFA). Such actors advise, enable, and support local statecrafter involvements with commercial finance.

External actors developed their strategies and services to cultivate and shape this growing local public sector market. Their knowledge, analysis, and experience are sought by local statecrafters formulating financial

---

[1] Quoted in Rudgewick (2021a: 1).
[2] Peck and Whiteside (2016: 255), Möller (2021: 188), Dörry (2022), Weber (2015).
[3] Brooks (2018: 199).

Financialization and Local Statecraft. Andy Pike, Oxford University Press. © Andy Pike (2023).
DOI: 10.1093/oso/9780192856661.003.0005

strategies and arrangements. Local governments needed the legal cover of commissioned expert advice to underpin their due diligence, risk management, and accountable decision-making. The UK government and professional regulation and guidance require and encourage such engagement.

Initially outlining the origins and rise of external actors, the analysis zooms in on five key types: accountants and consultants; financial consultants; TMAs; property consultants; and professional and sectoral advisors, associations, and consultants. For each, it explains their strategies for local public sector market (re)construction, activities, and implications.

External actors now play more integral and prevalent, though differentiated, roles across local governments in England since 2010. This growth results from local statecrafters' denuded capacity owing to staff reductions and increased demand for advice on new activities amidst fiscal stress and more active financial management.

5.1 The origins and rise of external actors in local government

Local statecrafters in England have long histories of engagement with external actors. As large, multifunctional, and complex organizations, local governments have sought independent and specialist knowledge to support their decision-making. Many external actors are long-standing, undertaking key functions and roles in municipal finance. Such actors are distinct from wider local state bodies in not delivering policy or public services. Some are from or have relations with commercial finance.

Independent expert advice is required by UK government and professional association in the accountability system. CIPFA guidance requires demonstration 'that all decision making is supported by sound professional advice'.[4] Ultimately, the local political leadership and officers are accountable for decisions taken.

External engagement has underpinned reorganization episodes. Political-economic agendas marked key periods, influenced by think tanks including the Institute of Economic Affairs in the Conservative governments' 1980s market-oriented reforms and the then New Local Government Network (NLGN) in New Labour's 2000s modernization agenda. These external actors formulated, promoted, and encouraged debate and experimentation with new concepts, models, and strategies.

---

[4] CIPFA (2019: 134).

Various UK governments formalized elements of such knowledges into policy. The then department of Communities and Local Government's *Developing the Market for Local Government Services* viewed local government as strategic commissioners of services 'shaping and leading markets, rather than responding to them'.[5] Intensifying during the 2000s, UK government encouragement of diversity of provision stimulated public sector divisions of accountancy and management consultancy firms more actively to engage, enter, and construct the local government advisory market. PricewaterhouseCoopers's (PwC) (2006) 'sub-optimal markets' report is a key example.[6]

Fiscal pressures in England from 2010 changed the extent and nature of engagement with external actors as local statecrafters moved towards more strategic and active financial management. Reductions in staff numbers, especially senior positions, cut capacity and capability. Denuded in-house resources compelled local statecrafters' turn to external service providers to 'outsource their thinking'.[7] Amidst concerns about undue reliance, the costs of commissioning external advice vied with other budgetary claims.

Reduced capacity and capability were differentiated by local government type. Recognizing strategic financial planning's importance and with larger revenue and capital budgets, counties, metropolitan, and London boroughs tried to retain in-house capacity.

The need to address funding gaps stimulated demand, increasing expenditure on external 'third-party' inputs.[8] Lack of expertise for especially more commercial activities underpinned growth: 'If Finance Directors grew up in local government finance in the 90s and the noughties … [they] just wouldn't have had the kind of relevant technical skill'.[9] As local statecrafters moved into new areas, they sought analysis of risk to support their due diligence.

In novel areas where there is uncertainty and even controversy, officers engage external advisers to provide 'assurance' to council members, since they 'tend to trust their advice', and avoid suspicions officers are trying to 'hoodwink them'.[10] Further external advice has also been commissioned as additional affirmation.

Local statecrafters and external actors have interacted in (re)constructing the market, demand for advice being configured by service supply. A 'market place … of advisers and institutions' evolved through actors selling services

---

[5] Communities and Local Government (2006: 65–67).
[6] PricewaterhouseCoopers (2006: 1).
[7] Civil servant 2, local government department (2021).
[8] EY and Oxygen Finance (2021).
[9] Financial Consultant 1 (2020).
[10] CFO, District Council (2021).

'trying to help councils', meeting demand for 'creative ways of doing things', seeking to 'stay close' to understand local government needs via conferences, seminars, and trying to 'bring products and services to … try and meet demand'.[11] Integral to external advisors' strategies was developing more specialized and lucrative services embedded within longer-term relationships rather than one-off transactions. Their ongoing diagnosis of issues and 'solutions' sought constantly to stimulate demand and opportunities for the 'never ending kind of circus'[12] of further sales and fees: 'there's always somebody trying to sell them something new'.[13]

Local statecrafter and external advisor relations and interaction shaped how the process operated and its outcomes and implications. Political leaderships and councillors originated new, 'wacky' and 'not always wise' ideas from their contact networks and introduced them to their CFOs.[14] Signalling uneven shifts in risk appetites, while CFOs typically 'don't come up with … wheezes',[15] they have been compelled to change outlooks and behaviours by fiscal stress and have not needed 'an awful lot of encouragement' to 'look to their peers' and, 'desperate for income', become 'quite opportunistic'.[16]

The incentives for engaging external advice and new ideas across England since 2010 are diverse. Local statecrafters reluctant to cut services had to 'find new ways of raising money', requiring external advice on 'relatively straightforward stuff' and ideas considered 'a bit innovative and risky'.[17] Demonstrating local statecraft peer influence, external advisors suggested emergent practices or those working elsewhere that could be adaptable to local circumstances.

5.2 Accountants and consultants

Accountancy firms have long-standing involvement with local governments in audit and consultancy. Integral to the accountability system, local statecrafters require independent assessment of their finances by auditors. Underpinned by professionalization and professional associations defending their interests and regulating their expertise,[18] the legal requirement for

---

[11] Associate Director, professional association (2020).
[12] Researcher, campaign group (2021).
[13] Former Director, public audit body (2021).
[14] Partner, Top 6 accountancy firm (2020).
[15] Partner, Top 6 accountancy firm (2020).
[16] Local government financial consultant 2 (2020).
[17] Partner, Top 6 accountancy firm (2020).
[18] Willmott (1986).

audit creates a national state-guaranteed market and statutory role for the accountancy profession.

Historically, accountants were characterized as 'bean counters' and the 'watchdogs of capitalism' in the private sector.[19] Recently, they have been interpreted as shifting towards a more aggressive commercial and US-style consultancy culture and away from the 'British profession's gentlemanly traditions of self-regulation and indulgent discipline'.[20]

Mirroring other business service sectors including the so-called 'magic circle' law firms, increased concentration through mergers and acquisitions created a smaller number of larger full-service firms. The 'Big 8' in 1987 became the 'quadropoly' of the 'Big 4' of PwC, Deloitte, Ernst and Young (EY), and KPMG in 2020, above lower tiers of medium-sized and smaller firms including BDO, Grant Thornton, and RSM.[21]

The reduced number of larger firms prompted the UK Competition and Markets Authority investigations of competition and conflicts of interest from cross-selling audit and consultancy services. Concerns originated in the demise of former Big 5 member Arthur Andersen following its involvement in US energy firm Enron's 2001 collapse.

Controversy surrounding these large firms selling consultancy services and compromising their accounting scrutiny independence and quality spread into the public sector. Such issues affected local governments in England, including construction firm Carillion's 2018 collapse. Experiences led the UK audit industry regulator the Financial Reporting Council to recommend stronger operational divides between accountancy firms' activities.

Underpinned by the CIPFA and the Local Authority (Scotland) Accounts Advisory Committee (LASAAC) code and IFRS, a legally required accountability is the publication of an audited annual statement of accounts providing a 'true and fair view' of the local government's 'financial position and transactions'.[22]

External and internal financial audits are required to demonstrate to the UK government and the public local government's management of taxpayers' money.[23] The local government's Audit Committee manages and oversees both audits. Separate from executive decision-making and scrutiny arrangements, this committee comprises governing and opposition members and relevant officers with an independent Chair.[24]

---

[19] Brooks (2018: x, 1).
[20] Brooks (2018: x, 1, 88).
[21] Brooks (2018: 283).
[22] CIPFA (2019: 104).
[23] Sandford (2019).
[24] CIPFA (2019).

Demonstrating its local statehood as a democratically accountable public institution, there is public right of access to local government's reported finances. An exception is where local statecrafters deem it commercially sensitive and/or discloses confidential information that provides 'some unfair commercial advantage'.[25]

Before the 1980s, audit was conducted by the localized District Audit Service (DAS) covering thirteen regions across England. Critics have questioned this system's independence, quality, and cost.[26]

Absorbing the localized system, the Audit Commission was established in 1983. It was part of then UK Secretary of State Michael Heseltine's aim to open up a local audit market to private sector firms.[27] Local statecrafters perceived further Thatcherite centralization. Based in London with regional District Units, the Audit Commission's in-house team independently commissioned external auditors for each local government. Approximately 70 per cent of contracts went to its District Units and the remainder to six of the largest accountancy firms.

From 2010, then UK Secretary of State Pickles' localism agenda sought greater market competition and the injection of private sector skills and expertise into the local public sector. Amidst firm lobbying, the Audit Commission was depicted as a 'creature of the Whitehall state, soaking up increasingly and unaccountably vast sums of public money'.[28] It was abolished in 2010 and wound up by 2015.

Aiming to reduce external audit costs by further opening-up the market for firms, the UK government introduced a new system. Reinforcing its national management of local statecraft, it combined tight central prescription with limited local discretion. A new statutory framework was formalized in the Local Audit and Accountability Act 2014 and NAO Code of Audit Practice.[29] Local governments could opt out of appointing their own external auditors and opt in to the new system managed by Public Sector Audit Appointments Ltd (PSAA) established by the LGA.[30] Almost all (98 per cent) local governments use the PSAA route.

Local statecrafters worried about propriety in audit appointments and losing the Audit Commission's sector-wide research and value for

[25] CIPFA (2019: 104).
[26] Campbell-Smith (2008).
[27] Clarke and Cochrane (1989).
[28] Wilson and Game (2011: 156).
[29] National Audit Office (2015a).
[30] Sandford (2019).

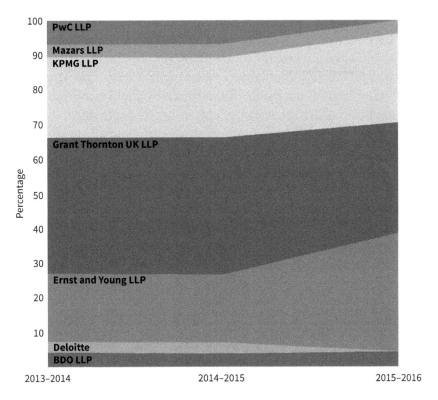

Figure 5.1 Audit contracts in local government by company, 2013–14 to 2015–16
Source: Public Sector Audit Appointments Ltd.

money studies.[31] With a narrower remit, PSAA reports annually on the results of auditors' work and established a forum to share good practice.[32]

Responding to the new system, accountancy firm strategies aimed to provide high quality, rigorous, and robust services demonstrating local government's value for money and compliance with statutory requirements. The market is structured around two- to three-year service contracts. The highly regulated structure has fostered relative continuity and stability across England since 2010 (Figure 5.1).

Market entries and exits have occurred. New firms entered, including EY. Many were pushed by the market contraction amongst national public sector bodies facing expenditure controls on using external consultants in austerity and drawn by local opportunities.

---

[31] Wilson and Game (2011).
[32] Sandford (2019).

Participants exited for several reasons. Since 2010 in England, local governments have become 'significantly more complex than private sector organisations',[33] involving hundreds of functions and service areas and myriad public and private relationships in a widening local state. The UK government funding system changes and fiscal stress introduced further complexity and uncertainty as local statecrafters engaged in new activities. Firms faced reputational risks in cost effectively meeting legal requirements to provide high quality audits and demonstrate compliance with national, professional, and international financial reporting standards.

Increased staff inputs to undertake more complex audits and relatively low fees paid by local governments reduced profit margins. Local audit fees fell by 40 per cent from 2015, while those for the UK government and FTSE100 firms rose by 20 per cent.[34] Declining fees and reduced market participants and competition questioned the system's viability. Critics argue standards have fallen relative to the private sector and inexperienced accountancy 'graduates get thrown in' despite growing complexity.[35]

Larger firms exited, including Big 4 members PwC and KPMG. By 2020, the market was divided between Big 4 and medium-sized firms Grant Thornton (~40 per cent), EY (~30 per cent), Mazars (~18 per cent), BDO (~5 per cent), and Deloitte (~5 per cent).[36] These remaining firms sought to balance their less profitable audit work with more lucrative advisory and consultancy services. Audit maintained their relationships with local statecrafters, replenishing their sectoral knowledge.

Market exits, falling fees, and concerns about local government financial sustainability and resilience prompted UK government attention. The Redmond Review identified problems with systemic operation, leadership, and market fragility, recommending a new supervisory body to reinstate some overall governance functions and increased fees to prevent further market exits.[37]

Auditors have been concerned with the management and impact of financial innovations and risk. They act as an assessor of, rather than advisor for, financialization. Indeed, some claim better audits would have revealed any financial problems earlier and created pressure for their timelier resolution.

Under the 2014 Act, public interest reports must be published when 'things have gone wrong'.[38] Originating in municipal *and* commercial finance,

[33] Senior Partner, Top 6 Accountancy firm (2020).
[34] Redmond (2020).
[35] Researcher, campaign group (2021).
[36] Partner, Top 6 accountancy firm (2020).
[37] Redmond (2020).
[38] CIPFA (2019: 112).

problems include failure to comply with statutory requirements, deficiencies in key funds, failed commercial ventures, and qualified opinions on annual report and accounts from auditors.

Demonstrating local governments' differentiated financial predicaments across England since 2010, qualified opinions on arrangements to secure value for money rose from 3.3 to 19.3 for single-tier councils and counties and from 2 to 4.8 for districts between 2010–11 and 2017–18.[39] This includes local statecrafters pursuing vanguard, intermediate, and long-tail approaches. Public interest reports were rare but are being published more regularly, including Grant Thornton's on the London Borough of Croydon, Northamptonshire County Council, and Nottingham City Council.

As accountancy firms developed full-service businesses, consultancy has been grown into a lucrative part of their strategies for the local government market in England. Critics even argue they are now 'consultancy firms with auditing sidelines, rather than the other way around' given most of their income and growth is now generated by non-audit and assurance consultancy services.[40] Others note the incentives for firms to provide a 'soft audit' to avoid compromising existing and potential consultancy business.[41]

The consultancy market in England opened up in the 1980s as local statecrafters sought advice on contracting out service delivery to generate efficiencies and reduce costs. This engagement mirrored the growing use of external consultants by the UK government and construction of a public sector market.[42] Deploying NPM, UK governments considered private sector expertise and skills essential to public sector modernization and efficiency improvement.

Critics highlighted the 'long reach of the bean counters', extending 'into the hearts of governments', and questioned their position as 'insiders', the independence of their advice, and prescription of public service 'marketization' generating further future service demand.[43] A link was drawn between the 'financialized world economy' becoming a 'theme park' for practices including 'false accounting, tax avoidance and regulation-dodging' with the 'bean counters marshalling their customers from one ride to another'.[44]

Before 2010 in England, consultants were typically commissioned to review operational management or oversee reorganization.[45] From 2010,

[39] National Audit Office (2019a).
[40] Brooks (2018: 11).
[41] Researcher, campaign group (2021).
[42] Campbell-Smith (2008).
[43] Brooks (2018: 6).
[44] Brooks (2018: 84).
[45] CIPFA (2019).

local statecrafters were focused on reducing costs and generating income. Consultancy addressed internal reorganization, service delivery (re)design, back-office activities, shared services, and the interface with local residents and businesses for payments and transactions.

External consultancy and its high cost were squeezed in UK government in early austerity. Then Conservative Prime Minister David Cameron promised 'an end to government by management consultant'.[46] This meant the focus of the largest accountancy firm consultancy businesses 'fundamentally shifted ... from Whitehall to town hall'.[47]

Overlapping with the accountancy ranking, lead firms were KPMG, PwC, and Deloitte. Boston Consulting Group and McKinsey undertook more strategic, shorter-term work for UK governments. EY entered the market from 2010. Rather than what EY UK chair Hywel Ball termed 'body shopping' the client by overproviding consultants,[48] specialist advisory work is lucrative because it can be priced on an individual basis securing 'proper resource to do a proper job'.[49] Contrasting regular, longer-term, and lower margin audit work, consultancy was irregular, shorter-term but higher margin. Even as firms exited local audit, they retained a consultancy presence. Others continuing audit provided consultancy advice to other local governments.

The local government consultancy market in England grew from 2010, propelled by reductions in local government capacity in austerity. While staff costs were reduced, capability was eroded to address the challenging tasks facing local statecrafters. As revenue budgets were squeezed, procuring albeit higher cost external consultancy for specific tasks was considered more cost effective than retaining in-house capacity.

As well as reducing costs in existing activities, local statecrafters increasingly needed external expertise to manage risk because they were considering new activities. These were often areas where any financialization was advised. Influenced by their relationships in audit, the consultancy divisions of the large accountancy firms became key sources of advice, especially for larger local governments.

This growing local market in England since 2010 remained differentiated. Consultancy was especially evident in local governments with substantial budgets and capital programmes including London and metropolitan boroughs, counties, and unitaries. Consultants were less evident or absent in smaller districts with limited budgets and potential local political difficulties

---

[46] Quoted in Brooks (2018: 195).
[47] Lead Partner, Big 4 accountancy firm (2020).
[48] Quoted in O'Dwyer (2021: 1).
[49] Senior Partner, Top 6 accountancy firm (2020).

procuring expensive services from high-profile international consultancy firms. Some local statecrafters drew upon peer group experience and networks rather than paying for external advice.

In early austerity from 2010, the focus was saving money. Advice was commissioned on temporary, project-based, and one-off activities. This involvement supported expenditure reduction strategies involving changing organizational structures, designing efficiency generation plans, and later transformation programmes. It included 'implementation consultancy' involving technology and 'bricks and mortar ... something tangible'.[50]

Advice was used by some local statecrafters to push through changes within the council and organization by deploying consultants' brand reputations for high-cost and high-quality work. Especially for large-scale and long-term decisions, council members sought companies with the 'brand or recognition for being experts' and the political cover of 'saying X advised us on this'.[51]

As austerity wore on into the mid-2010s, the focus intensified on reducing costs, increasing income, and managing risks. In the 'change to a price ... or cost-conscious environment', large consultancies saw opportunities to help deliver the UK government's 'real drive for vfm [value for money] and cost-down' and 'balancing government's books' locally.[52]

As straightforward efficiency improvements were exhausted, consultancy firms moved into root-and-branch reviews and organizational transformation programmes. This work involved 'payment by results' contracts and 'gain share' and 'risk and reward' models where advisers were only 'paid from the value they created'.[53] Strategies were formulated as part of long-term, multi-service partnership arrangements with large, internationalized firms.

Later austerity involved some outsourced activities being brought back in-house by local statecrafters to control assets and revenues, especially when projected savings failed to materialize. Recognition grew that local governments could not rely on a single partner and instead an 'ecosystem' was needed.[54]

Configuring the local public sector market in England through their interaction, consultancies sought longer-term relationships with local statecrafters to create call-off contracts and generate pipelines of repeat business and platforms to sell additional services. More profitable bespoke work remained prized relative to updates of existing advice. Consultancy moved

---

[50] Lead Partner, Big 4 accountancy firm (2020).
[51] Local government financial consultant 2 (2020).
[52] Lead Partner, Big 4 accountancy firm (2020).
[53] Lead Partner, Big 4 accountancy firm (2020).
[54] Lead Partner, Big 4 accountancy firm (2020).

towards securing outcomes rather than only providing time inputs. Where successful, the firms benefited from reduced transactions costs and increased trust as local statecrafters procured services from existing partners.

Accountancy firm consultants have been central in articulating, enabling, and supporting local statecrafters' more active financial approach and changing risk appetites. The increasingly sophisticated consultancy market has been shaped by its participants in 'how and what is bought from the sector' alongside a 'maturing of … capabilities … on the local government side to service some of their own needs better.'[55]

As the decade unfolded in England from 2010, market growth continued as more local statecrafters were forced to seek external advice to deal with fiscal stress and balance budgets. While evident in specific cases, consultants have not simply advised engagements with commercial finance and financialization across the sector. The landscape of local statecraft is differentiated. Amidst ongoing financial pressures, concerns persisted regarding costs and the larger firms' high prices, delivery record, and audit and consulting activity relations.

5.3 Financial consultants

Specialized local government financial consultants operate in England among the larger accountancy and consultancy firms. They are organized as small and medium-sized firms, partnerships, and self-employed freelancers. Some provide interim cover and secondment support for finance functions, especially during political leadership and management transition or structural reorganization. Many are former employees of local government and/or the large accountancy and consultancy firms.

Before 2010, these smaller, more specialized financial consultants faced less competition. Accountancy firms' consultants were engaged in larger scale and more lucrative work with UK government nationally before the 2008 financial crash.

Since 2010 across England, the number and range of these specialized financial consultants have expanded, creating a 'broader … wider mixed economy … of advisers.'[56] Their relative agility and lower day rates compared favourably to larger firms for cost-conscious local statecrafters seeking advice in austerity. Provision of tailored support was preferred rather than larger firms with a 'glossy brochure' selling their 'product.'[57]

---

[55] Lead Partner, Big 4 accountancy firm (2020).
[56] Associate Director, professional association (2020).
[57] Sector finance adviser (2021).

Competition has increased since 2010 but smaller consultants benefitted from increased specialization and segmentation as local governments sought advice from a range of advisers. Changes resulted from local statecrafters with reduced in-house capacity undertaking more active and strategic financial management.

These specialist financial consultants aim to provide tailored advice to local governments. They seek to add value by generating substantial additional resources above the costs of their services: 'forecasting and increasing the resources available over booking keeping or cuts off as savings'.[58] Each differentiate from larger consultancy firms selling services claiming large scale (~30 per cent) cost reductions. Layering external actors' involvement in local statecraft, some are commissioned to scrutinize and model claimed efficiencies from other external advisors.

Growing risks and uncertainty increased demand for specialist forecasting and modelling to assist local statecrafters constructing financial scenarios under different assumptions and decisions. From 2010 across England, strategies evolved from replacing capacity to providing more specialized advice 'providing a value added … [by] understanding complexity', supported by being 'steeped in local government history' and deep understanding of the funding system.[59] These consultancies are not advising financialization for its own sake.

Deciphering complexity and providing external understanding and validation of current knowledge and uncertainty are valued by local statecrafters. Some use advice to check their own projections, others frame it as external challenge. Independent analysis helps settle politically sensitive issues, such as revenue distributions in local business rate pooling schemes.

Some consultants use a subscription-based business model for member local governments. General sectoral advice builds profile and reputation alongside new service development and specialized projects. Examples include forecasting scenarios for local tax revenues and cash flow, peer benchmarking, and modelling new development revenues and their local service demand implications, and UK government financial settlements.

Given their size and limited capacity, districts are important clients. But, as austerity bit, local governments including counties and London boroughs purchased these services. Larger metropolitan districts and London boroughs undertook such work in-house. While not geographically limited since finance staff move around and can be brought in as required,

[58] Financial consultant 3 (2020).
[59] Local government financial consultant 2 (2020).

the consultants' customers tend to be regionalized around an initial core set and then broadening unevenly.

These smaller, more specialized consultants have advised local statecrafters on the potential risks, benefits, and costs of financial innovations. Advice has been provided at organizational and functional levels especially in care, housing, and regeneration. Specific advice has been provided on a case-by-case basis rather than promoting wholesale moves towards financialization.

Innovations originate in the ongoing relations and regular, even weekly, interactions between these consultants and client CFOs. Wider information sharing occurs amongst local finance community networks.

5.4 Treasury management advisors

TMAs have played a long-standing role in local government finance in England. Historically, they provided advice including macro-economic outlooks, interest rate forecasts, counterparty creditworthiness assessments, technical accounting inputs, and cash deposit placements. TMAs operated at the interface of local statecraft's engagements with commercial finance and financialization.

In the accountability system, TMAs are formally embedded in the treasury management statements required for every local government under CIPFA guidance. Around 90 per cent of local governments purchase treasury management advice, increasing in England amidst fiscal stress since 2010. Larger local governments retained some in-house capacity, but treasury management was only part of CFO roles in smaller districts.

Since 2010 and mirroring accountancy and consultancy firms, concentration reduced TMAs from seven to two firms (Figure 5.2). Sector Treasury Services' acquisition of Butler's for an undisclosed fee in 2011 prompted an UK Office of Fair Trading (OFT) competition inquiry before its authorization.[60] While the deal value was relatively small for national regulator attention, it was reviewed because the firms were selling services to local governments managing public money.

Revealing undisclosed relations with commercial finance, the OFT inquiry exposed how some TMAs were earning more in 'introductory fees' from commissions from third parties, mostly banks, to encourage uptake of their financial products by local governments than they were from

---

[60] Office of Fair Trading (2011a).

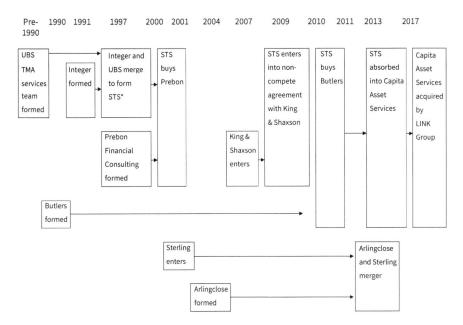

Figure 5.2 Mergers and acquisitions in the treasury management sector, pre-1990–

Note: Sector Treasury Services (STS).
Source: Adapted from Competition Commission (2011: 54) and Marrs (2017).

advising local governments.[61] As a downside of hitherto hidden financialization advice, this was problematic for local statecrafters if their TMA was getting paid for advising what was in the advisor and banks' interests 'rather than the [local government] clients'.[62] Tightened regulation and greater transparency followed the inquiry.

Further concentration and internationalization occurred through LINK's £888 million acquisition of Capital Asset Services to create LINK Asset Services in 2017. By 2020, the ~£10 million annual market was a duopoly between Arlingclose (~40 per cent) and LINK Asset Services (~60 per cent). Each are active across the UK with some geographical variations, shaped by historical contracts and referrals by neighbouring local governments. Both sell their services to private and civic sectors too.

While fees for local governments can be £20,000–30,000 annually, key for local statecrafters is advice that is 'going to help you save massively more than their own fees'.[63] Contracts are three years on average. While some local statecrafters prefer one- to two-year contracts, others buy lower-cost

---

[61] Office of Fair Trading (2011b: B3).
[62] Director, treasury management advisor (2020).
[63] Local government financial consultant 4 (2020).

seven-year deals, and some purchase discounted advice in geographically adjacent groups.

Given the duopoly, concerns lingered about firm strategies, pricing, and competition. Each firm sells similar services but is trying to upgrade from basic, standardized provision to more bespoke and higher margin advice that incurs higher fees—similar to the larger consultancy firms. TMAs' provision of more strategic and specialized services reflects and stimulates local statecrafters' more active financial management.

With growing complexity across local governments since 2010, interpreting evolving codes, guidance, and standards and translating them into options for local statecrafters is a core service. Examples include investments, debt, and balance sheet management. Working at the interface of local statecraft and financialization, maintaining close relationships with the Department and commercial finance actors are critical for TMAs.

TMAs encourage local statecrafters' openness to new ideas, especially what they do not realize they want. Reflecting the municipal and commercial finance intersections of financialization, new services include strategic debt management, innovative financial instruments, financial modelling, and capital financing. Reinforcing more active and integrated financial strategies and moving in a more financialized direction, TMAs have grown in importance in England since 2010 especially in areas new to local governments. Examples include helping local statecrafters to borrow cheaply then decide what to invest in.

Local governments in England already engaged with commercial finance have deepened their relations. Specifically, more active cash management gained prominence given low interest rates following the 2008 crash. This activity has become critical for those with substantial cash reserves, especially more prosperous counties and districts. For these local statecrafters, making cash work harder to reduce inflation exposure and generate returns has become more important given their value for money responsibilities and the opportunity costs of cash deposited in the bank at very low interest rates.

In the tight financial situations across England since 2010, even the relatively small-scale contributions to overall finances from interest rate arbitrage between locations for cash deposits are deemed worth pursuing by local statecrafters. TMAs have challenged the traditionally risk-averse strategies of treasury management staff focused on the UK government and CIPFA guidance principles of security, liquidity, and yield since 'they're kind of stuck in that mode.'[64]

---

[64] Local government financial consultant 4 (2020).

TMAs have encouraged use of MMF. These are mutual and pooled funds managed by financial institutions offering investors high liquidity, low-risk, and short-term investments in cash, cash equivalent securities, and debt-based securities with short-term maturities and high credit ratings. Total UK local government investments in MMF increased sharply, especially in England, from £0.7 billion to £7.7 billion between 2008 and 2019.[65] Stimulating relations with other external financial actors and the process of financialization, such moves have been met by financial institutions promoting new products.

More active cash management and TMA advice has been shaped by the Icelandic Banks episode. During the 2000s, under national government pressure to generate returns on their cash, local statecrafters across England made deposits with Glitnir, Kaupthing, and Landsbankinn in Iceland. Each bank pursued fast growth strategies following privatization and liberalization, rapidly expanding their balance sheets with government guaranteed deposits and tapping international wholesale money markets to offer relatively higher and market leading interest rates on their products.[66]

Amidst low interest rates, local councillors and officers were attracted by 6 per cent returns on deposits, and mindful of their fiduciary responsibilities to ensure value for money for their local government's finances. By 2008, 123 local governments had deposited £920 million.[67] The 2008 crisis precipitated the banks' failure. They were too large to be bailed out by Iceland's national government without a sovereign default. The banks' collapse left the local governments exposed with deposits in failed banks and concerned about getting their money back. Sector commentators aired concerns about 'bad advice' from TMAs.[68]

While around 90 per cent of the deposits were recovered by 2014,[69] this experience fuelled the 'councillors at the casino' narrative that local governments were unable effectively to manage risk and steward public money when engaging with external financial actors and financialization. The Audit Commission concluded 'a substantial sum of public money was put at risk' and local statecrafters had not responded effectively to 'warning signals'.[70] Campaigners interpreted 'a speculative local authority Iceland carry trade, where money was borrowed from UK banks like Barclays at low teaser rates

[65] Dagdeviren and Karwowski (2021).
[66] Wade and Sigurgeirsdottir (2011).
[67] Treasury Committee (2009).
[68] Sector journalist (2021).
[69] Bridge (2014).
[70] Audit Commission (2009: 30).

by UK councils, to invest at higher rates of interest in Icelandic banks—pocketing the 3–4% interest rate spread'.[71] The episode exposed substantial financial risks of fiscally stressed local statecrafters engaging with external financial actors in financialization.

The UK government viewed the local governments involved as responsible for making autonomous financial decisions. The Prudential Code and CIPFA guidance was subsequently updated to emphasize the security, liquidity, and yield principles governing local government investments. Similar to the chilling effect on financialization in local government in England of the Hammersmith and Fulham swaps affair from the 1990s, the Icelandic banks episode cast a shadow on conceptions of risk and 'reduced the number of banks councils are prepared to invest with'.[72] This experience further increased rather than reduced local statecrafter demand for specialist advice in managing cash deposits to avoid a repeat.

Working the boundary of municipal and commercial finance, TMAs have been integral in the introduction and encouragement of financial innovations as engagements with financialization. While investment in hitherto untried asset classes such as bonds, equities, and property might be considered 'quite racy' for local governments,[73] TMAs have sought to embed assessment and decision-making methods into more balanced, strategic and longer-term approaches to treasury management. TMAs claim to provide informed advice for local government rather than promoting novelty for its own sake. Their argument is that many things local statecrafters might class as 'innovative' are actually 'tried and tested elsewhere' in the public sector, including derivatives to hedge risk in UK government and housing associations.[74]

TMA roles in financial innovation vary in the differentiated landscape of local statecraft engagements with the relations and process of financialization. TMAs are especially evident amongst vanguard statecrafters receptive to new and potentially riskier approaches and instruments. The Director of Corporate Resources, London Borough of Newham, Conrad Hall described its history as 'almost a text book case of initiative overload' with its 'share of every passing trend in local government finance over the last decade or two' including vanilla and 'exotic' LOBO loans, 'over a dozen' subsidiary businesses, several 'complex PFI deals', 'joint venture arrangements with multiple partners', 'public inquiries into deals with the owners of local sports stadiums',

[71] Benjamin (2018: 1).
[72] CIPFA (2019: 82).
[73] Director, treasury management advisor (2020).
[74] Director, treasury management advisor (2020).

and 'an ambitious shared arrangement, OneSource, for all of our back office services'[75]. TMAs' role is also scrutinizing other external advice amidst local government's growing openness to the increased 'flow of innovations' to close funding gaps in England since 2010.[76]

Nuancing accounts of widespread local state financialization, these potentially riskier innovations are not simply instruments enabling local statecrafters to chase yield—i.e. earnings generated and realized on an investment over a specific period. Reflecting local government's wider economic, social, and environmental responsibilities and the Environmental, Social and Corporate Governance (ESG) agenda, specific arrangements including Real Estate Investment Trusts (REITs) have been used to finance social infrastructure including housing with integrated social care.

Beyond the vanguard approaches, many local governments in England remain risk-averse, although this is often concern about 'doing something different to everyone else'.[77] Financial innovations originated and stimulated by TMAs have spread across the sector since 2010, including LOBO loans and sale-and-leaseback deals. TMAs act as a 'time saver', interpreting what changing regulations mean for local governments and providing scale economies in knowledge diffusion.[78] Yet there is still around 10 per cent, albeit declining, of local statecrafters suspicious of TMAs as operating like 'insurance salesmen'.[79] These local governments use in-house capability, drawing upon informal networks and peer knowledge.

The role of TMAs in local statecraft's engagements with financialization reached a new point in a high profile and contentious financial innovation in 2020. Arlingclose advised Plymouth City Council on an interest rate swap deal. The first use of this type of derivative instrument since the Hammersmith and Fulham swaps affair in the late 1990s.

Amidst uncertainty over the legal basis for entering such arrangements and UK government concerns about 'sharp accounting',[80] the City Council's Head of Financial Planning and Reporting Paul Looby argued 'at a time of adversity, you look for new innovative ideas'.[81] The £75 million deal with Santander aims to hedge against the city council's exposure to rising interest rates in refinancing £468 million of short-term debt by fixing lower borrowing costs for twenty years and mitigating the risk of expenditure or investment reductions.

[75] Hall (2020: 1).
[76] Director, treasury management advisor (2020).
[77] Director, treasury management advisor (2020).
[78] Director, treasury management advisor (2020).
[79] Director, treasury management advisor (2020).
[80] Civil servant 1, local government department (2021).
[81] Quoted in Stubbington (2020: 1).

Arlingclose advised that the 2011 Localism Act's general power of competence overrides the precedent from Hammersmith and Fulham, supported by legal opinion obtained by Plymouth City Council and Santander.

This innovation proved controversial amongst local statecrafters and other external actors. Advocates argued it was a common derivative contract used for hedging that allowed the exchange of floating for fixed interest payments and was appropriate for Plymouth City Council given its relatively high levels of short-term borrowing, especially from other local governments, that were exposed to interest rate risk when refinancing.[82] Critics claimed the deal was ultra vires beyond the local government's legal powers, arguing that 'ultimately it's services to the public that can suffer when this sort of recklessness occurs.'[83]

5.5 Property consultants

As integral actors in local property markets, local governments in England have long-standing engagements with property consultants. Advice on land, building, planning, and physical regeneration has long been sought by local statecrafters. Legal and professional guidance requires such input in due diligence. Historically, such services were focused on local government activities within their areas.

Property consultancies are of three types: 'big and global, medium and regional, and local and niche'.[84] Large, internationalized firms in residential and/or commercial property dominate the market including CBRE, Jones Lang LaSalle (JLL), and Savills. Similar to accountancy and consultancy, concentration is ongoing through mergers and acquisitions with medium and smaller sized firms in lower market tiers. Larger firm consultancies are part of wider property services firms including planning, regeneration, surveying, and valuation. Each are plugged into and seeking to shape highly internationalized flows of property investment.[85]

Reconfiguring the local government market in England since 2010, property consultancies have evolved from valuing current land and buildings to formulating revenue generation strategies based on existing asset utilization and commercial property acquisition. Local statecrafters have engaged such consultancies in more active financial strategies to deliver

---

[82] Stubbington (2020: 1).
[83] Rob Whiteman, CIPFA Chief Executive, quoted in Public Finance (2020: 1).
[84] Executive Director, property company (2021).
[85] Brill (2020).

cost reductions and income generation. First is more active utilization of existing property assets within local government areas. Activities include sale of unused or assets deemed surplus to generate capital receipts, and asset retention, redevelopment, and integration within local regeneration strategies.

Demonstrating geography's critical role in structuring and shaping local statecraft and financial strategies, much activity concerns addressing local opportunities. This includes using UK government department land asset disposals for housing developments and responding to disinvestments including local retail centres being sold by owners.

Growing substantially to generate income across local governments in England since 2010, formulating property-based investment strategies is the second main area. Critical is this now includes existing in-area activities and, increasingly, out-of-area strategies beyond the local government's boundaries. The local statehood underpinned by the Localism Act 2011 has been used to justify this local statecraft.

Local statecrafters' increased interest in property since 2010 resulted from low interest rates and returns in other asset classes and their higher risk profiles. As local governments and their advisors considered potential asset classes in which to invest: 'historically, properties are a pretty certain investment … better than putting it into equities or things like that.'[86] Given local statecrafters know their own patch, investing outside their areas necessitated external advice to identify opportunities and manage risks.

Demonstrating the related agency of external actors *and* local statecrafters, advisors, politicians, and officers have all been actively constructing the market for such property investments. Local government's income generation imperative from 2010 translated into growing demand for property assets able to produce revenues greater than their costs. Financial benefits have been sought amidst risks of especially commercial property investments including factories, logistics hubs, offices, and retail parks.

Property consultants provide the supply-side advice for local government investors, identifying potential properties and assessing their fit and contributions as part of portfolio investment strategies. While advisors have been 'sending lists of properties to local governments', they 'don't need much tempting.'[87] Changing local statecraft and its geographies in England from 2010, consultants are being commissioned 'with the brief … to find me something I can invest in either in borough or anywhere.'[88]

[86] Partner, Top 6 accountancy firm (2020).
[87] Local government financial consultant 2 (2020).
[88] Local government financial consultant 4 (2020).

Concerns have been raised about the independence of advice provided by some consultants when 'they've often got a vested interest in the scheme.'[89] Local statecrafters have had to ensure compliance with guidance on independence, transparency, and accountability. This responsibility is acute in mitigating risk of loss of revenue, income, and/or asset value.

Forging new local statecraft geographies across England from 2010, property consultants have innovated by introducing and promoting the distinction between in and out-of-area investment strategies. Advice has changed the focus of local governments only investing in their own areas, extending local statecraft's investment landscape. It has enabled local governments with limited local investment opportunities to expand their spatial reach and manage risk by diversifying their investment portfolio beyond their areas.

Financial innovations have been utilized too, engaging local governments in the financialization process. Property consultants have worked with commercial financial institutions on funding and financing arrangements, including income strips and sale-and-leaseback deals. Working with a growing number of local governments enabled sharing of peer group practice amongst local statecrafters across England.

Contributing to the 'councillors at the casino' narrative, the rapid growth and value of commercial property investment by local governments attracted attention from Parliament, the NAO, national and sectoral media, and campaign groups.[90] Disquiet was evident among sector professionals of all being 'tarred with the same brush' as the small number of local statecrafters pursuing such vanguard strategies.[91] UK government concerns focused on prioritization and whether local governments were borrowing at less than commercial interest rates from the PWLB to invest to generate yield ahead of security and liquidity, distorting local and other property markets through their access to relatively cheaper credit.[92]

The Department issued new statutory guidance on local government investments in 2018.[93] Reflecting their growing role and influence, it was explicit on whether and how local statecrafters in England were using external advisors and monitoring and maintaining the quality of their advice. This stipulation reflected UK government suspicion that local governments were

---

[89] Associate Director, professional association (2020).
[90] National Audit Office (2020), Davies (2018), Marrs (2018b), TaxPayers' Alliance (2020).
[91] Associate Director, professional association (2020).
[92] Plender (2017).
[93] MHCLG (2018).

commissioning independent advice to confirm their existing decisions and underpin due diligence.

Amidst this national regulatory tightening, local statecrafters built internal capacity as property investment strategies became more important in their finances. High-profile property consultants were expensive and attracting unwanted media attention. In-house teams often included ex-private sector property specialists and learnt from commissioning external advice.

5.6 Professional and sectoral advisors, associations, and consultants

A further key category of external actors working with local governments in England is professional and sectoral advisors, associations, and consultants. While having sectoral origins, they operate externally to individual local governments. Their formal and informal activities, services, and networks remain important for local statecrafters seeking trusted views to close funding gaps since 2010. Advice is often used in complementary ways alongside more commercial external advisors.

The Department commissions external actors to undertake specialist reviews. These occur in local governments facing financial difficulties and/or failing to meet statutory responsibilities for specific services or overall. While non-statutory, criteria guide their commissioning within the broader accountability system.

Reviewers are sector leaders with senior executive experience and trustful reputations. Demonstrating the effects of fiscal stress, reviews have increased since 2010, including Bristol City Council, Croydon Borough Council, Northampton County Council, and Nottingham City Council.

Reviews can precede national intervention in local statecraft, including the appointment of temporary external managers by the UK Secretary of State. The negative impacts of new activities and their mismanagement have been evident since 2010. Reviews at Croydon, Bristol, and Nottingham focused on new commercial initiatives and financial management and governance.

New external relations with commercial finance actors and engagements with the financialization process have been used as fixes for particular local statecraft predicaments. One illustrative example is the Best Value review of Northamptonshire County Council. Its CFO issued two S114 reports in 2018. Concerns about 'financial failings' in management and governance and compliance with its best value duty began emerging in mid-austerity 2016.[94] Auditor KPMG reported adverse value for money opinions on its annual accounts and an advisory notice that an unlawful unbalanced budget was about to be set by the council in 2018.

The Department announced an external review of the County's published financial information and the LGA led a peer review of its financial planning and management. At the start of 2018, then UK Secretary of State James Brokenshire commissioned a formal Best Value inspection. Rather than recommending improvement of the County's financial management and signalling more structural, even unfixable, financial management problems, the inspection recommended the County's abolition and replacement with two unitary local governments.[95] As its financial situation worsened through 2018 and trust in the County's financial management competence declined further, the Department appointed commissioners to run the local government until its replacement in 2021.

Responding to problems the Best Value review identified, local statecrafters turned to financial innovation and financialization. In the municipal finance world, the Department allowed the County to use £70 million of capital receipts for revenue expenditure. Engaging commercial finance actors, £42 million of this capital receipts total was generated from a thirty-five-year sale-and-leaseback deal with Canada Life Investments worth £64 million for the County's recently opened new headquarters building in Northampton. Local media bemoaned service cuts while the local government spent £554,000 on consultancy advice from PwC.[96] Relaxing centralized controls on local statecraft, the UK government allowed the County to raise an extra 2 per cent on CT without holding a referendum.

The Northamptonshire County Council's experience demonstrates the related roles of different external actors in addressing this local government's particular financial difficulties, involving external auditors, the Department appointed Best Value inspectors and commissioners, LGA peer review, Canada Life Investments, and PwC. Whether deemed a rogue mismanaged element or victim of a dysfunctional system, external actors were pivotal in explaining this instance of local statecraft's municipal finance innovations and engagements with financialization.

For their sector-led improvement agenda, the LGA provides advisory and support services in local governments. These comprise challenge through finance peer review, financial health check, efficiency and income generation

[94] Sandford (2020c: 17).
[95] Sandford (2020c).
[96] Ward (2018).

support programmes, peer support events, councillor and officer training and development, and data analysis through LG Inform.

Financial peer reviews are conducted by former or current senior local government officers, typically Chief Executives or functional directors, and CFOs for financial management reviews. Peer review provides independent and constructive external challenge and support for the political and organizational leadership and management. The LGA is often invited in by local governments experiencing challenges. Reviews provide general and specific advice, including new financial approaches and innovations, monitoring, and follow-up activities, but decisions remain with the local statecrafters responsible.

CIPFA is the professional membership association, standard setter, regulator, and provider of commercial advice to the local government sector. Services include consultancy on efficiency improvement, process transformation, and income generation. Specific areas cover strategic and technical advice including financial resilience reviews and accounting assistance. Financial modelling and benchmarking are provided with Grant Thornton and CIPFA's own financial resilience index and resource forecasting model. Further services are provided on counter fraud, service areas, governance, and data and intelligence analysis and research, networks and publications, professional qualification, and training and recruitment with Penna Recruitment Solutions.

CIPFA advises on financial innovations, aiming to inform local statecrafter decision-making rather than advocate specific instruments. Some see CIPFA's multiple roles as problematic given their national professional, regulatory, and commercial roles effecting market power and competition in the local government consultancy market.

Further key networks shaping local statecraft and financialization in England are the finance officer-led associations for local government types: Society of County Treasurers; Society of District Treasurers; Society of London Treasurers; Society of Municipal Treasurers; and Society of Unitary Treasurers. Each are run by volunteer officers and represent member interests on finance issues, organizing events, networking, and providing support. All are represented within the Association of Local Authority Treasurers Societies. These associations act as important channels for dissemination, sharing and networking on financial issues and innovations affecting their local government type.

Interest groups are a further set of external actors that influence local statecraft in England. They include the County Councils Network, District Councils Network, London Councils for London Boroughs and the City of London, SIGOMA (Special Interest Group of Municipal Authorities) for metropolitan boroughs, and the Unitary Councils' Network. Other interest groups organize around specific agendas and themes, including the Co-operative Councils' Innovation Network, larger Core Cities, mid-sized Key Cities, and local authority pension funds.

Several are organized as Special Interest Groups within the LGA and pro-vide voice for their members. Often concerning financial issues, they provide advocacy and lobbying, and cross-party/non-partisan political representa-tion, research, media, and public affairs work for members, and networking events and support services. Larger organizations such as London Councils have specialized finance units producing research and analysis for London boroughs and seeking to influence UK government policy.

These groups act as vehicles to articulate and mobilize around collective concerns on financial affairs, such as annual financial settlements, reforms to specific grant funds, local tax arrangements, and financial innovations. They also serve as channels for dissemination and networking around mem-ber experiences across England, underpinning the local government finance community's sharing culture.

Staff-based organizations for local statecrafters operate across local gov-ernment in England. General membership-based associations—such APSE (Association for Public Service Excellence)—provide advice, research, and information sharing on public service areas especially in-house provision and in-sourcing as well as advocacy, campaigns, lobbying, and training for coun-cillors and officers. APSE Solutions is an in-house consultancy and interim management support service. More specialized is SOLACE, the membership-based UK network for public sector and local government professionals that undertakes advocacy and representation work. Subsidiary SOLACE in Busi-ness provides personal and organizational development and interim and executive recruitment services. SOLACE deals with financial affairs but it is not their core focus.

The last group are think tanks offering various services concerning local government issues. Many use a subscription model for members. They provide assorted advice and consultancy services, research, project imple-mentation, evaluation, events, publications, and training. Some have political alignments and ideological agendas such as the Centre for Local Economic Strategies' (CLES) community wealth-building[97] and Localis' neo-localism.[98] The main organizations are CLES, Local Government Information Unit

[97] CLES (2021).
[98] Localis (2017).

(LGiU), Localis, and New Local, formerly the NLGN. While their work sometimes covers financial issues, none are specialized in this area.

5.7 Conclusions

While long-standing, the role and reach of a widening array of external actors in local government in England extended and deepened since 2010. In more active financial management to reduce costs and generate income, local state-crafters were compelled into new strategies and activities. Needs for specialist advice grew markedly.

Seeking to stimulate and grow such demands, various external actors worked with local statecrafters to construct and configure this local public sector market. Existing commercial actors sought closer, longer-term relationships, and service upgrading into higher margin activities. New actors emerged, drawn by market opportunities.

The national governance of local government funding structures and shapes the growing need for and involvements of external advisors. As a long-standing, highly centralized, and multilayered municipal finance system in England, it has become increasingly complex since 2010. Ongoing changes involve minor modifications punctuated by radical shifts. This situation forced local statecrafters to seek the advice and support of external actors with deep knowledge of the system and close relationships with the Department. The specifics of the local public sector market in England favours existing external actors, although many have reconfigured and extended their long-standing roles.

The growing role and influence of external advisors and promotion of the relations and process of financialization have not been a homogenous roll-out across local governments in England since 2010. While elements of normalization of a 'new financial culture' are evident involving prominent external actors,[99] the picture is institutionally, geographically, and temporally differentiated; determined by local statecraft. This landscape is explained by differences in local government type and size, risk appetites, attitude and openness to external advice, strategies, locations, local economic conditions,

---

[99] Deruytter and Möller (2020: 408).

and tax bases. Local statecrafters undertaking vanguard approaches are more open than those exhibiting intermediate and long-tail behaviours. The complexity and uncertainty of the local government funding system in England since 2010 means it is not straightforward for commercial finance actors to financialize, even with the help of external advisors.

6

The local statecraft of borrowing and debt management

6.0 Introduction

Periodic accounts emerge of spendthrift local governments in England with a 'debt addiction' on a borrowing 'spree' in the 'councillors at the casino' narrative.[1] These somewhat superficial interpretations lack depth, context, and referents for their claims. Borrowing and debt are long-standing, integral areas of local statecraft where municipal and commercial finance intersect.

Borrowing and debt management strategies grew in importance for local statecrafters across England addressing funding gaps from 2010. A national system governs local government borrowing. From 2003, the UK government encouraged greater local autonomy and responsibility while retaining control within the highly centralized funding system.

Reflecting the use of specific loan types and new, more complex debt instruments as evidence of local state financialization,[2] more active strategies are evident. Local statecrafters interpret and work with and around the centralized national codes and guidance in devising their borrowing and debt management.

Borrowing has grown overall and in particular ways since 2010. Underpinning the differentiated landscape of local statecraft engagements with financialization, vanguard, intermediate, and long-tail approaches are evident. The local political and officer leaderships' strategic vision, aims, and responses to closing funding gaps determine strategies, reflecting external advice and involvement (or not) with financial institutions developing loan products for the local public sector market in England.

Examining who local governments are borrowing from and on what terms reveals the widening range of lenders and instruments, including internal resources, each other, the PWLB, and external financial institutions

---

[1] Ford (2020: 1), Hammond (2020: 1).
[2] Deruytter and Möller (2020), Lagna (2016).

Financialization and Local Statecraft. Andy Pike, Oxford University Press. © Andy Pike (2023).
DOI: 10.1093/oso/9780192856661.003.0006

and investors. Financial innovations and financialization are evident amongst those pursuing vanguard approaches but are a relatively small proportion of overall borrowing.

6.1 The national governance of local government borrowing

Amidst fears of profligacy, weak public money management, and perceptions of financial incompetence, historically the UK government has controlled local government borrowing. The UK government is 'umpire and player' in financial markets as a borrower, regulator, and monetary policymaker.[3]

National governance of local borrowing has persisted within the highly centralized funding system in England. Legislation provides the framework alongside codes and guidance. Utilizing the UK sovereign guarantee and the PWLB's dominance as a lending source, HMT sets the interest rates and limits, exerting central national discipline over borrowing. Further influence is expressed through ministerial speeches and departmental policy documents. Local statecrafters engage, navigate, and formulate their borrowing and debt management strategies in this evolving national setting.

Demonstrating the institutionalization of limits,[4] the UK government retained tight control before 1981 through mandatory codes and approvals of loan and borrowing allocations. Since 1981, borrowing limits were set nationally for capital programmes. National credit controls were used between 1990 and 2004. Local statecrafters circumvented UK government controls by funding capital projects through capital receipts from asset sales, revenue, and leasing rather than buying capital goods.[5]

The introduction of prudential borrowing through the Local Government Act 2003 remains the legal and regulatory framework in the early 2020s. This Prudential Code (hereafter the Code) increased local government autonomy and responsibility for borrowing from any willing lender within the centralized system. It reduced the risks and uncertainties resulting from UK government ministers deciding on borrowing controls and credit approvals. Local statecrafters bemoaned such decisions as arbitrary, political, and detrimental to strategic and longer-term financial planning.

The Code sets the framework for overall debt levels based on affordability. Introducing 'wide freedom to borrow and invest' matched by local decisions

---

[3] Sbragia (1986: 311).
[4] Sbragia (1996).
[5] Sbragia (1986).

and accountability[6], it required 'councils to determine and keep under review how much money they can afford to borrow'.[7] It stipulates that appropriate revenues are available for servicing and repaying debts, and consideration is made of the borrowing's wider financial, legal, economic, and social implications. Reinforcing the national structuring of local government debt management and limits on financialization, borrowing is only allowed in sterling without HMT authorization to borrow in other currencies.

The Code requires local governments to determine, review, and 'not to exceed their prudential borrowing limits, or any national limits imposed by central government'.[8] It continues the circumscribed autonomy of local statecrafters to determine capital investment and levels of borrowing to finance it based on their current and future affordability assessments.

The Local Government Act 2003 gives local governments a general power to borrow 'for any purpose relevant to its functions … or for the purpose of the prudent management of its financial affairs'.[9] Short-term borrowing is permitted for cash flow management. Medium and longer-term borrowing is only for capital investment. Local governments cannot mortgage their assets as collateral to secure borrowing against their properties. Borrowing can be secured against future revenues.

The Code contains treasury management indicators requiring local statecrafters to monitor and report on external borrowing and connect to their risk management. The capital financing requirement estimates the underlying borrowing need. Set by the full council, the authorized limit for external debt is the maximum a local government can borrow. The operational boundary for external debt is set by the full council and is the 'estimate of most likely, ie [sic] prudent, but not worst case scenario' of the maximum external debt.[10] Each indicator relates to the local government's capital expenditure plans and annual estimates of capital financing and cash flow requirements. A further requirement is the MRP stating the minimum amount charged to the annual revenue budget for the repayment of external borrowing associated with capital expenditure.

While affording relatively more autonomy than before 2003, the Code remains a nationally controlled framework, albeit one which deliberately avoids 'hard' limits or ratios on borrowing.[11] Further, the UK government retains a reserve power to impose borrowing limits and override local

[6] Civil servant 2, local government department (2021).
[7] CIPFA (2019: 83).
[8] CIPFA (2019: 35).
[9] CIPFA (2019: 82).
[10] CIPFA (2019: 87).
[11] Civil servant 2, local government department (2021).

governments' own determinations of borrowing under the Code for national economic reasons. The UK Secretary of State's power to introduce such restrictions remains as yet unused.

The Code has been revised in response to evolving local statecraft in England since 2010. New income generation strategies have led many local statecrafters to borrow to invest in assets to deliver financial returns to close funding gaps and offset reductions in revenue expenditure on services. Fearing the reordering of the municipal financial management principles of security, liquidity, and yield, the UK government and CIPFA's concerns were that fiscal stress and borrowing for investment was putting yield ahead of security and liquidity. Such changes were rewiring and rescaling incentives and risks in local statecraft.

Debate and bargaining between local statecrafters, the UK government, and CIPFA around regulation is long-standing.[12] CIPFA highlighted the growing risks involved in 'borrowing significant sums in advance of when they needed the finance' with 'these sums … being invested, increasing the credit risk faced'.[13] TMAs highlighted the ambiguities between CIPFA and HMT guidance on borrowing in advance of need and the unusual situation of having two national regulatory bodies covering local government activities that 'sometimes use the same word to mean different things'.[14] The revised guidance now states that 'local authorities must not borrow more than or in advance of their needs purely in order to profit from the investment of extra sums borrowed'.[15]

Local statecraft evolves amidst UK government controls and circumscribed autonomy. External advisors are used to support due diligence and demonstrate Code compliance. TMAs have increased their role in explaining what the rules mean, what is 'generally accepted', and what other local governments are doing and thereby constitutes 'normal practice'.[16]

6.2   Borrowing and debt management strategies

Local statecraft strategies in this realm have changed from a 'highly technical … arcane, activity' since 2010.[17] From the breakdown of the US dollar-based monetary system in the 1970s, financial markets became more

---

[12] Sbragia (1986).
[13] CIPFA (2019: 92).
[14] Director, treasury management advisor (2020).
[15] CIPFA (2019: 86).
[16] Director, treasury management advisor (2020).
[17] Sbragia (1986: 311).

unpredictable and volatile generating demand and supply of new instruments to manage risk including derivatives, futures, options, and swaps.

Before 2010 in England, administrative and entrepreneurial local statecraft was evident.[18] The Code prompted an increase in the importance and size of treasury management functions in local governments to manage increased borrowing levels. Engagements with financialization were initiated as some treasury managers contracted with external financial actors for their borrowing needs. Approaches largely focused on packaging loans to finance capital projects.

Reflecting international public financial management practice,[19] strategies shifted towards a portfolio approach. This debt management involves more strategic analysis and deliberation of the rationale, selection, prioritization, optimization, and control of borrowing and its instruments, and closer alignment with overall financial management strategy.[20] Supporting local statecrafters in England, TMAs provide 'better analysis of what people actually need' using techniques including long-term cash flow forecasting.[21] More active and strategic debt management enables local governments to borrow and reduce its costs—including fees and interest rates—across all their loans from different sources, connect to revenue generation strategies, and manage risk.

Borrowing has three main purposes: capital expenditure; investment; and refinancing existing debt. Local statecrafters in England typically utilize all three rationales simultaneously, although many struggle to balance short-, medium-, and longer-term borrowing.

Austerity and fiscal pressures across England since 2010 have constrained borrowing by reducing the revenues available to arrange, service, and repay debt. CIPFA acknowledged many local governments had already borrowed up to their capital financing requirement by 2019 even before the pandemic.

Identifying and mitigating risk, especially interest rate and credit, have become more central to borrowing. More active and strategic risk management involves relating borrowing and debt management more closely to the local government's overall financial condition and resilience to unforeseen changes. CIPFA emphasizes balancing overall borrowing, outstanding debt, revenue, and general reserves 'adequate to deal with unexpected increases' including PWLB interest rate hikes.[22]

---

[18] Sbragia (1986).
[19] Fastenrath et al. (2017a).
[20] Deruytter and Möller (2020).
[21] Director, treasury management advisor (2020).
[22] CIPFA (2019: 61).

Once the decision is taken to borrow, there are several strategic dimensions for local statecrafters. First is the amount. This relates to the local political leadership and CFO's assessment of borrowing needs within the Code. Assessments of affordability and financial condition are central, especially the level and type of existing debt.

The amount relates to the borrowing source. Typically, the PWLB and public debt markets are used for loans of £250 million or above, whereas those below £30–40 million are 'private placement territory'.[23] Although the PWLB still dominates lending, local statecrafters in England have diversified since 2010 to manage risk through 'optionality' and avoid becoming a 'price taker' of market offers.[24]

The timing of when to take out new debt or refinance existing debts is important and determines borrowing costs and terms. Drawing upon external advice on interest rates, inflation, and other market factors, local statecrafters seek to optimize their debt management strategies through the timing of borrowing.

Amount, source, and timing connect with the structuring of borrowing. Maturity is the length of time over which the loan is taken out, ranging from short-term (overnight to a year) to long-term (up to fifty years). Local statecrafters in England use different terms for different purposes. Short term borrowing is for cash and liquidity management, while longer-term borrowing finances capital programmes.

External market conditions are pivotal. Before the 2008 crash, an inverted yield curve incentivized local government deposits in the Icelandic Banks and short-term borrowing strategies. Inversion occurs when yields on longer-term debt fall below those of short-term debt with the same credit risk as investors expect interest rates to fall with economic contraction and/or recession. Historically, HMT was nervous of short-term debt levels given the need for constant refinancing and its costs and risks with volatile financial markets and interest rates.[25]

Closely related to maturity is interest rate type. This is either fixed at a specific rate or variable and changing for the loan term. Exotic instruments provide more varied and sophisticated elements including derivatives. Forecasts of interest rates are critical and provided by TMAs.

Since 2010, few local governments have tried to 'lock in' low rates over thirty to forty years due to their relatively short-term orientation and focus

---

[23] Director, bank (2020).
[24] Director, bank (2020).
[25] Sbragia (1986).

on security, liquidity, and yield.[26] Seeking certainty on borrowing costs for annual budget setting, some local statecrafters secured long-term borrowing at fixed rates. Low interest rates since the 2008 crash supported this borrowing strategy, although this is under review following Brexit, the pandemic, Ukraine conflict, and rising inflation and interest rates.

Inflation expectations influence local statecrafters' selection of interest rate type. Rising prices introduce risks but enable borrowers to pay lenders back with money worth less in real terms than when it was initially borrowed. Credit demand increases too, enabling lenders to charge higher fees and interest rates, potentially exposing local governments to higher costs and further risks.

As local statecrafters in England since 2010 sought income generation and utilized borrowing to finance capital investments, arbitrage between potential return rates relative to interest rates charged on borrowing and timing have become critical. Some local governments have been engaging in a carry trade by borrowing at relatively low rates and investing at higher rates making a return on the difference.

This strategy led to increased long-term fixed rate borrowing and short-term variable rate investing. Considered a 'crazy way of dealing your money' by TMAs,[27] this approach bore a cost of carry by generating potential risks of rates of return on investments falling to or below the interest rates at which local statecrafters were borrowing and eliminating the returns.

Overall, total gross external borrowing by local governments in England increased from under £60 billion to over £80 billion between 2012–13 and 2019–20. Borrowing growth is a central local statecraft response to funding gaps because of the need to finance capital investment programmes to reduce costs (invest to save) and generate income (invest to earn).

Constituting the differentiated landscape across local governments in England, short and long-term borrowing sources varied since 2010. Short-term borrowing is mainly from other local governments followed by other financial intermediaries.[28] Longer-term borrowing is largely from the PWLB with other sources including UK banks, other sources including non-UK banks, unknown sources, negotiable bonds and commercial paper, and other local governments.

While there is active dissemination due to the 'culture of innovation and sharing amongst councils',[29] borrowing is differentiated across local

[26] Local government financial consultant 4 (2020).
[27] Director, treasury management advisor (2020).
[28] MHCLG (2021).
[29] Associate Director, professional association (2020).

government in England. Smaller local governments including districts and some unitaries with relatively small treasury teams tend to 'keep doing what you know', including PWLB and inter-local government borrowing since, they are 'only a phone call away', whereas larger London boroughs, metropolitan districts, counties, and some unitaries have larger teams 'able to look at different ways of doing it'.[30]

While dominated by PWLB lending, several districts and unitaries demonstrate vanguard approaches with the highest levels of gross external borrowing (Figure 6.1). This 'small number of local authorities' are more active in what are perceived as more risky activities by the rest of the sector.[31] Most local governments in England are following intermediate approaches at a range of lower borrowing levels with long-tail activities mostly amongst districts. Complicating interpretations of Labour-welfarist higher borrowing,[32] vanguard behaviour is evident under NOC, Labour, and Conservative control. Labour and NOC lead those pursuing intermediate approaches, while NOC and Conservatives dominate long-tail activities (Figure 6.2).

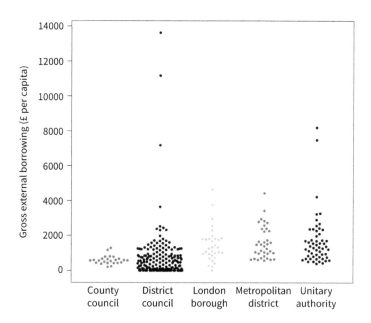

Figure 6.1 Gross external borrowing by local government type, 2019–20

Source: MHCLG (2021).

[30] Director, bank (2020). Mertens et al. (2020).
[31] Director, bank (2020).
[32] Cf. Deruytter and Möller (2020), Mertens et al. (2020).

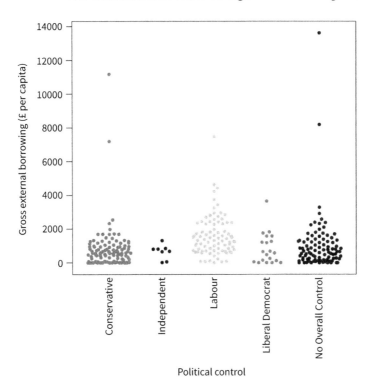

Figure 6.2 Gross external borrowing by political control, 2019–20
Source: MHCLG (2021).

Geography structures and shapes local statecrafters' borrowing across England.[33] This is not a simple explanation that local governments in more prosperous economies with stronger tax bases are more able to borrow. Given the differentiated local statecraft involved, it is not possible to read off borrowing and debt management strategies from location. Mirroring the varied geography of interest and investment income, vanguard approaches are situated in the outer South East and North West, while the higher levels of intermediate behaviours are in the South West, Midlands, and North (Figure 6.3).

While borrowing and debt have become central to more active financial management across England since 2010, many local governments following long-tail approaches 'have never borrowed before' and require advice to support their strategy.[34] Such local statecrafters typically consider debt as a temporary finance source that must be repaid.

[33] Dagdeviren and Karwowski (2021).
[34] Director, treasury management advisor (2021).

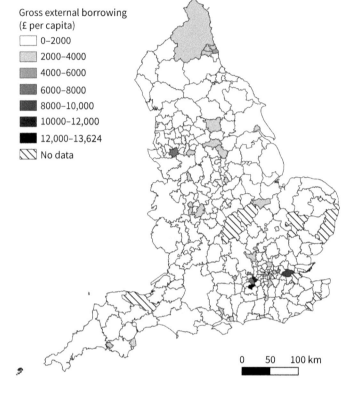

Figure 6.3 Gross external borrowing by location, 2019–20
Source: MHCLG (2021).

Local governments in England are servicing and repaying their borrowing through several strategies and funding sources. Mostly they utilize their main revenue streams to pay fees for external advice and arranging and delivering loans, interest costs, and debt repayment.

How much is borrowing costing local governments in England? The NAO identified three elements of non-service expenditure related to borrowing.[35] Between 2010–11 and 2019–20, interest payments were the largest of these, and growing. As a proportion of spending power between 2010–11 and 2019–20, debt servicing rose from around 7 per cent to over 8 per cent. MRP was reduced from 2013–14 by being calculated differently to make savings and free up revenue cash following national guidance change. Last were capital expenditure charges to the revenue account, which increased and then fell.

---

[35] National Audit Office (2021a).

6.3 Who are local governments borrowing from and on what terms?

Borrowing strategies by local statecrafters in England since 2010 are more sophisticated, especially amongst those pursuing vanguard approaches, and involve a wider range of sources and financial instruments in debt portfolios. Evolving from '"plain vanilla" deals',[36] loans terms and conditions are more complex, including repayment periods, interest rate types and levels, fees (e.g. origination, early repayment, refinancing), and other special conditions (e.g. balloon payments due at repayment term ends).

Reflecting engagements with the relations and process of financialization, the array of actors lending to local government in England, their rationales, and terms has widened since 2010. While the main borrowing sources are long-standing, some diversification is evident with increases in bonds, listed securities other than bonds, and more international and alternative sources, although borrowing from banks has decreased.[37] Rather than a wholesale shift to external actors, local statecraft engagements with financialization are uneven and involve relations with existing and new municipal and commercial finance actors.

6.3.1 Themselves

Borrowing from their own internal resources within local governments rather than external institutions increased in England from 2010. Internal borrowing is long-standing, whereby local governments 'lend their surplus funds to the capital accounts of their spending departments, and those departments repay the authority with interest'.[38] By 2019, 'temporarily surplus internal resources' were 'being used initially to finance capital expenditure before borrowing externally' and such financing was considered 'most appropriate when interest rates are expected to fall or at least remain static'.[39]

Avoiding engagements with financialization, using internal resources avoids external borrowing and its costs. It affords local statecrafters a degree of autonomy and flexibility, especially for commercial property investment.[40] Internal borrowing is highly differentiated amongst local governments across England because it is only an option for those with accumulated resources

---

[36] Hendrikse and Sidaway (2014: 196).
[37] MHCLG (2021).
[38] Sbragia (1986: 316).
[39] CIPFA (2019: 92).
[40] National Audit Office (2020).

where local statecrafters 'finance [capital] expenditure effectively through cash'.[41] Interest rates on internal lending are influenced by the PWLB and market rates to ensure financial transparency and discipline in resource allocation appraisal and decision-making.[42] Internal lending also generates revenues from borrowing department debt service contributions to overall income.

Reflecting disaggregation and growth of the local state, internal borrowing has supported on-lending to other related bodies including arms-length entities, subsidiaries, partners, and local companies. Liverpool City Council's invest-to-earn strategy, for example, included on-lending of a PWLB loan worth £280 million to Everton Football Club to help finance a new stadium, dovetailing with the city's docklands regeneration plans in north Liverpool.[43]

In this way, local government is leveraging its local statehood and using internal resources to lend to wider local state and other actors. Market failure rationales are used to justify such finance provision, including lending to developers and housing associations to progress local schemes and local SMEs when bank credit dried up following the 2008 crash. Local statecrafters use external advice in their due diligence given the novelty of this lending and their limited capacity. Key issues include the interest rates to charge and, before Brexit, compliance with EU state aid rules.

The local statecraft of internal borrowing and on-lending imports new credit risks. Given local government's integral role locally it can face pressure to act as lender of last resort, especially for local actors with locally embedded assets struggling to raise capital from more commercial sources. Avoiding engagement with external commercial finance actors, internal borrowing is not financialization but standard municipal finance practice. Widening the frame, such agency helps explain the differentiated landscape of local statecraft and financialization across England.

6.3.2 Public Works Loan Board

The PWLB remains the dominant source of local government borrowing in England. Formed in 1817, it is a distinctive institution unlike other national development banks. The PWLB is an arm of HMT's national Debt Management Organization (DMO). Reflecting increased national

---

[41] Director of Finance, Metropolitan Borough Council (2021).
[42] Sbragia (1986).
[43] Wilson (2018).

government attention to more strategic sovereign debt management, such DMOs have been established internationally.[44]

Embodying a key element of local statehood, the PWLB provides local governments and public bodies in England with a source of UK HMT-backed and low-cost borrowing to finance their capital programmes. The PWLB is the long-standing lender of last resort in providing 'long-term loans to authorities at interest rates somewhat below the market'.[45]

In the nationally centralized system, HMT sets the interest rates of PWLB loans based on the trading price of UK bonds. These UK government liabilities are issued in sterling by HMT, listed on the London Stock Exchange, and sold with varying maturities. They are known as gilts or gilt-edged securities because they are backed by the UK sovereign guarantee and its historical record of due interest and principal payments. The return investors realize on these bonds—or yield—is determined by its price and interest payment— or coupon—paid by its issuer the UK government. Since the late 1990s and varying by type and maturity, gilts prices have broadly risen and yields fallen.

These UK government bonds are bought by international investors seeking a relatively secure, low-risk investment.[46] Purchasers include large banks, financial institutions, and the Bank of England in its quantitative easing programme to increase money supply and lower interest rates to support lending and investment following the 2008 crash.[47] Gilts are also sold to pension funds, other banks, insurance companies, and individual investors. Given the UK's high credit rating, this bond market's size and liquidity means it is considered the lowest cost and most efficient source of national and hence local government borrowing.[48]

Given its national macro-economic policy remit, HMT historically sought to control gilts issues and local government debt instruments and their issuance within the international public debt market. The aims were reducing competition with gilts and ensuring the long-term borrowing market remained favourable to UK national rather than local government objectives.[49]

Demonstrating the worth of a key local statehood attribute, credit rating agencies recognize the value of the implicit UK sovereign guarantee and lack of a legal framework for local governments in England to go bankrupt unlike elsewhere including the US. In 'extreme financial distress', the UK

---

[44] Fastenrath et al. (2017a).
[45] Sbragia (1986: 315).
[46] Carr (2012).
[47] Stubbington (2021).
[48] National Audit Office (2015b).
[49] Sbragia (1986).

'government would step in.'[50] When local governments 'run out of money', the external perception of financial actors is that the UK government 'stands behind it.'[51] There is an *implicit* rather than *explicit* guarantee that some argue would further reduce borrowing costs. But HMT has been unwilling to formalize the guarantee fearing moral hazard, generating credit risk, and encouraging unnecessary and risky local government borrowing.

Reflecting macro-economic shifts since the 2008 crash, interest rates on PWLB loans have fallen across maturities. For local statecrafters in England, using the PWLB is an accessible, straightforward, and tried-and-tested borrowing source. The PWLB operates on trust with local governments in England without due diligence: 'it's almost like going to a cashpoint and you put your card in the wall and you type in 20 million quid.'[52] With local statecrafters governed by the Code, the PWLB does not ask about the purpose of the borrowing. The only downsides are having to begin repayment immediately, uncertainties about HMT's interest rate–setting, and existing loan refinancing penalties.

Alongside internal borrowing, the PWLB has limited local statecrafters' use of alternative external lending sources. Most local governments in England rely upon this long-standing and readily available source for low-cost loans of flexible maturities with limited risk and scrutiny. Straightforward access to low-cost credit has stymied engagements with the relations and process of financialization in borrowing and debt management strategies. The PWLB's size and dominance dissuaded UK and foreign banks' market entry 'because of the cheapness of funding elsewhere.'[53]

Since 2010, however, HMT's ultimate control and changing management of PWLB has opened-up the local government debt market in England. Continued uncertainty over interest rate increases and the PWLB's future generated increased governance and interest rate risk. Amidst fiscal stress, local statecrafters were forced into re-assessing their borrowing and debt management strategies.

In early austerity, HMT's fiscal consolidation limited local government borrowing. It sought to sharpen market discipline and diversify borrowing sources beyond the UK government while balancing the loss of debt service payments. Interest rates on PWLB loans were increased from 0.15–0.20 per cent to 1 per cent above the UK government borrowing rate 'to

[50] Senior analyst, credit rating agency (2021).
[51] Director, treasury management advisor (2020).
[52] Associate Director, professional association (2020).
[53] Möller (2017); Director, bank (2020).

create downward pressure on council borrowing and to make councils more market facing.'[54]

Raising the cost of new loans forced local statecrafters across England to review their borrowing and debt management strategies and affordability assessments. It rewired and rescaled their incentives and accountabilities, pushing them towards engagement with external commercial finance actors as a UK state-led financialization of local statecraft.

In later austerity, without warning HMT increased PWLB rates further from 1.81 per cent to 2.82 per cent on a fifty-year loan.[55] HMT explained this was because the lending limits of the PWLB were nearly reached following sharply increased borrowing. A UK government department generated this interest rate risk rather than wider macro-economic or external financial actor changes.

The 2019 increase in borrowing costs and uncertainty compelled further strategic reviews. Local statecrafters were forced 'to think very carefully about … funding their capital investment programmes' with projects 'potentially put at risk because the business cases can be quite marginal' because local government was investing where 'the private sector couldn't do it on its own' and an 'interest rate rise of hundred basis points appears to have killed … or delayed some schemes.'[56]

HMT's rate hikes since 2010 prompted local statecrafter consideration of alternative borrowing sources. The LGA established the Municipal Bonds Agency (MBA) in 2014 collectively to issue bonds. Financial actors more actively developed new loan products tailored to this changing local public debt market in England.

In addition to unplanned interest rate increases, local statecraft since 2010 prompted further changes in HMT's management of PWLB. Challenging national regulation, what HMT considered borrowing in advance of need and for investments and yield outside local government areas stimulated debate and further revisions.

Since 2003, the PWLB was used for borrowing compliant with the Code to finance capital expenditure on service delivery and economic development and regeneration primarily *within* local government boundaries. Local statecrafters' use of PWLB borrowing has evolved since 2010 given the 'push from central government to increasingly encourage' local governments 'to be more

[54] CIPFA (2019: 92).
[55] Marrs (2019a).
[56] Associate Director, professional association (2020).

commercial' for income generation and investment strategies especially for commercial property *outside* their areas.[57]

Caricatured as 'councillors at the casino', such local statecraft prompted HMT to consult on the use and future of PWLB lending in 2020. HMT described the 'minority' of local governments using low-cost loans from PWLB to 'buy investment property primarily for rental income' as a 'debt-for-yield' activity that introduces risks.[58] Locally, HMT argued 'it exposes ratepayers' if the income does not materialize and the local government retains the 'inflexible commitment' to service and repay the loans.[59] Nationally, 'it diverts money from core services' and makes it harder for the private sector to compete, potentially crowding out public investment and distorting property markets.[60]

Financial actors questioned local government use of UK sovereign-backed lending for financial purposes other than or in addition to local public service provision, especially commercial property investment within *and* outside their areas to generate income. Tensions grew for the UK government as local statecrafter incentives in England were rewired and rescaled.

The treasury responded to the consultation with revised lending terms, a new requirement for a three-year plan for capital spending, financing, and PWLB use, formal confirmation of 'no intention to buy investment assets for yield', and penalties for deliberate misuse.[61] Local statecrafters argued that increased PWLB borrowing was split equally between borrowing for investment in commercial property, new projects, and refinancing as routine financial management investing to save and earn as well as reducing borrowing costs.

By 2020 and the pandemic, the new PWLB rules reduced borrowing to invest with local statecrafters unwilling to attract adverse attention and scrutiny. Yet, local government's key pandemic response and recovery role was acknowledged to need access to low-cost PWLB lending. The effects of tightening restrictions on PWLB borrowing were accentuated by the loss of European Investment Bank financing following Brexit, the delayed EU funds replacement the UK Shared Prosperity Fund, and the new UK Infrastructure Bank launch in 2021.

---

[57] Director, bank (2020).
[58] HM Treasury (2020: 2).
[59] HM Treasury (2020: 2).
[60] HM Treasury (2020: 2).
[61] HM Treasury (2020: 4).

6.3.3 Other local governments

Borrowing between local governments grew from 'virtually nil' until 2011 to over £9 billion by 2019 across the UK.[62] Lending to each other was mostly short-term and part of treasury management strategies for security and to 'keep their cash liquid'.[63] Following the Icelandic banks episode and Basel banking reforms, CIPFA tightened the treasury management code to emphasize security over liquidity and yield. With the cash build-up by local statecrafters in response to austerity and uncertainty in England since 2010, such changes made working with other UK sovereign-backed parties low cost and low risk. Such on-lending provided local governments with reserves opportunities to generate returns from sectoral lending. It was 'always going to be a good bet for the money', charged at slightly above PWLB rates but less than commercial market rates provided financial advantage for both parties.[64]

Post-2008 banking system regulations to 'bail in' rather than 'bail out' failing banks meant local governments in England would be 'bottom of the pile' in the liability structure, making lending to other local governments more attractive than cash deposits in banks 'since they can't go bust'.[65] This borrowing growth is another internally oriented change in local statecraft and municipal finance, demonstrating lack of engagement with external commercial finance. For critics, it reveals how local governments are behaving more like financial institutions whereby 'the Council has become … like this financial investment banking type layer completely below the radar of regulation and scrutiny'.[66]

Inter-local government lending is central to more active cash management by local statecrafters in England since 2010 as a means for those with reserves to earn returns. Differentiating the landscape, net lenders are concentrated in England, reflecting austerity impacts, economic growth, and varying risk appetites, and in larger cities and towns with metropolitan and unitary authorities in the North East, Yorkshire, and North West regions.[67]

---

[62] Dagdeviren and Karwowski (2021: 11).
[63] Director, bank (2020).
[64] Former Director, public audit body (2021).
[65] Director, treasury management advisor (2020).
[66] Researcher, campaign group (2021).
[67] Dagdeviren and Karwowski (2021).

6.3.4 External financial institutions

Demonstrating long-standing engagements with the relations and process of financialization, local statecrafters in England have borrowed in the market since the 1960s[68]. Shaped by macro-economic conditions and Sterling's value, international investors historically loaned to local governments. Their 'huge cash flow' and local statehood attribute of implicit UK sovereign guarantee made them attractive to commercial finance.'[69] Yet, such international 'hot money' has proved highly mobile, for example during the capital flight and ensuing crisis and high interest rates in the UK in the early 1960s.[70]

Since the 1970s and 1980s, local government loan officers in England have dealt with commercial finance actors to access borrowing and circumvent national limits. Local statecrafters cultivated City of London relations with stockbrokers, money brokers, and merchant banks that were 'interested in helping authorities circumvent any treasury regulations local officials may find too irksome.'[71] City financial actors were reputed for ingenious and tailored financial instruments that were technically compliant with prevailing regulations 'but neutralize if not actually subvert them.'[72] International, national, and local contacts—the 'bankers' grapevine'[73]—as well as knowledge and experience made City relations with local government strong, functional, and transactional.

Local government borrowing in England in the 1980s was 'extremely fast-paced, by comparison to the staid and deliberate practices found in other local authority activities.'[74] The loan officer role was technical and specialized for local statecrafters able to 'cope with substantial uncertainty and stress', leading to recruitment of people with reputations of being an 'outstanding market operator' from the sector or, in a marker of financialization, external financial institutions.[75] Situations varied by local government type across England with larger, often urban, authorities with sizeable debt portfolios attracting the most ambitious loan officers.

Local governments in England broadened their borrowing sources throughout the 1990s and 2000s. PWLB interest rate increases accelerated diversification after 2010. HMT, CIPFA, and the LGA encouraged

---

[68] Bank of England (1966).
[69] Labour Councillor and Finance Cabinet Member, London Borough (2021).
[70] Sbragia (1986: 326).
[71] Sbragia (1986: 330).
[72] Sbragia (1986: 330).
[73] Sbragia (1986: 331).
[74] Sbragia (1986: 318).
[75] Sbragia (1986: 318).

local statecrafters to consider new borrowing sources and instruments.[76] Commercialization advocates argued local governments should engage with 'private capital' and diversify risk by using a range of borrowing instruments including 'bonds, derivatives and TIF [Tax Increment Financing]'.[77] This setting created opportunities for commercial finance actors to engage local statecrafters 'to leverage the capital markets'.[78]

Responding to local statecrafter demand, financial actors formulated new products at differential rates to the PWLB. As a loan market worth around £115 billion in 2020,[79] local government borrowing provided a UK sovereign guarantee and confidence to lenders who did 'not need to worry about a potential New York-style bankruptcy'.[80] While investors were not typically knowledgeable about specific local governments in England, they were willing lenders given the low credit risk.

Following the 2008 crash, financial institutions embarked on a 'search for yield' in a macro-economic setting of national state quantitative easing, low interest rates, and low returns from traditional asset classes. Finance actors pursuing new markets (re)engaged with municipal finance.[81] Attempts to balance investment portfolios led them into safer, longer-term as well as more alternative, less liquid or illiquid and harder-to-sell assets and private markets.

Engaging local statecrafters with financialization, counterparties lending money to local governments in England innovated on this sell-side of the debt market. Rather than 'de-financialisation',[82] it involved differing financial actors using existing and new instruments. For short-term borrowing, other financial intermediaries and private non-financial corporations grew, while banks declined and then recovered.[83] For longer-term borrowing, negotiable bonds and commercial paper, other listed securities, other financial intermediaries, private non-financial corporations, rest of the world banks, and unknown sources increased as UK banks declined.

Banks provide accounts, overdrafts, and working capital facilities for local governments in England. Shifts towards fees-based business models and new income sources were evident post-2008.[84] In early austerity, banks focused on transactional banking, deposits, lending, and asset financing. Strategies have

---

[76] Möller (2017).
[77] Carr (2012: 43).
[78] Director, bank (2020).
[79] Department for Levelling Up, Housing and Communities (2021b).
[80] Sbragia (1986: 315).
[81] Möller (2017).
[82] Dagdeviren and Karwowski (2021: 688).
[83] MHCLG (2021).
[84] Bhatti and Manley (2015), Deruytter and Möller (2020).

evolved into a 'far more strategic relationship' and 'partnership' on longer-term issues including social value and green agendas.[85] Larger banks have public sector and even dedicated local government teams focused on getting close to and supporting the sector's needs across England.

Pension funds were other long-term lenders, often at fixed rates. Traditionally, pension funds bought gilts which local statecrafters saw as a potentially 'uncomfortable' encroachment in the debt market.[86] Although an earlier financial innovation, the droplock loan was designed to make local government debt more attractive to pension funds. It had a variable interest rate until it drop locked into a fixed rate at a specified time point.

Other sources of borrowing for local governments in England included lending from the lightly regulated Eurodollar market of US dollar-denominated deposits at foreign banks or overseas branches of US banks. Banks brought together foreign lenders into syndicated loans using non-negotiable bonds denominated in Sterling to avoid UK government controls on foreign borrowing.[87]

Local government lending in England remains a challenging market for financial institutions. The sector is known for its caution and risk aversion given its accountability for spending public money,[88] and the legacies of its previous engagements with commercial finance and financialization. Borrowing from external financial institutions has higher costs and is more time consuming for local statecrafters because of the due diligence required. It is 'costly and expensive on both sides' and for 'alternatives to fly they will need to be quick, easy, simple, cheap to access'.[89] Given the PWLB's dominance, the net position is key. Interest rate savings over the life of the loan need to be enough to offset the higher costs of borrowing from commercial finance institutions, although the 2019 PWLB interest rate increase stimulated new product development. Innovations were based on lower interest rates and loan structures including tailored maturities and terms such as penalty and refinancing clauses.

Uptake of new loan products is differentiated across local governments in England since 2010. Financial institutions see that traditionally the sector 'has been quite risk-averse' and 'change hasn't always come naturally' but that is 'slowly evolving' with 'more desire to look at innovation because 'the whole commerciality of it has been forced upon them because of austerity.'[90]

---

[85] Director, bank (2020).
[86] Sbragia (1986: 330).
[87] Sbragia (1986).
[88] Carr (2012).
[89] Associate Director, professional association (2020).
[90] Director, bank (2020).

Once used, dissemination and sharing of existing and new loan products amongst local governments supported financial institutions' sales strategies. Word of mouth and recommendations mean receptive local statecrafters 'borrow with pride or copy'.[91]

One controversial example is LOBO loans from the 2000s. LOBOs were designed by international banks for borrowing by local public sector institutions. They represented 'a dabble in the market' by local statecrafters.[92] The top five largest LOBO lenders were banks: Barclays; Dexia; Depfa; Royal Bank of Scotland; and Dresdner.[93]

LOBOs were structured around a Lender Option allowing the bank to change the interest rate on the loan upwards or downwards at agreed dates while giving the borrower notice. The Borrower Option enabled the borrower flexibility to accept the new terms or repay the total outstanding liabilities. Each loan could be renegotiated between borrower and lender or the borrower can pay to cancel the loan.

Differentiating their product and opening up the market, banks marketed LOBOs to local governments in England using a teaser rate set below PWLB levels.[94] Mimicking the selling strategies for subprime mortgages in the US that underpinned the 2008 crisis, this initial period of lower interest rates would then increase at an agreed future point. LOBOs were mostly long-term loans of forty to seventy years.

LOBOs were introduced when interest rates were relatively high in the UK between 2003 and the 2008 crash. They provided lower than prevailing rates and 'there was no perception that there would be anything like the banking crisis.'[95] For some local statecrafters, LOBOs 'made perfect sense' and were 'the best you could get in the market' at the time.[96] Over 250 (~75 per cent) of local governments borrowed around £11 billion using over 450 LOBO loans, differentiated between those following vanguard and intermediate approaches (Figure 6.4). Demonstrating rapid financial innovation dissemination, LOBOs spread throughout the sector across England.[97]

Following the 2008 crisis, interest rates fell in the UK amidst recession and faltering economic recovery. The LOBOs were now at higher than market or PWLB rates. Exposing their relatively costly position, local statecrafters' accountability for prudent stewardship of public money forced them into

[91] Associate Director, professional association (2020).
[92] Labour Councillor and Cabinet Member for Finance, London Borough (2021).
[93] Debt Resistance UK (n.d.).
[94] Möller (2017).
[95] Director of Finance, Metropolitan Borough Council (2021).
[96] Local government financial consultant 4 (2020).
[97] Mertens et al. (2020).

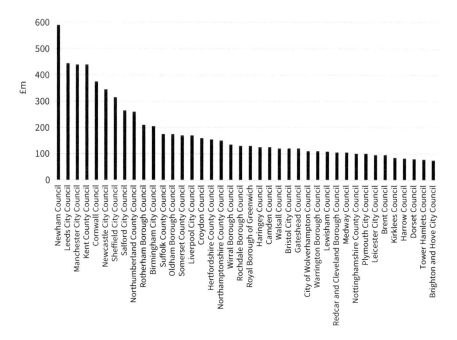

Figure 6.4 Top forty local governments borrowing in LOBO loans by value, 2018
Source: Debt Resistance UK (n.d.).

refinancing this borrowing. Typically, this meant local governments paying costly fees to their bank lenders to exercise their option to turn their LOBO loan into a lower and fixed rate product with a longer maturity. London Borough Newham paid nearly £200,000 to refinance £249 million of LOBOs from Barclays and Dresdner Bank.

Campaign group Debt Resistance UK's analysis identified 35 per cent of LOBOs being sold on beyond the originator, concentrating amongst thirty-two rather than the original forty lenders with a new Top 5 banks comprising Barclays, Dexia, FMS Wertmanagement, Royal Bank of Scotland, and Hypothekenbank Frankfurt.[98] Hit by the 2008 crash, Dexia Credit Local and Depfa were bailed out by the Belgian, French, and Irish national governments respectively and parts were designated bad banks holding loss-making assets and unwound by financial regulators.

Local statecrafters in England turned against LOBOs in the lower interest rate situation post-2008. Concerns were fuelled by the high profit margins the lender banks posted. Some even interpreted a 'bonfire of the LOBOs'.[99]

---

[98] Debt Resistance UK (n.d.).

CIPFA expressed concern about such 'market loans' and encouraged reviews of contract terms amidst fears about bad deals and poor value for public money.[100]

Debt Resistance UK mobilized around this financial innovation and instance of local government engagement with financialization. Utilizing the 'councillors at the casino' narrative, they argued LOBOs were 'speculative decisions ... to gamble on interest rates' at a 'margin over and above PWLB rates' that had led to substantial annual premiums being paid by local residents to banks for decades into the future.[101]

Further controversy emerged after Barclays' conviction in the UK in 2012 for manipulating the LIBOR benchmark for bank lending.[102] In the volatile late 1970s, LIBOR loans were variable rate and longer-term borrowing products enabling local governments in England to roll-over shorter-term loans.[103] Given the banks involved and use of LIBOR in setting LOBO loan interest rates, eight local governments brought a legal claim against Barclays. The local statecrafters sought loan cancellation because the bank was 'tainted' in its representations given its fraudulent manipulation of the LIBOR.[104] Their claim was thrown out of the UK High Court in 2021 following a ruling that they would be unlikely to be successful at trial.

As a specific financial innovation for local government borrowing, LOBOs have been interpreted as evidence of 'financializing town halls' through local government relations with global financial actors through the international derivatives market.[105] The argument is that local statecrafters were bamboozled by the banks into taking out the loans and only belatedly realized they were a bad deal.

The LOBOs episode reflected the differential expertise between the banks and local governments in England. Some felt local statecrafters didn't 'understand the risk' and expressed concerns this was a 'bad innovation because it's being tested on the public sector first'.[106] LOBOs emerged when the UK macro-economic situation was relatively strong with interest rates relatively high and expected to rise. They were a local statecraft engagement with the relations and process of financialization at a particular geographical and temporal moment. Conditions changed post-2008 exposing local governments

---

[99] Marrs (2018c: 1).
[100] CIPFA (2019: 92).
[101] Debt Resistance UK (n.d.).
[102] Ashton and Christophers (2015).
[103] Sbragia (1986).
[104] BBC News (2021: 1).
[105] Möller (2017: 1).
[106] Director, treasury management advisor (2021).

to rate increases. While LOBOs were substantive in specific local governments, they were only ever around a fifth of total sector borrowing.

6.3.5 Bond investors

Seeking to borrow from investors in the international bond market and diversify their debt portfolios, local governments in England made individual and collective bond issuances. A bond is a tradeable security bought at a price with a yield or coupon paid to investors by the issuer. Investors buying bonds are lending to the issuers in return for set levels of interest paid regularly on the bonds over their lifespan and repayment of the bond's face value at maturity.

For local statecrafters engaging this instrument of financialization, bonds provide an alternative borrowing source offering potential flexibilities, bespoke design, and savings. Their use has been limited amongst local governments in England by the need to buy in technical expertise and the costs of securing a credit rating (estimated at £50,000), arrangement, commission, sales, and transactions fees.[107]

Local governments have long held powers to issue bonds, but they remained unused since the 1990s. Dissuasion by the UK government, the PWLB's dominance, the chilling effect of the Hammersmith and Fulham swaps affair, and disinterest from financial institutions limited bond use. Local governments in England were effectively insulated from external rating of their creditworthiness and did 'not need to worry about how the financial community perceives their particular authority's finances'.[108]

Financial pressures since 2010 renewed local government interest in bond issues. Compelled to engage with external financial actors and financialization by fiscal stress, local statecrafters have sought alternative, diversified, and lower-cost borrowing sources and more flexible deals than PWLB especially for refinancing.

Commercial finance institutions on the investment supply-side touted bonds as low-risk lending in a bond market able to 'inject more discipline into local authorities and add an extra layer of scrutiny—in terms of ratings agencies, bond analysts, investor roadshows and pricing metrics—that might punish wayward councils'.[109] Fees could be earned by finance actors from selling advice and delivery services, including underwriting and marketing. International investors bought the local government bonds as relatively

---

[107] Sandford (2016b).
[108] Sbragia (1986: 320).
[109] Gore (2020: 1).

low-risk fixed-income assets within wider portfolios, backed by the UK sovereign guarantee. Purchasers include major institutional investors such as asset managers and insurance and pension funds.

The use of bonds is highly differentiated across local governments in England. Only vanguard local statecrafters have secured credit ratings and issued their own bonds (Tables 6.1 and 6.2). Not many have sought to 'take long-term cash'.[110] Demonstrating the limits of this vector of financialization, bonds have grown but remain small-scale, increasing from 1 per cent to 4 per cent of total borrowing between 2007 and 2015.[111]

Responding to uncertainty about PWLB rates and UK government encouragement to diversify borrowing sources, the LGA and fifty-six local governments established the MBA in 2014. Modelled on the *Kommuninvest* in Sweden, the MBA aimed to support collective or pooled bond issuances from local governments at a larger scale and value underpinned by participant cross-guarantees. The idea was to secure higher credit ratings, reduce set-up and servicing costs, mitigate default risks, and attract international investors.

Table 6.1 Local government credit ratings, 2020

Local government	Credit rating	Credit rating agency
Cornwall Council	Aa2—'High quality, very low credit risk'	Moody's
Guildford Borough Council		
Lancashire County Council	Aa3—'High quality, very low credit risk'	
Warrington Borough Council	A1—'Upper-medium grade, low credit risk'	
Woking Borough Council	A—'susceptible to the adverse effects of changes in circumstances and economic conditions, obligator's capacity to meet its financial commitments on the obligation are still strong'	Standard and Poor's
Royal Borough of Kensington and Chelsea	AAA—'highest rated, obligator's capacity to meet its financial commitments on the obligation is extremely strong'	
Wandsworth Borough	AA+—'Very high credit quality'	Fitch

Source: Carr (2015), UK Municipal Bonds Agency (2020).

---

[110] Local government financial consultant 4 (2020).
[111] Carr (2015).

Table 6.2 Local government bond issues, 1994–

Local government	Purpose and year	Value (£ million)	Interest rate (percentage)
Salford City Council	Housing PFI, 1994	100	7.25
Warrington Borough Council	Town centre redevelopment, 2015	150	0.85–3*
Birmingham City Council	National Exhibition Centre refinancing, 2005	200	–**
	'Brummie Bonds' for housing, 2017	45	2.36
Lancaster County Council**	Refinancing of short-term debt and other general purposes, 2020	350	Floating rate linked to SONIA at a spread of 80bp***
Leicester City Council	Housing and regeneration****	80	7.25

Notes: * Consumer Price Index–linked.
** Via the UK Municipal Bonds Agency.
*** SONIA (Sterling Overnight Index Average) and bps (basis points). Basis points are 1/100th of 1 per cent or 0.01 per cent (i.e. 1 per cent change =100 points and 0.01 per cent change =1 basis point).
**** Year not disclosed.
Source: Carr (2015), Sandford (2017), and UK Municipal Bonds Agency (2020).

Like individual bond issues, MBA bond uptake is differentiated across local governments in England. The MBA made a slow start because local statecrafters opted for less complex and short-term borrowing from each other given prevailing interest rates and uncertainty. The local statehood dimension of local party politics has intruded too, dissuading external financial actor involvement. Explaining their lack of engagement, a bank advisor argued that 'it's doomed to failure. It's based on a principle of cross-guarantee, which is crazy. Can you imagine a Tory council cross guaranteeing the debts of a Labour council?'[112] Such political risks are hardwired into the local statecraft of such borrowing arrangements and engagements with financialization.

The MBA's first issuance was six years after its establishment in early 2020: a £350 million, five-year SONIA-linked floating rate note for Lancashire County Council to refinance short-term debt and finance its capital programme.[113] Like other exotic loan products, bonds are another

---

[112] Quoted in Gore (2020: 1).
[113] Gore (2020). The SONIA interest rate benchmark has been administered by the Bank of England since 2016 as a replacement for the LIBOR. Floating rate notes are debt instruments with variable interest rates tied to a relevant benchmark rate.

engagement with commercial finance and financialization at the edge rather than centre of local statecrafters' financial management.

6.3.6 Against their assets and revenues

Reflecting international ambitions for more 'professional' public asset man-agement,[114] local statecrafters have been compelled by fiscal stress and the UK government more actively to manage their assets and related revenue streams. Such 'creative accounting' is long-standing in local municipal finance in England, dating back to 1980s innovations including lease and leaseback deals and factoring.[115] Generating cash from existing assets in place became more appealing to local statecrafters in austerity from 2010.

Borrowing and debt management strategies have sought financial innova-tions to enable new sources of borrowing against such assets and revenue streams. National rules on asset use and the lack of tried-and-tested financial instruments to undertake such manoeuvres initially limited their develop-ment and uptake across England.

External financial actors were engaged to formulate approaches and arrangements, attracted by local public asset markets opening-up amidst austerity. Reflecting the national legal basis and guidance, such products were designed and adapted for local governments as often asset-rich, cash poor borrowers. Local statecrafters were enabled to borrow against their assets, leases on their assets, and future revenue streams when securitized. Instruments were treated as debt in the accounts. Techniques such as capital-ization and leasing were imported and adapted from other national settings, especially the US.[116]

Such instruments aimed to use—leverage—existing assets to generate immediate and more flexible cash. 'Monetizing value' from fixed capital otherwise locked up in immobile and illiquid assets was the rationale.[117] This financing was then used for multiple purposes including repairing balance sheets, servicing, and repaying existing debts, offsetting service pro-vision reductions, and securing ongoing revenue streams from rents and leases. Such techniques enabled local statecrafters in England to avoid claims of privatization of assets and irrevocable transfers from public to private sectors.

---

[114] Detter and Fölster (2017: 7).
[115] Campbell-Smith (2008).
[116] Ashton et al. (2016).
[117] Detter and Fölster (2017: 125).

Engaging the relations and process of financialization, however, the instruments introduced new objectives, incentives, autonomies, accountabilities, and risks into local statecraft. Local fixed assets were rendered liquid, tradeable, and open to new ownership and funding, financing, and governing arrangements over time. Geographically and temporally differentiated, local statecrafter control over assets, revenues, and finances was rewired and rescaled.

Sale-and-leaseback deals involved local government selling an asset to an investor and leasing it back from this purchaser for a predetermined, often long-term, period. These arrangements enable local statecrafters to raise finance and generate rent and fees from the asset. In return for their up-front payment, investors secure a rent, often index-linked and inflation protected, and potential appreciation in the asset's value over the length of the lease,[118] backed by the local government and its implicit UK sovereign guarantee. Promoted by TMAs, lease procurement is allowed under national borrowing rules. Demonstrating the differentiated local statecraft in this novel financialization, examples were limited in England from 2010. Northamptonshire County Council addressed its particular financial situation with such a deal on its newly built headquarters building.

Income strip deals are similar, although newer and untried. Here, the local government sells the asset but retains a right to repurchase it at the end of the lease for a predetermined amount. The investor still secures the index-linked returns but is not exposed to changes in the asset's value. Similarly promoted by TMAs, income strips were limited to those undertaking vanguard approaches in England because of novelty, risk, and lack of experience.

Portsmouth City Council agreed a £73 million strip lease for forty-one years with Canada Life for the Wightlink Ferry terminal connection to the Isle of Wight. Part of a wider £45 million refurbishment programme, the strip lease generates a £2 million annual rent—double the existing revenue from the ferry service.[119] Portsmouth City Council retains the freehold while generating revenue to offset pressure to reduce service expenditure and support its commercial property investment strategy. Canada Life secures an income stream to match its long-term income annuity liabilities. The income strip structure provides a 'novel way for the private sector to provide financial support to the public purse whilst leaving the reversionary value in public sector hands'.[120] As purchaser of the lease, Canada Life relies upon the city council's

---

[118] Swallow (n.d.).
[119] Buckley (2016).
[120] Michael White, Property Investment Director, Canada Life, quoted in Buckley (2016: 1).

local statehood attribute of a relatively higher covenant strength compared to ferry operator Wightlink for payment of the ferry service rent.

While income strips provide short-term cash, they are relatively risky for local governments longer-term given their duration and potential for adverse changes in asset values and inflation. While they take the legal form of leases, they are effectively borrowing. Income strips have even been described as 'son of LOBOs'.[121] Articulating the 'councillors at the casino' narrative in a different national setting, in the US they have been interpreted as where 'some of the biggest bets are being placed'.[122]

Incentives and risks are rewired and rescaled for local statecraft in financialization in England by these new asset-based approaches. Undervaluing and underpricing assets and revenues is a risk. Differences between anticipated and realized revenue streams can emerge, especially in multi-decadal deals. Assets and revenue streams are locked-in to external actors over the long term with corresponding loss of control over key local assets and wider planning, regulation, and governance.[123] Deals can be costly with limited room for manoeuvre for local statecrafters if high penalty clauses are involved. Criticisms of selling the family silver have been made, albeit unlike outright privatization only for the long-term, fixed-lease periods.

In addition to deals with external commercial finance actors, innovations for borrowing against future revenue streams have been introduced through bespoke and negotiated adaptations to central–local fiscal relations in England since 2010. These new arrangements were related to business rates localization, including tweaks to tax revenues distribution between the UK national and local government such as 'earn back' and 'gain share' models.[124] In early austerity, the Department and HMT introduced New Growth Deals allowing local governments in large cities to securitize and borrow against projected uplifts in future business rate income within demarcated areas to finance up-front infrastructure investments.

This TIF-type arrangement meant 'future business rates growth as a result of a new development is retained by the council in order to fund the development.'[125] It is 'borrowing against different elements of retained business rate income', whereby the UK Secretary of State 'designates an area (and revenue stream) which is outside the Business Rates Retention Scheme.'[126]

[121] Marrs (2019b: 1).
[122] Peck and Whiteside (2016: 246).
[123] Farmer (2014).
[124] Pike et al. (2019).
[125] CIPFA (2019: 41).
[126] CIPFA (2019: 41).

Such municipal finance innovations provided another borrowing source for specific, nationally determined local governments in England. They rewired and rescaled incentives for local statecrafters by tying these local governments' financial fortunes more closely to their local economies. Local government strategy and planning were skewed towards maximizing commercial property floorspace and business rates revenues as a result.

6.3.7 Refinancing existing borrowing

As more active financial strategy and management was pursued amidst fiscal stress and debt increased amongst local governments in England from 2010, refinancing existing borrowing grew in importance. Managing existing debt is a long-standing and core task of treasury management for local statecrafters: "'turning over' debt keeps loan officers busy."[127] HMT have long-standing concerns about the debt maturity structure and need for refinancing given the costs involved and potential competition for investors between the UK and local governments.

Refinancing aims to reduce costs and restructure the timing and level of debt service and repayment profiles. It has also been necessary for local governments in England involved in PPP programmes (e.g. PFI (Private Finance Initiative), PF2 (Private Finance 2)) financing capital projects for local infrastructure including hospitals, schools, and street lighting. Following concerns about their high costs during austerity from 2010,[128] such long-term (more than twenty-year) arrangements were being refinanced in secondary markets and, by the 2020s, were ending.

As the range of lenders, sources, and types of borrowing widened in England since 2010, local statecrafters have been mixing different refinancing approaches and instruments. Some sought to reduce costs by changing the level and type of interest rate, through reductions and/or shifting between fixed and variable rates and moves from existing loan products onto new ones. Other techniques included rescheduling maturities from short to longer periods to spread out the payments for debt service and repayment, consolidating multiple loans into a single loan on different and renegotiated terms, and reorganizing repayment schedules. Inflation and rising interest rates following Brexit, the pandemic, and Ukraine conflict have prompted further review.

---

[127] Sbragia (1986: 317).
[128] National Audit Office (2018b).

6.4 Conclusions

Investigating a key area of local state financialization,[129] borrowing and debt management reveal the engagements of local statecrafters in England since 2010. Reflecting local government diversity, the landscape is differentiated. The interrelated factors explaining financial strategies and external advice configure this picture too: political and officer leaderships, local government types, financial conditions, risk appetites, locations, and time periods.

Borrowing and debt management innovations are relatively small-scale even in local governments pursuing vanguard approaches. Certain instruments are taken up and disseminated amongst local statecrafters across England through municipal finance staff associations and community networks. Responsibility for prudent public money management amidst austerity is compelling consideration of financial instruments formerly perceived as risky. Yet innovation has been uneven, conditioned by differential expertise and risk appetites, and lack of legal clarity. Memories of the financial downsides from 1980s creative accounting, the 1990s Hammersmith and Fulham swaps affair, and 2000s LOBOs endure.

New approaches to borrowing and debt management by local statecrafters are integral to the uneven shift towards more active and integrated financial strategy and management in local governments in England. Arranging, servicing, refinancing, and redeeming debts are now greater parts of local statecraft than hitherto.

Some vanguard local statecrafters leverage their local statehood, moving towards behaving as financial institutions. Using financial innovations as 'statecraft tools',[130] local governments in England have established banks, undertaken on-lending, and pursued asset-based strategies since 2010.

In certain cases, new approaches contribute to the financializing ratchet. Yet further innovations are deployed to manage growing debt portfolios, especially when conditions change and the costs of specific loan products rise.

Commercial finance lenders quickly identify demands for further local government borrowing, formulating loan products to meet demand amidst austerity. But such debt fixes are not only more complex, innovative, and financialized; risking the bamboozlement of local statecrafters.[131] As

---

[129] Lagna (2016).
[130] Hendrikse and Lagna (2018: 19).
[131] Kass et al. (2019).

downsides of novel instruments become apparent, solutions are sometimes more straightforward, simplifying measures with reduced risks.

Funding gaps created by the UK government are displacing risk onto local government in England, forcing it to take on increased debt. Critics see a 'perpetual state of borrowing from Peter to pay Paul'.[132] Increased and more complex borrowing has implications for local government financial sustainability and public services provision across England.

Evolving and new debt relations and claims are contributing to the rewiring and rescaling of local statecraft's objectives, incentives, autonomies, and accountabilities towards lenders. As agents and objects of financialization, local statecrafters in England are internalizing market incentives, economic, and investment yardsticks. The actors lending money to local governments are widening to include other local governments, banks, bond investors, and other financial institutions.

[132] Journalist (2021).

7

In-area and out-of-area statecraft

7.0 Introduction

Local statecrafters in England investing to generate income to offset fiscal stress face fierce criticism. Such strategies are guided by 'bad incentives to gamble on commercial assets' encouraging 'councillors to behave recklessly' and seeking 'to gamble to preserve services without the electorally unfriendly expedient of hiking council tax'.[1] In this interpretation, local statecraft across England since 2010 is driven by the 'dangerous mixture' of a 'debt addiction' to 'cheap government-subsidised' borrowing from the PWLB and engaged in a 'pro-social carry trade' but running 'eye-watering risks'.[2] Lacking oversight, scrutiny, and transparency, this endeavour demonstrates local governments 'can't be trusted with taxpayers' hard-earned cash'.[3]

Such depictions are especially pointed when local governments in England invest outside their areas. Engaging commercial, sometimes international, financiers and their more spatially open and mobile worldviews, more locally rooted statecrafters in municipal finance have established new geographical relationships and arrangements since 2010.

Examining this local statecraft, a distinction is drawn between in-area and out-of-area. Existing work on England largely focuses upon local government and other local state actor strategies and activities *within* their local administrative areas. Given their founding local purposes, the national governance of local government activities addresses their powers and responsibilities *within* their local boundaries.

New financial strategies and arrangements emerged in-area across England since 2010. Initiatives include more active asset management covering land, property, and infrastructure as well as extension or initiation of commercialization activities in wholly or jointly owned businesses.

Intensifying fiscal pressures forced local statecrafters in England to extend activities beyond their local areas. While long-standing in geographically

---

[1] Ford (2020: 1).
[2] Ford (2020: 1).
[3] Ford (2020: 1).

Financialization and Local Statecraft. Andy Pike, Oxford University Press. © Andy Pike (2023).
DOI: 10.1093/oso/9780192856661.003.0007

dispersed local government pension fund investments and other limited areas, new out-of-area strategies and arrangements are evident. These involve shared management and service collaborations, local pooling of business rates revenues, investment strategies involving commercial properties and other projects, and commercial activity extension outside their territories.

These new geographies of local statecraft within *and* beyond local administrative jurisdictions in England extend and forge new relations. Objectives, incentives, autonomies, and accountabilities are being rewired and rescaled. Amidst austerity and local financial self-sufficiency, the UK government, professional and sector bodies, and commentators articulate concerns about local government activities and what it means for their purpose, financial resilience, and sustainability.

7.1 The geography of the national governance of local government activities

Expressing local statecraft's centralized setting in England, national governance historically covered powers and responsibilities *within* local areas. The 2011 Localism Act's general power of competence enabled local governments to pursue a wider range of interventions to improve their local residents' well-being. Amidst fiscal stress and the search for new income sources since 2010, local statecrafters were compelled to interpret this legal underpinning as licence to look for such opportunities within *and* beyond their administrative territories.

This rewiring and rescaling of local statecraft beyond its geographical boundaries were most evident in local government investments. Given a statutory basis in the Local Government Act 2003, the Prudential Code provides the governing framework for such capital expenditure. Capital budgeting is also regulated by the Department's statutory guidance.

Changing from historic control by the UK government, the code describes a broad purpose for local governments in England to 'invest both for the prudential management of their financial affairs and for purposes relevant to their functions'.[4] Such powers for capital expenditure seek alignment with local government's wider economic, social, and environmental responsibilities in their areas.

This governing system affords local statecrafters 'the freedom to determine how to invest their surplus cash balances'.[5] The central challenges are

---

[4] CIPFA (2019: 35).
[5] CIPFA (2019: 83).

'the effective management of risk and the balancing of security, liquidity and yield'.[6] In this order, these principles constitute the holy trinity of local municipal investment in England.

Encouraging more active financial strategy amidst austerity and localism from 2010, the 2017 Prudential Code update required local governments to produce a capital strategy. This approach aims to ensure longer-term views of capital investment plans, financing, and risks related to asset and project lifecycles. Underpinned by this strategy and three-year capital expenditure forecasts, each local government in England must produce a capital programme demonstrating its decisions 'have regard to' its overall strategic plan, service objectives, and asset management plan.[7] Importantly, the UK government has no desire to 'draw a big red line around a local authority' when cases can be made for 'doing something outside their area or in conjunction with other local authorities'.[8]

Complying with the code as a national accountability, the capital strategy must reflect value for money principles. This comprises formal options appraisal, prudence, sustainability, affordability, and practicality. The code requires local governments to assess the capital financing strategy's revenue implications and capital strategy, programme, borrowing, and investment's ramifications for its CT level. Local statecrafters must also report on a common set of prudential indicators.

Following the national legal framework, statutory guidance and code, the governance of local government investment remains with the full council to oversee and approve strategies and budgets prior to each financial year. Responsibility and circumscribed autonomy characterize the local statecraft and geographies of investment in England. In this highly centralized system, ultimate control over capital expenditure is retained at the national level. The UK Secretary of State can impose a national limit on specific local governments, although these powers were not used by 2020. Equipped with the general power of competence and under fiscal pressure to generate income within *and* beyond their areas, local statecrafters innovated unevenly across England from 2010.

7.2 In-area strategies and activities

Local statecraft's wider economic, social, and environmental responsibilities and objectives to improve conditions for residents combine through

---

[6] CIPFA (2019: 82).
[7] CIPFA (2019: 35).
[8] Civil servant 2, finance department (2021).

the in-area strategies and activities of local statecrafters and other local state actors. Local governments are historically bound to invest locally given their statutory purposes and well placed due to extensive local knowledge. The local statecraft of essential service provision connects with wider strategies including local regeneration.

Local statecraft innovations *within* areas in England increased amidst fiscal stress from 2010. In the UK government's localism and local financial self-sufficiency agenda, creating conditions conducive for growing local economic activities was hardwired into local statecrafters' incentives.

7.2.1 Asset-based approaches

New public wealth management argues that public authorities are underutilizing and undervaluing their assets, leaving untapped sources of local public wealth.[9] Key tasks are identifying, locating, and coordinating asset utilization more effectively to contribute to local finances.

This international agenda influenced the UK government and local statecrafters in England. It encouraged exploitation of public sector assets deemed underutilized and surplus. Promoted to cope with austerity, it claimed to enable local governments to plug funding gaps without having to reduce expenditure *or* raise taxes.[10]

Supporting shifts towards more active and strategic financial management from 2010, local statecrafters aimed to ensure asset management contributed more to cost reduction and income generation. Rather than only accommodating staff or delivering local services,[11] more commercial approaches sought strategic use of the assets on the local government's balance sheet and closer coordination with wider financial strategy.

For some local governments in England, new asset management approaches connected to more active place making strategies. Ideas such as place-based investing sought coordination with planning to promote locally mixed rather than single use and asset class strategies. Initial activities involved the centralization, integration, and more systematic approach to strategic asset management across the local government. Assets formerly the responsibility of individual service departments were drawn into overall organizational control.

---

[9] Detter and Fölster (2017).
[10] Detter and Fölster (2017).
[11] Christophers (2019).

Local asset registers and maps were created to provide local state-crafters with knowledge of their asset holdings. The geography of assets and opportunities across England was differentiated, revealing relatively asset-rich and asset-poor areas.[12] Identification of different asset types informed strategy on their potential utilization.

Local governments typically adopted the Corporate Landlord approach. This involved the introduction of a more strategic, commercial, and inte-grated policy towards their asset holdings. Yet, reflecting differentiation across England from 2010 and adaptation to local circumstances, a variety of institutional ownership, management, and governance models were used by local statecrafters. Property Boards and Land Commissions were estab-lished in larger areas in collaboration with adjacent local governments and the public sector including UK government departments and NDPBs.

Asset-based innovations in funding and financing were introduced. Local statecrafters pursuing vanguard approaches experimented with connecting land, property, and infrastructure to support capital investment schemes, informed by international value capture techniques and experiences.[13] Their activities sought new financial arrangements better able to capture part of the land value increases resulting from public investments alongside land owners.

Rather than only one-way outsourcing and privatization of local govern-ment functions and services,[14] in-area local statecraft with assets is more differentiated. Mixed approaches to selling, holding, and/or buying assets evolved across England from 2010.[15] Local statecraft encompassed com-mercial and entrepreneurial strategies alongside longer-term planning and place-making, working alone and with other private, public, and civic sector actors in the wider local state.[16]

Mirroring other local statecraft realms, differentiation is inherent amongst local government types. Counties with relatively large land holdings pursued different, typically in-area, strategies compared to geographically smaller and often spatially constrained districts and unitaries. London boroughs, metropolitan districts, and larger, more urban unitaries had substantial land holdings to work with especially brownfield sites connected to wider regeneration strategies.

---

[12] Pike et al. (2019).
[13] Leong (2016).
[14] cf. Latham (2017).
[15] Carr (2015).
[16] Pike et al. (2019).

Location is integral to local statecraft, especially in more prosperous local economies with more dynamic property markets, strong demand, and supply constraints. Local statecrafters in such geographies had more opportunities for asset management than in weaker and less buoyant places with limited demand and abundant supply. Indeed, this differentiated geography sometimes pushed these local governments in England to look outside their own areas where prospects were more promising.

Asset disposals are one-off financial transactions removing an asset from the balance sheet and generating a single capital receipt. This activity was important in early and mid-austerity with UK government support and incentivization. National guidance and specific programmes, including the Government Property Unit and LGA's One Public Estate, sought coordination between the national and local public sectors across England.

Rules where the UK government took all or most of the proceeds from local asset sales were changed. Local governments were incentivized for short-term gain by being allowed to retain 100 per cent of capital receipts. UK government policy compelled local statecrafters to identify underutilized and surplus assets and maximize capital receipts from their disposal to public, private, and civic buyers. This policy change fuelled a 'fire sale of public spaces' by some local governments in England.[17]

Reflecting geographically differentiated local statecraft across England from 2010, varied financial and ownership arrangements were used, including whole and partial sale and leases for various time periods. Asset valuations and capital receipts were weak in early austerity as financial institutions reeled after the 2008 crash and interested buyers were scarce.[18]

Utilizing municipal finance's flexibility, assets were also gifted by local governments as part of wider local development plans. New institutional arrangements were established. LABVs were joint ventures with firms and/or investors to enable asset commercialization and contribute to regeneration strategies.[19]

Such institutional and financial innovations became strategies for asset-rich, cash-poor local governments across England, especially for larger metropolitan districts with substantial urban sites and land and property assets.[20] These schemes typically included further public investments for

[17] Journalist (2021).
[18] Carr (2012).
[19] Carr (2015).
[20] Raco and Souza (2018).

site remediation to prepare areas for development, reducing or removing liabilities associated with specific assets.

Advocates argued LABVs provided private sector knowledge and support enabling local statecrafters to create asset portfolios with development potential and maximize wider economic, social, and environmental returns.[21] Critics interpreted LABVs as vehicles for commercialization, privatization, 'selling the family silver', and technocratic governance.[22] Local government's financial dependence upon property market uplifts increased as 'attempts to foster regeneration' became 'increasingly financialised, with the inflation of market values and returns becoming both the means and the ends of regeneration policy'.[23]

Demonstrating the distinctive local statehood of local politics in local statecraft in England, such asset strategies and institutions were contested locally. The Haringey Development Vehicle in London was a joint PPP between the borough and Australian property developer Lendlease.[24] Ostensibly focused on affordable housing development, it was protested by the local community and challenged by a Left faction in the ruling Labour group, leading to its demise and the council leader's resignation.[25]

While prominent in the 2011 Localism Act, there has been limited uptake of the Community Right to Challenge. This clause allowed local community bodies to express interest in running local government functions and services. Demonstrating geographically differentiated local statecraft, it is estimated over 1,700 transfers occurred across England between 2015 and 2020, especially in non-statutory services including libraries and swimming pools.[26] Transfers often occurred in relatively more prosperous places led by local groups with higher levels of social and other capital.

Moving beyond only asset disposal and 'selling off to the highest bidder' in early austerity and reflecting differentiated approaches,[27] local statecrafters in England renewed their interest in holding *and* acquiring assets and revenue streams from 2010. As fiscal stress deepened, more active financial strategy and balance sheet management turned CFOs against only selling assets to the private sector.

---

[21] Trowers and Hamlins (2013).
[22] Greenhalgh and Purewal (2015).
[23] Raco and Souza (2018: 161).
[24] Raco and Souza (2018).
[25] Williams (2018).
[26] Co-Op and Locality (2020).
[27] Professor of Real Estate, UK university (2020).

Earlier outsourcing was interpreted as hollowing out local government balance sheets and financial capacity, limiting scope for more active management. Reflecting local public wealth management, owning and better managing existing assets were increasingly seen by local statecrafters in England as ways to address local governments' multiple economic, social, and environmental objectives *as well as* financial constraints.[28] Local assets were reinterpreted by CFOs as contributing to generating direct and indirect local economic activity and business rate revenue.

Renewed interest in asset ownership did not herald a wholesale return to a fully public, insourced, and filled-in local government in England and reversal of the privatized, outsourced, and hollowed out local state.[29] Instead, local statecraft reflected the renewal of historical knowledge and experiences of municipal entrepreneurialism, countering outdated critiques of local public ownership.[30] More strategic and pragmatic local statecraft emerged in England from 2010, taking broader and more integrated views of regeneration and asset utilization for local employment, training, and housing. Property-based strategies were interpreted as catalysts stimulating achievement of wider local objectives.

This local statecraft involved a new institutional and financial innovation: housing companies. By 2021, 83 per cent of local governments in England had established such entities, up from 58 per cent in 2017.[31] Geographically differentiated across the country, housing companies were direct local responses to the national Right to Buy legislation introduced by the Conservative Government in 1980 affording local government tenants the right to purchase their council-owned houses at discounted prices. Right to Buy created strong incentives against local governments investing in building and owning housing to rent locally because their heavily subsidized sale translated into financial losses.[32]

Housing provision was acute for local governments in places facing growing populations and demand for affordable housing. As a historically core local government role, connections were made to invest-to-save strategies for cost savings and demand management on adult and child social care provision, and investment opportunities from asset ownership and guaranteed future revenue streams. Increased housing units also contributed to CT revenues by expanding the local residential property tax base.

---

[28] Carr (2015).
[29] Cf. Latham (2017).
[30] Cumbers (2012), Fenwick and Johnston (2020), Whitfield (2020).
[31] Morphet and Clifford (2017).
[32] Murie (2016).

Housing companies were established at arms-length from local government to circumvent Right to Buy. National legislative changes enabled some funding and financing autonomy and, in some cases, engagement with external financial actors and financialization.[33] With a mixed record across the sector, by 2020 several housing companies were disbanded and their activities brought back in-house to enable greater control over the assets and revenue streams.

Alongside disposals, holding existing, and building new assets, local statecrafters deployed new public wealth ideas to acquire assets in-area. While not differentiated between in-area and out-of-area categories, capital expenditure by local governments in England rose from around £13 billion to nearly £19 billion between 2010–11 and 2019–20 specifically in the 'acquisition of land and existing buildings'.[34]

Historically, asset acquisitions were connected to wider local regeneration aims. Common across England since 2010 were shopping centre purchases with local governments as backstop investors responding to local high street retail collapse and owner disposals even prior to the 2020 pandemic. Approaches sought to preserve local retail, economic activities, employment, and multipliers, and link to city and town centre regeneration strategies.

Asset acquisition included buying in through ground leases and retaining freeholds to provide local statecrafters with longer-term ownership and control. Repurposing was used to address local needs, including converting retail to affordable housing or mixed-use developments.

Funding, financing, and governing innovations were evident in some places in England to provide local statecrafters adopting vanguard approaches a strategic role in shaping longer-term local development and managing demands upon their finances. The London Borough of Southwark, for example, developed a lend-lease arrangement for the Canada Water regeneration in Rotherhithe. In this deal, the borough is the freeholder, with options to participate on development phases with the developer British Land. While attracting local contestation,[35] such deals have become part of some local statecrafters' in-area strategies and activities.

Under austerity and limited decentralization since 2010, a key challenge for local statecrafters' in-area strategies in England is assembling the local capital stack.[36] This is the package of internal and external resources required to fund

[33] Christophers (2019).
[34] MHCLG (2020b).
[35] 35% Campaign (n.d.).
[36] Bamberger and Katz (2019).

and finance capital investments including reserves, debt, equity participation, grants, and philanthropic contributions.

Amidst austerity from 2010, local statecrafters in England have sought to attract external financial investors to in-area assets. Embodying the relations and process of financialization, such actors have been drawn to local public assets in their search for yield amidst low returns from conventional asset classes, desire to balance investment portfolios, low interest rates, and quantitative easing. Attractions include the implicit UK sovereign guarantee, high investment grade credit ratings, relative stability (prior to Brexit, the 2020 pandemic, Ukraine conflict, and the Liz Truss prime ministership), strong and growing demand for local government services, and enhanced risk management and governance.[37] These conditions and situations have led investors to make a 'distressed bet' on alternative and less or illiquid 'harder-to-sell' assets.[38]

International ESG and Net Zero Carbon agendas have further encouraged commercial finance actors to consider formerly neglected areas of the investment landscape. Examples include social infrastructure and social housing in partnership with local governments and other local state actors in England and elsewhere.

Local statecrafters in England have sought funding, financing, and governance fixes for local assets generating revenue sources. Several local governments retain ownership of airports collectively (e.g. Manchester Airports Group) or in joint ventures (e.g. Newcastle Airport with seven north east local governments and AMP Capital). Such holdings are deemed strategic in critical local infrastructures and not for trading. These local statecrafters have worked with external private sector partners to provide expertise and finance. However, climate change and the 2020 pandemic impacts on air travel generated substantial losses and future uncertainty.[39]

Underexplained in local public wealth management, local statecrafter in-area strategies have to deal with the assets *and* liabilities associated with their local holdings of land, property, and other existing entities. Liabilities are future obligations including financial losses, maintenance, and site security. Such legacies are thorny for incumbent local governments. Local statecrafters cannot ignore such visible and often critical assets located in their areas. Yet many suffer from long-term underinvestment, especially if abandoned by failing commercial entities. They raise issues of finding new partial or full owners and/or arrangements to provide capital investment.

[37] Moody's (2017).
[38] Kumar (2019: 1).
[39] Knott (2021).

Local statecrafters are left holding assets and their liabilities struggling for viability that require major capital injections. These assets and liabilities include economic and social infrastructures such as ports and community centres, wholly or partly owned trading companies failing commercially and/or requiring recapitalization and/or new management, and locally embedded businesses grappling with commercial pressures including cultural venues and football clubs.

Local legacy assets led some local statecrafters in England to engage in relations with external commercial finance actors including developers and investors and become embroiled in financialization after 2010. Such forced in-area financial innovation has not always worked out positively for those involved.

Since the 2000s, Thanet Borough Council wrestled with its ownership of the listed but loss-making Dreamland amusement park in Margate. Connecting to financial actors' search for yield in illiquid investments post-2008, it attracted Arrowgrass Capital Partners to acquire this 'distressed' asset and local properties and sites in 2015, betting on its revitalization generating an financial upside from the town's regeneration.[40] However, the hedge fund closed following a 50 per cent drop in the value of its assets and around £750 million of redemption requests from fund investors. As 'one of the firm's most difficult to sell assets', the Margate investment attracted particular attention following an external valuation led to its writedown to £16 million, 70 per cent below its previous valuation.[41] As Arrowgrass folded, the Borough had to step in as the local owner of last resort, returning the asset and its liabilities to its balance sheet and undermining its wider regeneration plans.

Such engagements with financialization support interpretations of local statecrafters bamboozled by international investors and finance capital. Rather than a wholesale transformation, however, such local statecraft has only turned parts of the local public asset market into scenes for risky commercial finance actor plays and new, exotic financial schemes.

7.2.2 Commercialization

Local statecraft in England since 2010 has extended commercialization activities and the establishment of new ventures operating primarily within and, in some cases, beyond local areas. Commercial strategies have been supported by LGA guidance and the build-up and enhancement of staff

---

[40] Kumar (2019: 1).
[41] Kumar (2019: 1).

commercial skills.[42] Ventures have largely complemented and supplemented existing service provision. Distinct from financialization, much commercialization has developed without engagements with external financial actors and/or innovations.

Local statecrafters in England following vanguard approaches have pushed commercialization furthest in their local government's vision and strategy. Rationales focused on the acquisition or creation of assets and revenue streams to enhance financial situations and address multiple and interrelated local economic, social, and environmental objectives.

Since their legal authorization by the UK government in 2003, the number of trading companies operating within and beyond local government areas have increased. As a corporatization of local public entrepreneurship, across the political spectrum companies have been created by larger local governments in deprived and prosperous areas with higher levels of grant and debt dependence and varied managerial capabilities.[43] Growth and geographical extension have occurred across England since 2010 in search of new and expanding markets.

A specific area is the more than ten local energy services companies established over the decade. Such ventures sought to address multiple goals for local statecrafters in England: reducing utility service costs; ensuring residents' access to affordable energy; and supporting decarbonization and transition to renewable energy sources.

Experiences have been mixed. Nottingham City Council led the commercialization agenda with an in-house team to develop a more business-oriented and risk-based approach. Robin Hood Energy was established as a not-for-profit entity to address local fuel poverty.[44] It encountered problems including building a customer base from scratch, tight margins, limited liquidity to hedge against future price increases and purchase cheaper energy in advance, the limited scale of selling services in-area, and competition from larger private sector incumbents in the highly regulated and volatile energy market. Following a market price downturn and sustained financial losses, it was sold to Big 6 energy company Centrica for an undisclosed sum in 2020.[45]

Similar situations occurred with Bristol City Council's disposal of Bristol Energy to Together Energy (part-owned by Warrington Borough Council) and Portsmouth City Council's abandonment of Victory Energy before it commenced trading.[46] Critics highlighted the financial losses and questioned

[42] Carr (2012).
[43] Andrews et al. (2019).
[44] Cirell (2020).
[45] Cirell (2020).
[46] Cirell (2020).

whether local statecrafters had the business acumen and savvy successfully to manage such new commercial ventures as entrants into often highly competitive existing markets.[47]

Rewiring local statecraft's objectives, incentives, autonomies, and accountabilities in England since 2010, new decision-making structures were set up to manage commercial ventures. Concerns arose, however, about their management's closeness to political and officer leaderships and their ability to operate on a fully commercial basis given their ownership and organization within local government's orbit.

7.3 Out-of-area strategies and activities

Out-of-area is an increasingly important realm for local statecraft in England since 2010. This geography raises fundamental questions about how such strategies and activities relate to local government's statutory responsibilities in their areas. Operating outside their administrative boundaries challenges local statecrafters, compared to working in-area, since they lack definitive legal underpinnings and local knowledge. External advice is bought to fill gaps. Local statecrafter objectives, incentives, autonomies, and accountabilities across England are being unevenly rewired and rescaled as a result.

7.3.1 Cooperation

Historically, activities beyond local government boundaries in England were confined to specific areas and local functional and/or service cooperation. Local government pension funds have fiduciary duties to invest in asset classes without geographical bias to maximize returns to cover their long-term liabilities. Their strategies have carefully to manage any investments in their own local areas to avoid conflicts of interest and manage risk. Informed by the urban wealth fund model,[48] some regional pooling of local government pension funds has occurred across England to achieve greater scale, spread risk, and reduce management costs. This move involved local statecrafters working across wider geographical areas beyond individual local government territories.[49]

---

[47] TaxPayers' Alliance (2021).
[48] Detter and Fölster (2017).
[49] Pike et al. (2019).

Local functional and/or service cooperation has been extended across areas by local statecrafters in England since 2010. Reflecting NPM, these activities included shared services, staffing collaborations, and joint initiatives and responsibilities. Internal shared services aimed to reduce costs and generate efficiencies through consolidating and rationalizing routine administrative activities. Finance functions included payments and other transactions. Shared staff involved senior roles across smaller local governments especially districts. External shared services were used by typically geographically adjacent local governments often within broader and longer-term outsourcing contracts with large international firms.

Boundary crossing arrangements were used by local statecrafters for ownership and management of key assets and sites. Infrastructural systems were especially important, including airports, energy, key roads, and waste management. Integrated transport bodies incorporated local governments in larger urban areas into pan-local and subregional arrangements. Underpinned by local statehood, local statecrafters supported new cross-boundary initiatives—such as housing estates and industrial parks—through low or zero interest loans, guarantees, planning permissions, and, with UK government authorization, Enterprise Zone designations.

Before 2010 and in early austerity, there were relatively limited examples of investment and management strategies involving commercial properties and other projects outside their local government areas. Such activities were often particular local situations or the beginnings of more innovative approaches amongst local statecrafters adopting vanguard approaches.

Since 2010, out-of-area local statecraft became a more important and pressing task for local statecrafters across England. The aims being to generate income, close funding gaps, and make local government finances more sustainable.

Some out-of-area initiatives were prompted by local government funding system changes. The UK government authorized experiments with the local pooling of business rate revenues. Complexities and uncertainties, however, meant arrangements were often discontinued after local pilots.[50]

Linked to Enterprise Zone designations by the UK government, future business rates revenues over twenty-five years were pooled and borrowed against by several local governments in England to provide capital investment to create employment sites and infrastructure. Distinct from commercial finance and financialization, such municipal finance innovations echoed the

---

[50] Amin-Smith et al. (2018).

'councillors at the casino' narrative as local statecrafters were effectively betting on future economic activity realizing the tax revenues to service and repay the borrowing.

7.3.2 Commercial property investment

Most important and increasing amongst some local governments in England from 2010 is out-of-area commercial property acquisition. With a statutory responsibility to manage public money based on security, liquidity, and yield, this activity became integral to the income generation strategies of local statecrafters seeking returns through ownership of assets and related revenue streams.

Prior to the 2008 crash, local governments in England held ~70–5 per cent of their reserves in cash deposits in banks. This made less financial sense as interest rates fell following the crisis prompting a 'big shift away from cash balances' and reduction of cash deposits down to 40 per cent as local statecrafters got 'into other asset classes to try and generate that yield'.[51] Changing macro-economic conditions made it difficult to demonstrate value for money with cash sitting on their balance sheet or in bank deposits earning 0.1 per cent interest compared to potentially ~4 per cent from commercial investment. This situation compelled some local statecrafters to consider riskier options in search of returns.

Commercial property investment is long-standing in local statecraft in England. Historically, it was broadly in-area, relatively small scale, and related to wider development and regeneration strategies. This picture changed from 2010 to out-of-area, larger scale, differentiated by local government type and location, and focused on income generation.

Local government in England owns commercial property through several routes. Default ownership of land and property in-area results from development in place and/or as by-products of local capital investment programmes. Deliberate commercial property ownership occurred through commercialization strategies before 2010 and/or in relation to regeneration plans. It also includes local in-area assets with limited value and requiring investment such as vehicle garages, industrial estates, and neighbourhood shopping centres. Fiscal stress and income generation pressures from 2010 pushed local statecrafters to look beyond their own areas to secure assets and revenue streams to close funding gaps.

---

[51] Director, bank (2020).

Commercial property proved attractive to local statecrafters because of its potential returns and diversification of risk in investment portfolios in different sectors (commercial, industrial, residential, retail), tenants and tenancies ('blue chip' international corporates, medium-sized local businesses, long to shorter-term), locations (city centre, suburban), and places across the UK. Diversification reduced dependence on in-area investments and connected into wider opportunities within functional economic areas, including employment and housing sites within travel-to-work-areas. Land and bricks and mortar were seen as appropriate and long-term investments in assets made with calculated risks capable of generating steady incomes rather than shorter-term approaches of 'putting some of their money into the stock market or … trying to gamble it.'[52]

Increased local statecrafter demand has been supported and stimulated by the supply of external advice and investment opportunities by banks, TMAs, and property consultants. There has been increasingly active construction, expansion, and stimulation of a market for local government commercial property investment outside their areas in England since 2010.

While acknowledging their emphasis on yield, local statecrafters faced difficult strategic and operational decisions about the levels of returns and risks in relation to security and liquidity. Depending upon market conditions, property investments are relatively illiquid in the short-term and local statecrafters were keen to avoid forced sales and losses on their acquisitions.

While controversial, the local statehood attribute of relatively low-cost borrowing from the PWLB incentivized local statecrafters in England to undertake a carry trade: seeking net positive returns by borrowing at low interest rates to invest in assets generating relatively higher returns. Borrowing at ~2–3 per cent and acquiring commercial property yielding returns of ~6–8 per cent, local statecrafters sought benefit from the arbitrage while demonstrating value for money. For some, this was seen as a 'get out of jail free card' with a local political dividend of not having to make cuts or raise taxes and make themselves unpopular.[53]

Local statecrafters utilized the Localism Act to underpin their out-of-area strategies. This enabling legislation places the onus on local governments in England to justify their decision-making, prudent financial and risk management, and due diligence. Such governance underlines the local political and officer leaderships' key roles, especially those with property market knowledge and skills. External advisors have been integral to decision-making and

---

[52] Conservative Councillor and Finance Committee Chair, District Council (2021).
[53] Local government financial consultant 4 (2020).

risk management, especially when local 'politicians endorsed it as part of the plan'.[54] In other cases, council members were more risk-averse, concerned with 'stewardship' of local taxpayers' money, and keen to avoid the reputational risk and press coverage if it had 'gone off and bought a skyscraper down in Canary Wharf [in London]'.[55]

A common strategy and instrument involved establishment of a specific fund for property acquisitions. This approach evolved from an early focus on individual asset acquisition towards a more integrated and strategic portfolio approach to manage costs and risks. Sizeable funds are required to generate sufficient income to cover costs and provide worthwhile contributions to local government budgets. In early austerity, funds sought acquisitions in the £2–10 million range and struggled to interest the 'big capital markets boys in the City'.[56] As funds have been built up by especially local governments in England pursuing vanguard approaches, larger acquisitions have been made. However, balance is difficult to achieve in a £25–50 million fund with minimum £10 million lot sizes.

External advisors have been integral working with local statecrafters to establish their scoring criteria for prioritizing property acquisitions. Tempering the local in statecraft, advisors' rationale was to take out local sensitivities, making 'it less emotional', commercial, and objective.[57] Such approaches pushed acquisition decisions to out-of-area assets given their relatively higher potential returns and risk diversification beyond the local area. Critical has been anticipating and modelling unforeseen and uncertain additional costs resulting from property ownership and management including carrying voids, refurbishment, and repair.

Property advice for local statecrafters followed trends in categories. Timing was key to avoid the highest prices and lowest returns: 'in 2017, everyone was piling into offices … then "beds and sheds" in housing and distribution … latecomers tend to be caught out in those cycles.'[58] Engaging common advisors and seeking similar investments, local governments across England were often advised to target the same growth segments including premium office space and logistics centres. This situation led to secrecy and competition amongst local statecrafters for the highest quality assets.

Following decisions to invest in commercial property, local statecrafters pursued two main approaches. Direct acquisition necessitated external

---

[54] Director, bank (2020).
[55] Director of Finance, Metropolitan Borough Council (2021).
[56] Director, property consultancy company (2021).
[57] Director, property consultancy company (2021).
[58] Professor of Real Estate, UK university (2021).

advice since many were novices and investing in places where they lacked local knowledge. Specialists interpreted it as 'like running your own [property development] fund'.[59] Transactions-based business models incentivized external advisors to set up pipelines of potential properties to generate revenue from advice, commissions, and fees on deals. Some local statecrafters used real estate agents or other intermediaries to purchase 'off market' from existing owners to reduce costs.[60]

Reflecting differentiated engagements with financialization, some local statecrafters's financial arrangements contained innovations. Controversially, tax efficient shell companies located in offshore jurisdictions internationally were utilized.[61] Such practices created contradictions in local statecrafters using public money to pay for external advice and demonstrating value for money by minimizing the tax paid to the UK government on their property investments.

The local statehood underpinning local statecraft in the English setting enabled further financial innovation. An investment wrap used the local government's covenant or guarantee to enable low cost upfront borrowing to invest in property against its forecast future revenue streams. The covenant being the wrap around the investment scheme. Using the local government's guarantee, backstopped by the UK sovereign, reduced interest rates on the borrowing from 6–8 per cent to 2–3 per cent.[62]

Further innovations could then be layered on top of this wrap. The investment can be transferred to the lender and leased back to the local government in a long-term deal with a buy-back option at the end. The lender receives a guaranteed income index linked for the deal term. The local government agrees to pay a rent as a lower proportion, 40–60 per cent, of the total rent it will receive from the tenants it lets to. It then profits from the differential between the rent it receives from its tenants and what it pays to its lender. Index linking generates inflation risk over the deal term, potentially reducing this differential and requiring exit clauses if it turns negative.

The second main approach is indirect acquisition via a managed fund. Involving engagements with commercial finance actors and the relations and process of financialization, these arrangements place local government funds with a financial institution to acquire and manage property investments for a commission and/or fee. Property Funds and REITs were used to pool funds and risks. The rationale is such actors are more experienced and savvy

[59] Professor of Real Estate, UK university (2021).
[60] Director 1, property company (2021).
[61] Dhillon (2017).
[62] Director, property consultancy company (2021).

property market players able to read trends and offer foresight to support their clients' local government investment portfolios. These funds connected local statecrafters' finances into the volatile, internationalized dynamics of the property asset class.[63]

Demonstrating local statehood, local politics were critical in determining investment strategies across England. Elected to represent wards within local government areas, councillors have strong interests towards in-area investment to benefit local residents, taxpayers, and voters. Arguments focused on resource utilization for the good of the area and reservations about whether out-of-area property investment is what local government should be doing and the risks involved. Political leaderships and executives have these hard wired local electoral ties as a key accountability, but were compelled by fiscal pressure to generate income to close funding gaps and secure the overall local government's financial sustainability.

Rewiring local statecraft's incentives and accountabilities, local governments in England introduced institutional fixes to govern and deliver their strategies. Recommended by external advisors and often pushed by senior officers, delegated decision-making and higher value financial thresholds were sought to avoid 'political interference' and councillors' 'protectionism for their own areas'.[64] Local governments were considered insufficiently 'fleet of foot' in the sector and needed 'delegated power to buy and sell' to speed-up the acquisition cycle to two to three weeks 'not three months' and enable decision-making and approvals to work at the faster pace of commercial property markets.[65] Appropriate staff could then be more readily recruited from the private sector and afforded more operational flexibility.

Property investment strategies exposed contradictions integral to local statecraft in England where it engages with commercialized and financialized activities. Enabling local statecrafters degrees of commercial independence introduced the possibility of decisions conflicting with the local government's wider economic, social, and environmental objectives. As commercial property owners, local governments may cause local tensions because landlords must 'make commercial decisions' including increasing rents and foreclosing on struggling businesses.[66]

As more local governments across England invested in commercial property by late austerity, coverage moved from the trade press into the mainstream. Emblematic of vanguard behaviour and changing the paradigm

---

[63] Sanfelici and Halbert (2019).
[64] Director, property consultancy company (2021).
[65] Director, property consultancy company (2021).
[66] Director, property consultancy company (2021).

'for the whole sector' was Spelthorne Borough Council in Surrey, South East England.[67] This relatively small district attracted attention with its debt-led strategy of large-scale borrowing relative to its balance sheet to invest in high-value and high-quality assets within *and* beyond its area. Criticism and debate followed.

The main concern was the high level of borrowing financing the investments and, integral to the 'councillors at the casino' narrative, perceptions of speculative bets being placed on risky assets by inexperienced players.[68] Even before the pandemic, uncertain and volatile demand for commercial property generated risks of declining rents and rising vacancies potentially requiring funding from elsewhere in local government budgets.[69]

Finance commentators criticized local statecrafters' carry trade, borrowing cheaply from the PWLB then unfairly competing for assets and, reflecting the historic HMT view, crowding out more productive private investment. This local statecraft was described as a 'quirky and hazardous corner of British public finance' with local governments borrowing cheaply from the PWLB to compete unfairly with commercial banks and underpinning 'the creeping nationalisation of the UK commercial property market under a Conservative government'.[70] Contradiction was identified in local governments disposing of assets to close funding gaps resulting from UK government expenditure reductions while acquiring commercial property assets across the UK using lower cost borrowing from UK government.[71]

While stimulating and growing the market, property sector analysts acknowledged local governments 'are not real estate companies' and rely upon purchasing costly external advice.[72] In their sectoral view, local statecrafters lack expertise, skills, and experience on market structure, dynamics, and risk.

As its Chief Executive Rob Whiteman accused some local governments of 'going too far' and 'taking the piss',[73] CIPFA sought to guide local statecrafters to make informed decisions. They emphasized the need for prudence, affordability, and investments 'in proportion to the size and scale' of balance sheets, revenue budgets, and capital programmes.[74] CIPFA identified the risks from volatile revenue streams, unforeseen costs, reductions in asset values, and

---

[67] Former Director, public audit body (2021).
[68] Davies (2018), Ford (2020).
[69] Sandford (2017).
[70] Plender (2017: 1).
[71] Plender (2017: 1).
[72] Professor of Real Estate, UK university (2021).
[73] Peters (2021: 1).
[74] Associate Director, professional association (2020).

forced loss-making sales. The Department expressed concerns about investment in assets subject to macro-economic trends and overdependence upon commercial income providing revenues for statutory service delivery.

Local statecrafters argued local political leaderships had been forced into such income generation activities by austerity in England since 2010. Moreover, they were accountable for their decisions and had undertaken due diligence with external advice. Local governments were seen as 'willing partners' given the financial situation the UK government had created and their encouragement of local statecrafters to generate income.[75]

Concerns were expressed too. Sector finance consultants saw a 'level of foolhardiness in buying purely for yield' and small Districts doing 'hugely aggressive' and large-scale borrowing relative to their size to invest in commercial assets'.[76] While such behaviours were confined to a relatively small number of local statecrafters pursuing vanguard approaches, the disproportionate and negative attention meant all were 'tarred with the same brush'.[77]

Articulating the 'councillors at the casino' narrative, much coverage provided unbalanced accounts of local statecraft based upon vanguard activities rather than all local governments. More systematic views revealed a more differentiated landscape across England.

The NAO's study revealed steady growth from 2010–11 before a 'step-change in scale' of £6.6 billion spent on commercial property between 2016–17 and 2018–19: a more than fourteen-fold increase over the previous three-year period.[78] The majority (80 per cent) of acquisitions were by a small but growing group of 49 local governments, although over 100 had invested at least £10 million. Most of the purchases were office and retail properties. In the dramatic growth from 2016–17, in-area and out-of-area increased (Figure 7.1). The regional distribution was concentrated in South East England (Figure 7.2).

Mirroring the vanguard, intermediate, and long-tail approaches in local statecraft in England from 2010, based on their commercial property investments the NAO identified three groups differentiated by type: 'most active' (17 districts, 19 single-tier and counties); 'less active' (68, 75); and 'not active' (116, 57).[79]

[75] Local government financial consultant 2 (2020).
[76] Local government financial consultant 4 (2020).
[77] Associate Director, professional association (2020).
[78] National Audit Office (2020: 7).
[79] National Audit Office (2020: 69).

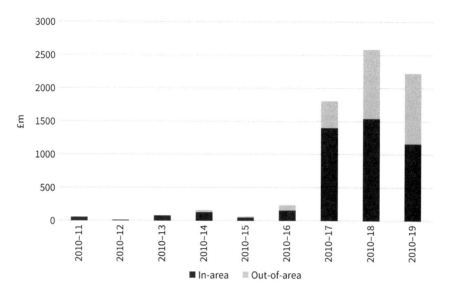

Figure 7.1 Location of commercial properties acquired by local governments in England, 2010–11 to 2018–19

Note: Nominal values.
Source: Adapted from National Audit Office (2020: 33).

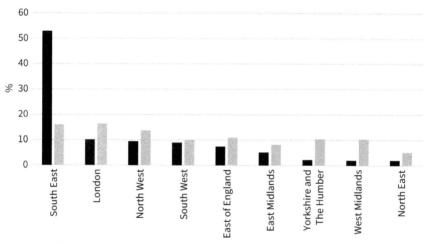

Figure 7.2 Regional share of commercial property acquisitions by local governments in England, 2016–17 to 2018–19 (cumulative)

Note: Share of national spend on commercial property shows the regional share of total spend from 2016–17 to 2018–19. Share of national spending power shows regional share of spending power from 2016–17 to 2018–19. This figure is included to give a sense of the financial scale of authorities in each region.
Source: Adapted from National Audit Office (2020: 28).

The most active were smaller districts in South East England, flush with cash reserves from buoyant property markets and tax bases and close to multiple property-led growth opportunities. Districts accumulated cash from business rates and New Homes Bonus grants but invested to generate revenue rather than use it for revenue expenditure given future uncertainty.

Reflecting local statecraft's geographical differentiation across England since 2010, varying financial strategies were explained by risk appetite, financial condition, political and/or officer leadership with property sector knowledge, and ability to design, develop and manage a property investment strategy. Councillors with 'financial backgrounds' were typical in local governments adopting vanguard approaches.[80]

Geographical settings in England directly structured and shaped the strategies of the different local government types. Larger metropolitan districts, counties, and sizeable unitaries with larger geographical areas, economies, and populations had more potential opportunities in-area. Smaller districts and unitaries with less potential were forced to look out-of-area.

Local economic conditions and prospects were important too. Certain London boroughs attracted attention for innovative schemes. Local statecrafters sought to capitalize upon international investors' interest in property-led development in the national capital city, sometimes triggering local campaigns against gentrification.[81] In less promising local economic settings experiences were different because it was: 'potentially easier to build a new business park in Surrey [South East England] than Knowsley [North West England]'.[82]

Demonstrating the local statehood underpinning statecraft in England, ideological and political elements were evident. Compelled by financial pressure, local statecrafters engaged in commercial property investments across the political spectrum. Those less or not involved were not only divided along party lines. Conservative and Labour leaderships considered commercial property investments as contrary to the local governments' purpose. Some claimed it was 'not our business' and 'not where councils should be' because they do not have the skills to 'run businesses in the commercial world'.[83]

As fiscal stress squeezed increasing numbers of local governments in later austerity, commercial property investment become more widespread across

[80] Director, property consultancy company (2021).
[81] Minton (2017).
[82] Local government financial consultant 3 (2020).
[83] Liberal Democrat Councillor, Deputy Leader, and Cabinet Member for Finance, County Council (2021).

England. Local statecrafter networks were key as the most 'risk-averse … like to see proof that it's been done' and 'it appears to work well'.[84]

Property sector actors continued to stimulate the market in England in response to continued demand. Working for multiple clients, property companies have been actively 'sending lists of properties' to local governments, 'but councils don't need much tempting.'[85]

By 2020, the market had become crowded. Local governments 'all wanted the same thing … a good yielding safe investment with growth' and ended up 'bidding against themselves'.[86] Enabled by lower cost PWLB borrowing, overvaluation and overpaying by some local statecrafters pushed up prices. Property companies even argued that the 'UK regional property investment market' was being 'held up by public sector borrowing [over the] last ten years' and strong local government demand 'put a premium on value of 5–10 per cent'.[87]

Market stimulus in England was multifaceted. External advisors were part of large property groups involved on both sides of the market and as intermediaries: advising on potential property asset purchases; developing properties for sale; and market making to build pipelines of projects, deal flow, and investor confidence.

Local statecraft engagements with financialization in commercial property investment across England was generating a classic speculative bubble involving local governments with external developers, investors, and property companies. Value was hard to find in the rush to acquire assets as more local statecrafters entered the market. The purchase of market lemons, including outdated and unlet office blocks and struggling shopping centres, occurred as agents and owners realized they could 'sell them [local governments] almost anything'.[88]

Lack of market understanding led some local statecrafters to acquire assets unlikely to fulfil revenue forecasts including first-generation business parks paying off set-up infrastructure costs. Local government investors focusing on premium market segments missed out on less attractive secondary markets with lower prices, risks, and easier escape routes in adverse conditions.

Secretive behaviours emerged as local statecrafters in England competed for the same asset types, especially with neighbouring local governments. Caution was urged by external advisors against an 'invest in commercial

[84] Director, property consultancy company (2021).
[85] Local government financial consultant 2 (2020).
[86] Director, property consultancy company (2021).
[87] Director, property consultancy company (2021).
[88] Director, property consultancy company (2021).

assets anywhere' approach since prudence, care, and risk consideration were needed in more balanced strategies to manage the geographical variations in risk.[89] Other local statecrafters following vanguard approaches sought 'not to overplay your hand' by sticking to their strategies, using high-quality external advice, and being prepared to walk away from potential deals.[90]

The rapid growth in local government commercial property acquisition in England from 2016–17 attracted UK government attention as a potential systemic risk, prompting review and intervention. The UK government tightened the rules as concerns about certain local governments' debt-based, risky statecraft mounted. The existing statutory guidance in the Local Authorities Investment Code was revised. Mirroring the need for a capital strategy, the Department now required an investment strategy approved by the full council. Demonstrating compliance with local public finance management principles, the strategy needed to disclose, explain, and justify investment plans in terms of security, liquidity, and yield.

Their strategy was also required to specify the contributions non-core investments would make to core statutory functions and service delivery and place-making objectives. This change sought more closely to connect strategic investment to the local government's overall strategy. Investments must now be justified where there is no market failure rationale, and they are competing against private sector and other investors. In addition, it 'should state the local authority's approach to assessing risk of loss before entering into and while holding an investment.'[91]

As more local governments in England beyond those pursuing vanguard approaches were 'becoming like a real estate company or doing lots of investments purely for yield',[92] the Department undertook further revision of the governing Code and HMT updated PWLB lending rules in 2019–20. Facing mounting fiscal stress, the sector bemoaned the clamp down on borrowing to invest as being unduly based on the minority of vanguard approaches in local statecraft in some local governments in England.

As the 2020 pandemic hit, the nature, scale, and pace of financial impacts in commercial property markets were uncertain.[93] Retail and high street investments were more adversely affected than logistics and supermarkets. Rent and business rates holidays were used as local business support

---

[89] Local government financial consultant 4 (2020).
[90] Deputy Chief Executive and CFO, District Council (2021).
[91] CIPFA (2019: 85).
[92] Local government financial consultant 4 (2020).
[93] National Audit Office (2021b).

measures. The UK government provided no compensation for loss of commercial income because local government's risk management was expected
to deal with any shortfalls.[94] Meanwhile, property sector actors argued falling
prices meant it was an appropriate time to buy to invest for the longer term.

7.4 Conclusions

Local statehood underpins the local statecraft realm of in-area and out-of-
area strategies and activities. Local governments in England hold powers and
resources that afford them authority and financial capacity, marking them
out from other economic actors. The implicit UK sovereign guarantee and
accountability as local democratic institutions with elected political leaderships means their agency is exercised in particular ways within *and* beyond
their local areas. Local statecrafters' visions and more than economic and
financial ambitions and objectives connect to wider social and environmental
responsibilities and aims.

Differentiation in such strategies and activities across local governments
in England since 2010 is evident. In common with financial innovation, it is
shaped by: type; political and officer leadership; risk appetite; organizational
structures, capacities, and capabilities; financial condition; and location.
In-area strategies involve asset-based approaches and commercialization.
Local statecrafters fund and finance investments to address local economic,
social, and environmental objectives and responsibilities.

Out-of-area strategies act like a spatial fix.[95] They enable local governments with weaker local economic and market conditions and opportunities
to enlarge, extend, and diversify their investment portfolio through geographical extension of ownership relations beyond their own area. Spatial
disconnections are created between custodians of local knowledge in one
area venturing into other local governments' territorial domains about which
they may know little. While a significant change and high profile in England
since 2010, such activities are highly skewed towards those following vanguard approaches. The municipal finance tactic of recalculating MRP is more
important financially.

In-area and out-of-area strategies can import the commercial finance
and risk rewiring and rescaling the relations, incentives, autonomies, and
accountabilities of local statecraft in England. Some local governments are

---

[94] National Audit Office (2021b).
[95] Harvey (1982).

drawn into often new, unfamiliar, and potentially financially riskier territory with substantive and longer-term implications for their financial resilience and sustainability. Transparency and accountability are under threat from commercial confidentialities and new delegated decision-making structures. Debt-led strategies reduce financial resilience as increased borrowing and risk extends amongst more local governments: 'when they go from being marginal to more important' there is a 'risk contagion … like a domino effect if one falls over'.[96]

The UK government is torn in its official mind and governing codes between encouraging local commercialism and entrepreneurialism for local government's financial self-sufficiency *and* the increased risks and potential costs involved with losses and failures deepening local fiscal stress. This situation creates tensions and contradictions generating further governance risks of UK government intervention and/or additional changes to local statecraft regulation in England.

---

[96] Associate Director, professional association (2020).

8

Conclusions

The differentiated landscape of financialization and local statecraft

8.0 Introduction

Struggling to balance their budgets since 2010, local statecrafters in England acknowledged 'we're not like Gordon Gekko [and] … really shouldn't be dabbling with complicated financial instruments', but are being compelled by national policy and fiscal stress 'to play in the market'.[1] As the UK government reduced expenditure and introduced local financial self-sufficiency, local governments were forced to find savings and new income sources. Innovative strategies and practices emerged, often untried and untested, combining municipal and commercial finance with unprecedented levels of risk.

Such instances attracted attention as departures from local government financial norms in England and, for some, evidence that new ways to fund local public services could be found. Critical characterizations followed of 'councillors at the casino' taking risks with local taxpayers' money and jeopardizing local service provision. At stake is a local tier of over 300 governments, managing £100 billion of revenue expenditure, and employing around 1.4m providing essential services to over 56 million people in England. This alleged local public service gamble raised fundamental questions about local government's role and funding.

Yet, the picture in England has been dominated by disproportionate attention given to the highest profile and leading cases deploying the most innovative financial strategies and instruments. Change and novelty have been highlighted over continuity and stasis. Local government engagements with commercial finance have been portrayed as leading to inevitable and necessary financialization, relieving dependency upon transfers from national government.

[1] Labour Councillor and Cabinet Member for Finance, London Borough (2021). Gordon Gekko was a financier character in Oliver Stone's 1987 film Wall Street notorious for his 'greed, for want of a better word, is good' speech.

Financialization and Local Statecraft. Andy Pike, Oxford University Press. © Andy Pike (2023). DOI: 10.1093/oso/9780192856661.003.0008

While contributing much to our understanding and a basis upon which to build, existing work has limits. Relations between general and financial strategies and activities are unclear. Municipal and commercial finance and their interactions are underspecified. Commercialization and financialization blur and are treated loosely. Studies have a relatively narrow and limited focus on specific cases, financial instruments, sectors, geographical scales, and places that are relatively small areas in the overall landscape. Questioning the 'councillors at the casino' narrative in England, this book aimed to provide a more balanced account of varying local government engagements with financialization and their impacts. It used a wider frame to outline and explain the hitherto missing account of the differentiated landscape across England.

Building and reflecting upon existing frameworks, a new theory of local statecraft was articulated to interpret and account for the case of England since 2010 and provide a means to understand and explain experiences elsewhere. Grounding statecraft in a theorization of the state endows local government with distinctive and underpinning local statehood attributes. Local statecrafters—elected councillors and appointed officers—exercise statecraft in specific realms, strongly framed by national constitutional, strategic and policy settings in particular times and spaces.

Local statecrafters in England pursuing vanguard, intermediate, and long-tail approaches with varying engagements with financialization were outlined and explained. Their differentiated local statecraft is accounted for by: local configurations of local government types and sizes with varying powers, responsibilities, and resources; local politics, political and officer leaderships, and experience; organizational models, expertise, and capacities; knowledge and openness to external advice and commercial finance; and local economic assets and liabilities, conditions, growth potential, and tax bases. Relatively small-scale engagements with financialization were evident in England, even amongst local statecrafters pursuing vanguard approaches, but these warrant attention because of their longer-term implications for local government and service provision.

Local governments' objectives, incentives, autonomies, and accountabilities in England are being rewired and rescaled by UK government policy and engagements with financialization alongside the relocation and displacement of risks. Such shifts prompt consideration of whether and how local government financial sustainability and resilience are being undermined by national policy and financialization in England since 2010. It raises foundational questions about what local government is for and how it can be funded? And asks whether the rewiring and rescaling of local accountability, transparency, and scrutiny of local statecraft's engagements with financialization in England are leading to depoliticized and post-democratic local governance?

8.1 For local statecraft

The book's main arguments and contributions are fourfold. First, local statecraft provides a meaningful way of understanding and accounting for the differentiated engagements of local governments with financialization and their wider implications. Local statecraft is the art of local government and management of state relations and affairs with national state, private, civic, and other public actors across and between different geographical scales and networks. Central to local statecraft are relations between local and national government and external financial actors.

This local statecraft is grounded in a theorization of the state as a social relation, constantly being remade and shaped by state actors' ongoing agency. Local statecraft is integral to this continuous state formation process as actors attempt to articulate, cohere, and stabilize its structures, imaginaries, strategies, and projects in specific geographical and temporal settings. National governments are central in framing the conditions for local statecraft in constitutional, legal, institutional, and policy terms.

The empirical focus was local government in England within the UK state since 2010. Over this period, national government actors constructed and pursued austerity and local government financial self-sufficiency through a highly centralized governance and funding system in a liberalized, financialized political economy. Local statecrafters were compelled to formulate strategies to close funding gaps by making savings and generating new income sources. Their agency brought local statecraft into varying engagements with the relations and process of financialization.

As part of the state, local governments are endowed with local statehood attributes manifest in their authority, powers, and resources to undertake statecraft within *as well as* beyond their administrative areas. Local government's territorial embeddedness and fixity are critical. It is underpinned by the legal basis of their powers, responsibilities, and statehood within and for their local jurisdictions. This geographical basis is integral to their local statecraft. Imparting intergenerational responsibilities and outlooks, geography and history structure and influence local statecrafters' variegated engagements with financialization.

Local statehood makes local governments distinctive from other economic and financial actors, underpinning their 'unique ability to "leverage" finance'.[2] Each attribute has material consequences for local statecraft: the legal basis to act in formulating local visions and strategies; authorizing developments and planning consent; levying, collecting, and using local tax revenues; charging fees for local services; receiving grants and transfers from national government; contracting with external service providers; borrowing with implicit sovereign guarantee; and demonstrating accountability for using public money. Local statecraft is largely undertaken in relations with other national and local state as well as private, civic, and hybrid actors. Varying in different countries, national government's central position determines the nature and extent of local statehood attributes.

Underpinned by this local statehood theorization, local statecraft is distinct from and extends beyond more narrowly focused financial statecraft because of local government's wider purposes, functions, and responsibilities. It performs different, multiple, and simultaneous roles: strategy developer; service provider; borrower; lender; regulator; and policymaker.[3] Funding and financing are integral to, rather than only and wholly determinant of, local statecraft. In any involvement with the relations and process of financialization, local governments do not simply 'respond' to the dominant 'logic of finance', nor are they *only* governing through finance[4]. Local statecrafters influence the rationales and agency of finance actors and vice versa. Finance is one of multiple local statecraft facets. Local statecraft histories and geographies predate contemporary manifestations of financialization, warranting further comparison of past and contemporary conjunctures.

Local statecraft is shaped by the intersecting worlds of municipal *and* commercial finance. Each world's specific actors, relations, aims and objectives, accountabilities, frames of action, and geographies engage, interact, and even conflict. Local statecrafters' engagements with financialization vary in degree and extent, resulting from their geographically and temporally variegated interrelations across space and time. This conjunctural interpretation of local statecraft is a complex, often messy, and pragmatic 'accumulation of expedient solutions assembled to tackle concrete problems'.[5]

The analysis of local government in England since 2010 reveals new municipal finance strategies and practices which are innovative and entrepreneurial but *not* financialized: undertaken by local statecrafters *within* local governments and *not* involving external financial actors. Exercising agency within national legal, regulatory, and advisory frameworks, such local statecrafter

---

[2] Wang (2020: 193).
[3] Sbragia (1986).
[4] Wang (2020: 197), Ashton (2020).
[5] Wang (2020: 190).

strategies included: generating efficiencies; invest-to-save initiatives; maximizing grant and tax revenue income; internal borrowing; recalculating MRP; reducing capital expenditure charged to the revenue account; reforming fees and charges; and lending to other local governments and related third parties. Challenging the 'councillors at the casino' narrative, these activities are more significant in generating financial benefits for local governments in England than their relatively smaller scale and more innovative financial and commercial activities.

Commercialization and financialization are evident in local statecraft but are not synonymous. Key is distinguishing internal, municipal finance strategies, activities, and innovations that may be commercially oriented but do not engage external commercial finance actors. Similarly important is clearly identifying external, commercial finance approaches, instruments, and novelties intersecting and being incorporated within municipal finance. A further important distinction is between using finance directly to deliver a policy or service objective and using finance indirectly to invest to generate funding for the same ends. Disentangling these distinctions in specific geographical and temporal settings helps understand and explain commercialization and financialization relations in local statecraft.

Commercialization and financialization reinforce each other in the vanguard approaches of local governments in England since 2010 but are less connected amongst local statecrafters adopting intermediate and long-tail behaviours. Commercialization has been pursued by local statecrafters without financial innovation. Financialization has been a by-product of commercialization. The UK government explicitly encouraged commercialization and new income generation since 2010, leaving local statecrafters in England few alternative strategies to exercise their agency.

This local statecraft theory's explanatory worth is enhanced by its recognition of risk. National policy and engagements with financialization generate multiple and growing risks for local governments. Critically, they emanate internally from within the state *and* externally from finance. Local statecrafters are now more focused and involved in managing and mitigating the distribution, transfer, and potential impacts of such risks. Further pressures were generated by the higher-level risk profiles and appetites evident amongst local governments in England since 2010.[6] A financializing ratchet is evident whereby ever more financial innovations are required by those engaged in the relations and process of financialization to manage the risks generated by

---

[6] National Audit Office (2019a).

previous and existing financial agreements. Financialization begets yet more financialization.

Specific and related realms are identified in which local statecraft is exercised: financial strategies and risks; external advice; borrowing and debt management; and in and out-of-area activities. Each realm provides a terrain to address the actors involved, their rationales, activities, arrangements, and impacts in their geographical and temporal situations. Their local statecraft is underpinned by specific configurations of authority, power, and resources within the national system of governance, regulation, and funding. This more spatialized understanding of statecraft builds upon and moves beyond existing work to strengthen its analytical and explanatory grasp of the differentiated landscape of local statecraft's engagements with financialization and its ramifications.

Future research can take several directions. Explore statecraft's explanatory value at different geographical scales including and beyond the local, especially the 'multi-scalar organization of political authority'.[7] Examine geographical and temporal settings where financialization is more internalized within municipal finance, where it is less evident, and where it is present in other statecraft realms including education, health, housing, and social care. Undertake international comparative work situating in-depth case studies within their wider landscapes, especially beyond the global North. Further engage other (sub)disciplines including local government studies, public accountancy, finance, and political science.

8.2 Explaining vanguard, intermediate, and long-tail approaches

Examining the experience of local governments in England since 2010 enabled the use, challenge, and further refinement of this local statecraft theory. This second main contribution revealed where local statecraft's varying engagements with financialization have occurred, accelerated, and flourished as well as where they have been absent, attenuated, stopped, and reversed. The picture is more complex than the binary interpretation of local state financialization or 'de-financialisation'.[8] It is better understood as a question of the degree and nature of local statecrafters' engagements with the relations and process of financialization. Financialization provides both

---

[7] Hendrikse and Lagna (2018: 24).
[8] Cf. Dagdeviren and Karwowski (2021: 688).

elements that need explaining *and* parts of their explanation. Local statecraft challenges outdated and stereotypical views of conservatism, ignorance, and risk avoidance in municipal finance. Local statecrafters in England have been compelled to act since 2010 because continuing with the status quo became a riskier path.

Local statecrafters' differentiated engagements with financialization in England from 2010 are characterized by vanguard, intermediate, and long-tail approaches. While central in the narrative of novel and high-profile activities as well as varying in specific activities, those pursuing vanguard approaches are relatively few. In terms of commercial property acquisition and acknowledging it is not necessarily financialized, the NAO's analysis estimated a 'most active' group of around 40 local governments in England, just over 10 per cent of the total.[9] Even for this vanguard, financial innovations are relatively limited in their overall finances.

These pioneering local statecrafters seek to operate at the leading edge, open to trying new concepts and arrangements and constructing their legal basis. Strong connections exist between commercialization and financialization. In commercial property acquisition, the NAO finds this vanguard behaviour equally split between local government types.[10] These local statecrafters are more risk prone and have been pushing the boundaries and exploiting flexibilities and loopholes in legislative frameworks, especially borrowing to invest for yield. External advisors are used to demonstrate due diligence and compliance with relevant legal requirements and guidance.

Strongly engaging financialization, local statecrafters in England pursuing vanguard approaches have formulated and used new financial concepts and novel instruments with external financial actors. These include income strips, investment wraps, and interest rate swaps for the first time since the 1990s. Their political leaderships interpret local government as a commercially oriented economic and financial actor with the agency and power to address its funding gaps. Broadly, politically Right-leaning administrations sought to reduce CT and diversify income, while Left-oriented leaderships pursued income generation in the local public interest. These local statecrafters focused on financial innovation, often drawing upon the knowledge, skills, and experience of senior councillors with experience in finance and/or property and were facilitated by commercially and financially savvy CFOs. Councillors elected from prosperous local wards with relevant employment experience reinforced such statecraft capacities.

---

[9] National Audit Office (2020: 69).
[10] National Audit Office (2020).

Attempting to get ahead of further UK government expenditure reductions was a key motivation for vanguard approaches. Openness to engagement with external financial actors and advisors and shifts towards risk seeking have been aligned with and supported consideration of new, often untried, ideas. Such local statecraft in England was shaped by financial condition and geographies of local tax bases and economic growth potential. Yet, even amongst these pioneering local statecrafters, in most cases the scope and scale of new activities is relatively limited in their overall finances.

Intermediate approaches are evident between the vanguard and long tail. From their commercial property acquisition study, the NAO estimate around 140 local governments in England are 'less active', just over 40 per cent of the total, and, like the 'most active' vanguard, roughly split between types.[11] Commercialization is evident but limited and not explicitly linked to financialization. These local statecrafters' risk appetites increased since 2010 but to a limited degree. They were less active in mostly using existing financial strategies and instruments, but were dabbling in novelties including property strategies, investment funds, and reprofiling capital projects to reduce borrowing costs. These are municipal *and* commercial finance innovations, often based upon adapting and copying approaches used elsewhere in vanguard approaches, and disseminated unevenly across England through sector finance networks.

Political leadership was mixed between those local governments willing to innovate and others pressured to engage in new arrangements as fiscal stress mounted in England from 2010. Differences in views were evident between political control, backbench councillors, and officers. Swing councils with changing political leaderships tended to be relatively more short-term in their financial management in relation to local electoral cycles, compared to longer-term approaches and legacy concerns in more stable situations. Where innovations were evident, external advisors and practice at peers were influential. In common with vanguard behaviours, local financial condition, tax bases, and growth possibilities were decisive in their local statecraft.

The remaining local statecrafters in England followed long-tail approaches characterized by relative caution and lack of involvement in financial innovations. Unwilling to reduce services and/or raise fees and charges, budgets were 'propped up significantly with reserves', drawing upon accumulated cash surpluses and raising questions of replenishment and sustainability.[12]

---

[11] National Audit Office (2020: 69).
[12] Director of Finance, metropolitan borough council (2021).

Local statecrafters adopting long-tail approaches have 'not really gone into that commercial world'.[13]

The NAO commercial property study estimates a 'not active' group at around 170 local governments in England, constituting the remaining 50 per cent of the total.[14] This long tail comprises just over 110 districts and fewer than sixty single-tier and county local governments. Political leaderships across the spectrum typically did not see local government's purpose as acting as a financial institution or competing in markets with businesses to trade and/or acquire assets. Commercialization and financialization were very limited, absent, and/or resisted.

These local statecrafters either did not consider or assessed and sought to avoid financial innovation, deeming it beyond the scope and/or capacity of local government and use of public money or less viable than existing and proven approaches. Or they concluded risks were too great and/or unmanageable relative to potential returns, following due diligence and alarm at negative peer experiences. Others had faced financial shocks from local assets generating unavoidable liabilities and priority in budget setting.

Risk appetites amongst those following long-tail approaches remained relatively conservative and limited, changing little across England since 2010. Less open to external financial actors, these local statecrafters relied more upon in-house expertise and resources only procuring occasional external advice for specific projects. They shared with those pursuing vanguard and intermediate approaches the influence of local financial condition and geographies of fiscal power and economic opportunity. These local statecrafters were unwilling to engage with financialization for principled and/or political reasons or were simply unconvinced of the rationales and evidence of novel instruments and arrangements in comparison to existing and tried-and-tested approaches.

Widening the frame for a more balanced account, local statecraft theory provided a way to explain this differentiated landscape of engagements with the relations and process of financialization. More active financial and risk management were evident across the sector in England from 2010, albeit spreading unevenly across local governments. The general trend was towards more proactive, integrated, and coordinated approaches, especially amongst those pursuing vanguard approaches. This moved local statecraft on from more passive, disconnected approaches that treated specific elements, including capital expenditure and treasury management, as separate local government finance subspecialisms.

---

[13] CFO, metropolitan borough council (2021).
[14] National Audit Office (2020: 69).

There is no clear geography to these varied local statecraft engagements with financialization in England since 2010. Reflecting the sector's inherent diversity and their varied financial strategies, the landscape is differentiated. Local statecrafters were working with key dimensions, combining in particular ways in specific geographical and temporal settings. Such configurations of 'generalized phenomena' and certain local factors align with those identified elsewhere, including funding systems, familiarity and histories of using financial knowledges and instruments, and declining financial condition.[15]

For local statecraft engagements with financialization in England since 2010, the dimensions explaining the differentiated landscape comprised, first, the specific kind of local government and their powers and responsibilities. Districts without social care functions to fund were especially active in new financial and investment strategies, especially out-of-area given their relatively smaller sizes and geographical areas. Their notional potential to achieve any degree of local financial self-sufficiency drove such income generation approaches.

The second dimension constituted the political and officer leaderships, backgrounds, and local politics involved in formulating the visions, strategies, and risk appetites of local statecraft. Reading-off from homogenized interpretations of party-political control can be misleading.[16] Greater differentiation is evident. A mix of categories exists: confirming political views (e.g. lower-tax Conservative, higher-tax Labour control); inversions (e.g. commercializing Labour-run administrations, public ownership in Conservative councils); evolution within *and* between party political factions (e.g. Red Tory, Blue Labour); claims of pragmatic, post-ideological views; and division, dysfunction, and instability (e.g. splits within ruling and/or opposition groups, leadership changes).

Organizational structures, capacities, and capabilities comprised the third dimension. Financial innovations were most evident where decision-making structures were streamlined to a core executive group of leader, senior councillors, and officers. Delegated arrangements and increased financial thresholds enabled quicker decisions and authorizations aligned with market dynamics. Capacity and capability to engage with internal staff and external advisors was critical, building confidence over time and repeating, adapting, and developing financial strategies and instruments deemed effective.

The fourth dimension constituted the local statecrafters' knowledge, experience, and openness to external advice and commercial finance. Understanding and being prepared to engage with new financial ideas by

---

[15] Kass et al. (2019: 1059), Christophers (2019), Singla and Luby (2020).
[16] Cf. Dagdeviren and Karwowski (2021).

the political and officer leadership was pivotal. Situations were typically shaped by previous jobs and contact networks and, amongst those following intermediate approaches, seeing what other local statecrafters were doing, and not wanting to be seen as distant from leading practice by sectoral peers.

The last dimension comprised local economic assets and liabilities, conditions, tax bases, and growth potential. These geographically particular attributes underpinned local statecrafters' potential to engage in the relations and process of financialization. Valuable local assets provided opportunities for new financial management approaches and arrangements, especially when liabilities were limited. Although high value incumbent assets forced local innovation too. The current and expected future financial condition of local governments were vitally important, especially levels of reserves, borrowing, and commercial and residential property tax bases. The nature, structure, and dynamism of local economies and their growth potential were integral to providing opportunities for increasing the number of businesses and houses to grow local tax revenues. Confidence and prospects were critical in attracting public and other investors.

Layering changes across this uneven landscape, the picture across England is likely to remain differentiated. A flattening of the terrain is improbable, even with continued diffusion of financial innovations following the pandemic, Ukraine conflict, inflation, and rising interest rates. Differentiation is hard wired by local governments' inherent diversity and the five key dimensions interacting and shaping the financial affairs and agency of local statecrafters in specific geographical and temporal settings.

8.3 Rewiring and rescaling local statecraft; displacing and relocating risks

The third main argument is that the objectives, incentives, autonomies, and accountabilities of local statecraft are being rewired and rescaled in uneven ways by national policy and varied engagements with financialization, and risks are being displaced and relocated onto local government and the local state.

Local statecrafters' responsibilities remain delivering statutory public services and balancing the budget in nationally and locally accountable ways. Yet, for local governments in England since 2010, the UK government reduced funding, compelled local financial self-sufficiency, and encouraged innovation and risk-taking *as well as* retained centralized control, constrained capacities to generate new income sources, and inhibited behaviours deemed too risky and speculative. These contradictory changes rewired and rescaled local statecraft aims and motivations towards prioritizing savings and income generation to balance budgets and strive for financial sustainability and resilience while struggling to maintain local service provision and demonstrate accountability for public money.

For local governments in England since 2010, this rewiring and rescaling of local statecraft are evident in several areas. The legal requirement for councillors to consult CFOs has supported the emergence of a cadre of commercially and financially savvy local statecrafters, especially those following vanguard approaches, with greater knowledge, contacts, and risk appetites than hitherto. They echo the rise of 'technical expertise' and use of approaches and discourses to legitimize and depoliticize commercial and entrepreneurial ideas across local government in England from the 1980s.[17]

New accountability, transparency, and scrutiny arrangements have been introduced in England. Formal structures were narrowed and weakened by the reforms of the 2000s, and austerity and organizational restructuring since 2010.[18] Delegated authority enables local statecrafters to decide and act more quickly and flexibly in line with external commercial and financial markets. These new, often less formal, arrangements are designed to overcome slower, less flexible but democratic and formalized structures.[19]

New institutional arrangements have been established *within* local government and *within* the wider local state across England since 2010. These aim to work around existing legal and advisory frameworks for local statecraft and incorporate external financial actors and innovations. Examples include arms-length trading companies, joint ventures, and partnerships. Where evident, innovations have introduced and, in some instances, embedded commercial finance interests more closely into local statecraft and complicated accountabilities.

In the central–local government dimension of local statecraft, relations between councillors, officers, national government ministers, and civil servants have changed in England since 2010. Mimicking commercial deal-making, the UK government utilized deals as a policy device to encourage innovation, new funding and financing arrangements, and tailored policy and governance responses to local issues.[20] Accountability, transparency, and scrutiny concerns have arisen from such informal arrangements.[21]

---

[17] Clark and Cochrane (1989), Pinch (1995: 48).
[18] Centre for Public Scrutiny (2017).
[19] National Audit Office (2019a).
[20] Pike et al. (2019).
[21] Ayres (2015), Moran et al. (2018).

The rewiring and rescaling of local statecraft across England amidst UK government policy change and financialization since 2010 are generating contradictions. Existing funding system complexities in who is paying who and for what at different geographical levels are further tangled. In some cases, local governments' responsibility to ensure value for public money is being compromised. While encouraging innovation, risk-taking, and local financial self-sufficiency, the UK government has simultaneously articulated concerns about commercial speculation, increased risks, rising indebtedness, and imbalanced knowledge and experience relative to external financial actors.[22]

The UK government cannot let local government in England go bankrupt given the loss of essential local service provision, but neither will it bail-out local statecrafters whatever the circumstances because of moral hazard. HMT used such arguments in its refusal to compensate local government's lost commercial income in the pandemic from 2020.[23] The UK government revised regulatory codes and guidance in response to local statecraft perceived as risky. Changes have, however, been based on vanguard behaviour rather than the more prevalent intermediate and long-tail approaches.

Relations between local statecrafters and external financial actors in England are being changed by the redirection and relocation of legal commitments codified in new financial arrangements and instruments. While finance is not at the US level of a fully-fledged 'second constituency' that local statecrafters must address, the geography and temporality of local accountabilities and power are being redrawn, albeit in differentiated and limited ways.[24] For critics, the 'culture of public service' is being lost in the 'drive to be commercial' and 'the gulf between public values and private sector values continues to shrink.'[25]

Neither local statecrafters nor financial actors are only in control; the relations and outcomes are subject to negotiation, accommodation, compromise, and settlement. This complex and differentiated substance of local statecraft-in-motion is manifest across the sector in England in risk appetite statements, terms of reference for consultants, borrowing terms with lenders, and so forth. Challenging broad level generalizations of transformations in the political economy of local governance, such shifts are changing local statecrafter aims and motivations and to whom they are answerable in geographically and temporally variegated ways.

[22] HM Treasury (2020).
[23] Williams (2020).
[24] Peck and Whiteside (2016: 245).
[25] Researcher, campaign group (2021).

Local statecraft's differentiated engagements with the relations and process of financialization have resulted from the UK government generally increasing, deliberately relocating, *and* inadvertently displacing risks onto local government in England. Moreover, it has been reducing local statecrafters' ability to manage and mitigate risks through expenditure reductions, continued centralization, and governance risk generation. Local statecraft demonstrated financial innovation and its risks are situated within the state *and* municipal finance rather than only commercial finance and financialization.

Consequently, increasing numbers of local governments in England have been exposed, rendered vulnerable, or weakened in dealing with the unprecedented and sustained financial stress since 2010. The impact of the pandemic from 2020 further intensified the fiscal pressures and uncertainty despite selective national government transfers and compensations.[26] Local statecraft helped some to cope but left others less capable and skilled to fail. Their ability and capacity to bear risk has been challenged, tested and, in some cases, undermined. Local statecrafters' varying ability to cope with fiscal stress across England suggests geographically unequal access to local public services will become more acute.

While not determining their agency and financial fortunes in direct and clear-cut ways, such systemic challenges are pushing more local governments to the edge of financial viability. In 2021, the Department was engaging almost half—150—of the local governments in England on their finances.[27] Countering the 'councillors at the casino' narrative, the outcomes of such varied engagements with the relations and process of financialization are not random or chance incidences. Failures are not only a story of unlucky statecrafters playing and losing at the financialization game.

This rewiring and rescaling of local statecraft and displacement and relocation of risk amongst local governments in England are being experienced unevenly by local residents and taxpayers. In certain financial strategies, arrangements, and instruments, the legally underpinned power and rights of external financial actors have been asserted above local populations. Manifesting a 'fiscal illusion', temporal dislocations are evident where current local statecrafters make short-term financial decisions that suit their interests and politics at that moment but shift the burden and costs onto future administrations and local taxpayers.[28]

Such local statecraft constitutes a deferred politics of financialization: upfront resources and investments are promoted, while complex financing

---

[26] National Audit Office (2021b).
[27] Kenyon (2021).
[28] Puviani (1897), Fastenrath et al. (2017b).

and risks are discounted and likely unrealized or forgotten.[29] Continued pressures to raise local tax rates, increase charges and fees for local services, reduce or remove exemptions, and rationalize and withdraw services, all have direct and material impacts and implications for people in their local area. They question local government responsibilities' as 'custodians for [your] residents' money'.[30]

Some are concerned that commercial finance's 'standards of risk-taking may take root in the public sector.'[31] Others fear 'the entry of financialized cultures in public institutions' affecting 'the distribution of power and resources' and transforming 'the character of statehood' and legitimizing 'financialization on a broader scale'.[32] Concerns are that such behaviours will subvert local statecraft's wider value and public purpose as local government morphs into a primarily financial institution that maximizes economic return rather than social benefit and delivers public services as a sideline.[33] The experience of local governments in England since 2010 suggest dangers exist of such changes sowing the seeds of a new and uncertain phase of local statecraft's engagements with finance marked by local state capture, risky innovation, and speculative tendencies.

8.4 Undermining local government financial sustainability and resilience in financialization?

The final main argument is that local government financial sustainability and resilience in the longer-term risk being undermined by national policy and the wider extension and intensification of its engagements with financialization. While relatively limited in scale and scope amongst local governments in England by 2022, fiscal pressures and incentives for local statecrafters to engage financialization remain and, in certain circumstances, have increased. From 2010, the UK government took the chance that local statecrafters could bear the new and weighty burdens of continuing to provide essential local services while reducing expenditure and generating new income sources. A decade on its local financial self-sufficiency agenda appears somewhat riskier than originally envisaged. Is it *national* rather than *local* government that has taken the local public service gamble?

---

[29] Kass et al. (2019).
[30] Labour councillor and Cabinet Member for Finance, London Borough (2021).
[31] Kass et al. (2019: 1043).
[32] Deruytter and Möller (2020: 408).
[33] Massey (1980).

Across the differentiated landscape in England, local statecrafters continue to face acute financial duress and uncertainty. The impacts and implications of financial innovations are challenging to discern. Beyond individual cases of financial problems and even failure where things have unravelled, many new local statecraft and commercial finance relations and arrangements are complex, long term, and mutable. The financializing ratchet demonstrates they are subject to renegotiation, rearrangement, and refinancing with shifting ramifications for their local outcomes and implications.

Rationales for local statecrafters in England trying new financial strategies and instruments remain. Fiscal stresses are likely to sustain and, for some, increase the incremental growth of financial innovations. Given the established and close, albeit geographically differentiated, dissemination networks amongst the local municipal finance community across England, these pressures may see more adopt vanguard approaches, increased innovation in intermediate behaviours, and shrinkage of those uninvolved or resisting engagement in long-tail approaches. Whether it is viable for all local statecrafters to undertake similar income generation activities or if further dysfunctions emerge remains to be seen.

Local statecraft's varying engagements with financialization in England are challenging local government capacity to meet legal requirements to account for the use of taxpayer's funds. Qualified conclusions published by external auditors on arrangements to secure value for money jumped from 3.3 to 19.3 for single-tier and county councils and 2 to 4.8 for districts in England between 2010–11 and 2017–18.[34] These increases demonstrate responsibilities for the stewardship of public money are being unevenly comprised by conditions and local statecraft amongst different local government types across England.

As more local governments are compelled to engage in financial innovations, a greater number will encounter difficulties and downsides. Local statecrafter knowledge, skills, and experience continue to be challenged in dealing with this rapidly changing, riskier, and more testing situation. Legal requirements to balance budgets remain alongside desires to avoid being labelled a failing council. The Department's diagnoses of particular and localized situations of weak governance and poor culture resulting in failures become less convincing. Differentiation will continue and even increase, reinforcing the uneven landscape of local statecraft and financialization across England.

Specific local statecrafters will cope in this conjuncture, including some following vanguard approaches. But others, including those with vanguard,

---

[34] National Audit Office (2019a).

intermediate, and long-tail behaviours, are likely to struggle and even fail. While a highly differentiated landscape in England since 2010, there are increased risks that commercial and more speculative ventures may crash incurring costs for the local governments involved and putting further pressure on balancing the books.

Such perils are evident in local statecraft realms. External advisors may provide inappropriate or mistaken advice, encouraging riskier behaviours. The financializing ratchet, embroiling local statecraft in ever more financial innovations, looks set to extend and deepen this process.

Increased borrowing makes debt a larger part of overall budgets. Debt service and redemption displaces local residents' and taxpayers' claims on uncertain local government finances, especially in extremis. Debt management demands greater resource as the borrowing stock expands and the complexity of lenders, loan types, interest rates, maturities, and refinancing options multiply. Interest rate risk becomes acute to manage as inflation and interest rates increase in the UK amidst Brexit, the pandemic, and Ukraine conflict.

Investments may sour as market conditions worsen, leaving local governments with rising costs and diminishing returns. Assets may end up worth less than local statecrafters paid for them, undermining their income generation plans.

Where is local statecraft heading on this path? Is the emergence of a new, more financialized local government putting public services at risk? How is long-term institutional degradation and weakened capacity related to voting behaviour and residents' declining expectations of what local states can provide?[35] The answers may be a local statecraft that is more risky, speculative, vulnerable, and lacking in financial sustainability and resilience in attempting to offset fiscal stress and pay for local public services. The differentiated landscape evident amongst local governments in England since 2010 defies more abstract framing as a newly cohesive political economy of local governance. Whether it is in the early stages of a more coherent period or continuing flux is as yet unclear.

While differentiated and limited amongst local governments in England by 2021 and combined with UK national policy change, engagements with the relations and process of financialization are responses to *and* causes of fiscal stress and crisis. It is yet to raise US concerns of commercial finance actors siphoning-off public resources to the detriment of local residents and communities with financial innovation distorting priorities and reducing rather

---

[35] Streeck and Mertens (2013).

than enhancing welfare.[36] But even in its more limited expression in England since 2010, local statecraft engagements with financialization still contain the capacity to erode, undermine and/or risk local collective provision, local economic renewal, democratic oversight, and social solidarity through service restructuring, rationalization and/or withdrawal. UK government policy and local statecrafters' riskier financial strategies may lose further public support and make people wonder why they are voting and for whom, and for what they are paying their local taxes.

8.5   What is local government for and how can it be funded?

The findings and arguments in this book raise fundamental questions of normative and political concern: what is local government for and how can it be funded? What should be done centrally and locally? Over a decade of austerity in England has renewed concerns about the 'scale and scope' of local government and the local state, and the social contract between state and citizen.[37] Finance actors too argue that 'innovation will take you a certain way', but there remains a 'fundamental need to have a grown-up conversation about what local authorities do' and how to fund them.[38] Accumulated challenges of inequalities, climate change, demographic ageing, digitalization, geopolitical tensions, inflation and rising interest rates and the Ukraine conflict in a post-Brexit and post-pandemic setting in the UK further complicate the situation.

Questions of purpose hinge on the distinction between local government *and* local administration.[39] Clarifying and enhancing local government's role requires establishing its constitutional position in statute, defining its basic powers rather than only specifying the services it provides or commissions for national government.[40]

Reconfigured local statehood with a stronger constitutional and legal footing and greater autonomies in powers and resources to underpin and bolster local statecraft is a way of giving expression to the 'the genius of place'.[41] This rounded view of local government's strategic purpose in 'place-shaping' across economic, social, environmental, political, and cultural dimensions

---

[36] Bhatti and Manley (2015).
[37] Gray and Barford (2018: 558).
[38] Director, bank (2021).
[39] Wilson and Game (2011: 30).
[40] Leach et al. (2017).
[41] Laski (1925: 412).

has received periodic attention in England.[42] It is integral to local government but requires more substantive constitutional and legal underpinning.

Fundamental to articulating what local government is for concerns whether the UK government is committed to universalism and common standards in local public service provision across England. This principle affords local government and its funding a central and supported role. Austerity is, however, part of a long-term political project of re-shaping and re-defining the welfare state nationally and locally, albeit in highly complex, fragmented, and incoherent ways.[43] Changes have been interpreted as 'residualisation' and 'increasingly selective and targeted concentration on low-income social groups who lack the financial capacity to access alternatives'.[44] Such outcomes risk local statecraft retreating to core provision of nationally determined and legally mandated services for only the most vulnerable people in places.

This Balkanization of local government and collective social provision will reinforce geographical inequalities and intensify competition between places for people and businesses and their economic and tax revenue contributions. Poorer places with weaker financial conditions and resources will be able to provide less or limited versions of statutory local public services and remain financially vulnerable. Richer places with stronger finances and situations can thrive, enhancing local service provision and strengthening their financial resilience.[45] Such outcomes may 'fuel a loss of support for council services (and taxes) from better off social groups—further driving and embedding the process of marginalisation'.[46]

Integral to its role, there is consensus that the local government funding system in England is 'broken'.[47] Fundamentally, 'no automatic link' exists 'between statutory duties' and the 'funding made available by the Government to enable them to carry out their duties', risking their ability to meet these legal requirements.[48] A structural gap exists between statutory responsibilities and rising service provision costs played out in central–local relations and statecraft: 'national politicians ... are unwilling to face the fact that local government can't deliver £100 worth of services for £70'.[49]

---

[42] Lyons (2007: 30).
[43] Gray and Barford (2018).
[44] Hastings et al. (2015: 617).
[45] Gray and Barford (2018).
[46] Hastings et al. (2015: 617).
[47] Hardingham (2021: 1).
[48] Sandford (2020b: 23–24).
[49] Tony Travers, LSE, quoted in Sandford (2020c: 12).

The impacts of Brexit, the pandemic, and Ukraine conflict, and inflation and rising interest rates are deepening this funding gap.

The 'fundamental underfunding of the sector' traps local statecrafters in England in short-term and reactive behaviours.[50] Their local statecraft is tactical and opportunistic rather than strategic, with many struggling to survive the next financial year. Indeed, the funding system has long been considered 'inherently unstable' in trying 'to balance a wide range of heavy and expensive duties on top of a remarkably narrow local tax base'.[51] Local governments have unfunded mandates: legal requirements to deliver local services without the necessary resources.

Since 2010, concerns have been articulated that for some local governments in England essential local public services are now being funded through property speculation.[52] Conservative political leaders in economically buoyant districts have even suggested abolishing CT and funding local service provision through 'radical strategies' including making efficiencies, selling services, and reaping investment returns.[53] Yet, such views confront long standing concerns that it is not the place for 'public entities' to be 'mucking about in private markets' because 'commercial markets are fickle' and 'stability is an essential feature of public financing.'[54]

UK governments have largely avoided changing this complex funding system due to its political and/or financial infeasibility. Local public services and taxes' high-level public visibility mean 'wholesale reform faces political difficulties' and 'consensus' has been lacking for more radical, longer-term changes.[55] Consequently, key issues—including the Fair Funding Review and CT and business rates revaluations—remain delayed, subject to ongoing consultation, and/or deferred. Brexit, the pandemic, Ukraine conflict, and inflation caused further disruption.

Guiding reform when local government's constitutional position and purpose are resolved, 'finance follows function.'[56] In short, local government is provided with appropriate funding and financing arrangements effectively to discharge its functions and responsibilities.[57] This principle for local government funding is, however, entangled with addressing unequal geographies

[50] Local government financial consultant 4 (2021).
[51] Newton and Karan (1985: 126).
[52] Travers (2017).
[53] Cowper (2018: 1).
[54] Hood and Young (2005: 572).
[55] CIPFA (2019: 7).
[56] OECD (2019).
[57] Sandford (2016a).

of need, especially when unmet, and the political and 'highly vexed question of how to pay for it'.[58]

Critical is the geographical political economy of tax and shifting the narrative from low local taxes and tax minimization to higher local taxes and tax base maximization to fund local government and the essential local public services it provides.[59] Taxes are the membership fee we pay to live in a civilized society; a force for good in funding things we collectively value.[60] The problem arises when 'tax liabilities are inadequately or inappropriately shared that they come to seem burdensome'.[61]

Central to new constitutionally embedded autonomies for local government are devolved fiscal powers. The ambition is lessening the UK government and Parliament's 'constitutional supremacy' and its 'power of the purse'.[62] The aspiration is rekindling the 'autonomous spirit' of local statecrafters that has been eroded and undermined by continued and accelerated centralization in England since the 1980s.[63]

Integral to such autonomies is increasing local statecrafters' fiscal policy space and its stability and predictability, created by the structures within which they operate. Changes require balancing a diversified set of elastic and inelastic tax revenue sources to enable better alignment of the local 'fiscal architecture' to the fiscal base and make the revenue system more predictable and resilient.[64] Basic elements include: revisiting the funding balance between national and local government;[65] increasing the proportion of tax revenue raised locally and maintaining equalization to prevent fiscal localization's negative distributional effects and competition between richer and poorer areas with different tax bases;[66] and providing multi- rather than single-year settlements to enable longer-term strategy, planning, and budget setting as well as demonstration of value for money.

In strengthening local government's constitutional position, powers, and funding in England, it is important to guard against local statecrafters' intensified engagements with financialization that extend and reinforce geographical inequalities in local service provision. Such moves are already rewiring and rescaling local statecraft and displacing and relocating risks. Fiscal localization is a particular concern because it ties local governments' financial

[58] Newton and Karan (1985: xiii), Phillips and Harris (2018), Sandford (2020b).
[59] Tapp and Kay (2019).
[60] Wendell Holmes Jr. (1927).
[61] Wilson and Game (2011: 232).
[62] Newton and Karan (1985: 128).
[63] Sbragia (1986: 336).
[64] Pagano and Hoene (2018: 18).
[65] Lyons (2007).
[66] Copus et al. (2017).

condition and local people's access to public services to the health of the local economy and tax base,[67] breaking the funding following duties principle.[68]

A key task is to better understand and situate financialization, putting it in its place. Tempering the inaccurate and 'blanket criticism' of it as always and everywhere regressive, undesirable, and inequality-generating, financialization in local government in England is interpreted as a problematic means being used for progressive and positive ends to offset austerity.[69] Critique is instead levelled at the UK government 'for shaping the financial context within which English local authorities are today operating' rather than 'those "financialisers" themselves'.[70] Sector commentators too question depictions of 'capitalist greedy enterprise' when local statecrafters are trying to generate 'money for services' and having to reduce provision or manage risks from income generation activities.[71]

Alternatives to financialized solutions to local statecraft's funding and financing predicaments need much further work. This is not just a story of simply reversing financialization through 'de-financialisation'.[72] How would any meaningful *reduction* in the power of finance, finance actors, and financial markets occur from its current starting point? Financialization has been attenuated, stymied, stopped, and reversed by local statecrafters in following vanguard, intermediate, and long-tail approaches. Experiences in England since 2010 challenge accounts of a one-way, inevitable, wholesale, and irreversible financialization of local government and the wider local state.

One path forward is widening the innovations and instruments from only the options presented by external advisors and commercial finance actors to create more public possibilities.[73] Critical too is countering the erosion and renewing local government accountability, scrutiny, and oversight.[74] This must include where engagements with the relations and process of financialization have extended into the local state in England in education (academies), health (private providers), housing (housing associations, housing companies), and social care (care home providers).[75]

---

[67] Gray and Barford (2018).

[68] Sandford (2016a).

[69] Christophers (2019: 581).

[70] Christophers (2019: 572).

[71] Sector journalist (2021).

[72] cf. Dagdeviren and Karwowski (2021), Deruytter and Möller (2020).

[73] Bhatti and Manley (2015), Brown and Jones (2021), Cumbers (2012), Pike et al. (2019), Whitfield (2020).

[74] Centre for Public Scrutiny (2017), Housing, Communities and Local Government Committee (2021).

[75] Christophers (2019), Beswick and Penny (2018), Burns et al. (2016), Horton (2021).

Enhanced financial education and literacy support for politicians and officers is required better to understand and question new and innovative financial strategies and arrangements. The worlds of municipal and commercial finance need to be rendered more visible and legible to the local statecrafters involved. Yet, while such activities may be 'risky and speculative and dangerous financially' they can also be 'very dull and boring and complex' for people to grasp.[76] If councillors and officers can more readily understand the risks involved then more robust scrutiny and decision-making should result.

8.6 Towards a depoliticized and post-democratic local governance in financialization?

Has weakened local accountability, transparency, and scrutiny of local statecraft amidst changing national policy and financialization introduced depoliticized or post-democratic local governance?[77] Any shift is characterized by the ascendance of finance's technocratic authority over that of locally elected politicians and the 'gradual withering' of democratic institutions, procedures, and norms.[78] Deepening reliance upon external advisors,[79] local statecrafters are actively using strategic opportunities afforded by national policy and engagements with financialization and its 'range of new tools' and 'a new style of governance' in attempts creatively to 'solve problems of a political nature'.[80]

Concerns have been articulated that following national policy changes local statecraft has become more instrumental and oriented towards commercial finance interests.[81] Financial strategies and regulatory functions have been interpreted as redirected towards narrower commercial objectives over broader public goals. Local statecraft here is 'redefining the public interest as one based on growth and rising market values' which 'represents the extension of processes of financialization into state and governmental practices'.[82]

The book presents a differentiated picture of such shifts towards depoliticization and post-democratic local governance in England since 2010. Where evident, change is manifest in several areas. There is informalization of

---

[76] Researcher, campaign group (2021).
[77] Crouch (2004).
[78] Hendrikse and Lagna (2018: 19).
[79] Möller (2021).
[80] Wang (2020: 190).
[81] Sanfelici and Halbert (2019).
[82] Raco and Souza (2018: 147), Brill (2020), Savini and Aalbers (2016).

governance and decision-making, operating without codified protocols and procedures through webs of social relations, influence, and patronage.[83] Such agency is led, determined, and influenced by the most powerful and resourceful local statecrafters in particular places. It is, in some cases, less accountable, transparent, and open to scrutiny.

Where speed of decision-making and initiative delivery have become critical due to financial pressures, appropriate governance is often viewed as a 'blocker', delaying decisions and undermining policy implementation.[84] CFO and external financial actor relations and contacts can be conducted in private via 'telephone calls and emails directly to a finance director who has access to hundreds of millions of pounds of public money'.[85] Greater use of exemptions and 'commercial confidentiality' by local political leaderships and officers in reporting in England makes details unavailable to other councillors, officers, and publics.[86]

Such local statecraft lacks scrutiny, rendering it problematic, especially for politically contentious, large-scale, and/or long-term issues and decisions. Reductions in resources to support accountability, scrutiny, and oversight arrangements compound the problem. Funding for corporate and democratic support was reduced by over 34 per cent in real terms in local governments in England between 2010–11 and 2017–18.[87] Changes within local government have been exacerbated by the erosion of local external scrutiny. The loss of local investigative journalism and media has further denuded local inquiry and accountability.[88]

The increased complexity of local statecraft in financialization has further complicated the situation. Local government finances in England are now largely beyond the understanding of all but the specialists. This sometimes incidental, occasionally deliberate, opacity or even 'mystification', means councillors and officers let alone the public do not understand and appreciate the changing and long-term risks involved.[89] For those so motivated, opportunities exist to 'blind' councillors 'with science' and 'present sixty pages of something that nobody really understands that goes by on the nod'.[90] Sufficiently sophisticated 'armchair auditors' of the kind envisaged by then UK Secretary of State Pickles in 2011 seldom emerged,[91] despite financial

---

[83] Ayres (2015).
[84] National Audit Office (2019a: 22), Hammond (2021). See also Pacewicz (2013).
[85] Journalist (2021).
[86] National Audit Office (2019a).
[87] National Audit Office (2019a).
[88] Baldwin (2018).
[89] Christophers (2015b: 2), Gray and Barford (2018). See also Bhatti and Manley (2015).
[90] Former Director, public audit body (2021).
[91] Communities and Local Government (2011b: 1).

reporting requirements, the UK Freedom of Information framework, and the Local Audit and Accountability Act 2024's public challenge provision.

These depoliticized and, at least weakened, if not wholly post-democratic practices are concerning. In the differentiated landscape of local statecraft in financialization, they are more evident in specific local governments and places. Together, they do not currently add up to a generalized or wholesale shift to a depoliticized or post-democratic local governance in England since 2010. Local governments are still democratically accountable bodies, even while in some areas local accountability, transparency, and scrutiny are being weakened and/or challenged. Amidst national policy change and financialization, local statecraft remains a site for political values, deliberation, and choices.

Where, then, does local statecraft go from here? Recovering recognition that local government finance is inherently political not just objective and technocratic is critical. Rather than putative solutions to political problems,[92] engagements with financialization must be reframed as potential causes of political and financial issues especially if local statecrafters do not understand the risks involved. Recalling Schumpeter's point that 'public finance is politics hidden in accounting columns' is vital.[93] 'A budget is a statement of values';[94] it is how the local political economy of collective provision is articulated. The budget is a "moral document" that expresses political choices over priorities and reflects local residents' and voters' preferences.[95]

Recovering local statecraft's moral and political dimensions means reinvigorating and clarifying codified, formalized, and structured systems and practices of accountability, and scrutiny. Measures for local government in England are manifold including: improving disclosure and transparency through more informative reports; reducing usage of commercial exemptions to prevent information release;[96] enhancing internal controls, monitoring, and audit;[97] improving councillor and officer education and training; and strengthening external audit through the new national Audit, Reporting and Governance Authority (ARGA).[98]

A further step is widening public participation and oversight. Greater recognition is needed of local statecraft's implications for different social groups in different places. How equality, diversity, and inclusion principles

[92] Wang (2020).
[93] Cited in Gray and Barford (2018: 541).
[94] Janette Williamson, Labour Councillor and Leader of Wirral Council, quoted in BBC Radio 4 (2021).
[95] Bhatti and Manley (2015: 66).
[96] National Audit Office (2019a), Bhatti and Manley (2015).
[97] National Audit Office (2019a).
[98] Redmond (2020: 1), Spokesperson cited in Rudgewick (2021b: 1).

inform local government finance in England is work-in-progress, including the LGA's Equality Framework for Local Government. Independent analysis and research are key. The Women's Budget Group (2021) pioneered analysis of local government finances in England and developed assessment tools including Equality Impact Assessments.[99] Operation Black Vote (2019) have championed greater racial justice and equality, revealing the underrepresentation of black, Asian, and ethnic minorities as local councillors even in areas with significant populations.[100] Inspired by positive evaluations of Participatory Budgeting,[101] popular engagement in budget setting can be built upon.

Transparency is key for campaign and lobbying groups, including Debt Resistance and Research for Action in the UK, and publics to scrutinize and render more accountable and transparent local statecraft in financialization. Examples include local coalition Fix L.A. and 'citizen debt audits' in France, Italy, and Spain working with the aim of 'making our money work for us'.[102] As objectives, incentives, autonomies, and accountabilities are rewired and rescaled and as risks are displaced and relocated by national policy and local statecraft's engagements with financialization, such views and voices are ever more needed.

[99] Women's Budget Group (2021).
[100] Operation Black Vote (2019).
[101] Communities and Local Government (2011c).
[102] Bhatti and Manley (2015: 83).

References

35% Campaign (n.d.) Canada Water regeneration, https://www.35percent.org/canada-water/; Accessed: 23 November 2021.

Aalbers, M. B. (2015) 'The potential for financialization', Dialogues in Human Geography, 5, 2, 214–219.

Agnew, J. (2002) Making Political Geography, Routledge: London.

Aldag, A. M., Kim, Y. and Warner, M. E. (2019) 'Austerity urbanism or pragmatic municipalism? Local government responses to fiscal stress in New York State', Environment and Planning A, 51, 6, 1287–1305.

Amin-Smith, N., Phillips, D. and Simpson, P. (2018) Spending Needs, Tax Revenue Capacity and the Business Rate Retention Scheme, Institute for Fiscal Studies: London.

Andrew, J. and Cahill, D. (2017) 'Rationalising and resisting neoliberalism: the uneven geography of costs', Critical Perspectives on Accounting, 45, 12–28.

Andrews, R., Skelcher, C., Ferry, L. and Wegorowski, P. (2019) 'Corporatization in the public sector: explaining the growth of local government companies', Public Administration Review, 80, 3, 482–493.

APSE (2019) Rebuilding Capacity: The Case for Insourcing Public Contracts, APSE: Manchester.

Ashton, P. (2020) '"City-fying" financial statecraft', Environment and Planning A, 52, 4, 796–797.

Ashton, P. and Christophers, B. (2015) 'On arbitration, arbitrage and arbitrariness in financial markets and their governance: unpacking LIBOR and the LIBOR scandal', Economy and Society, 44, 2, 188–217.

Ashton, P., Doussard, M., and Weber, R. (2016) 'Reconstituting the state: city powers and exposures in Chicago's infrastructure leases', Urban Studies, 53, 7, 1384–1400.

Audit Commission (2009) Risk and Return: English Local Authorities and the Icelandic Banks, Audit Commission: London.

Ayres, S. (2015) Assessing the impact of 'informal governance' on devolution in English cities post the Scottish referendum, Presentation, Regional Studies Association Annual Conference, May, Piacenza.

Ayres, S., Flinders, M. and Sandford, M. (2017) 'Territory, power and statecraft: understanding English devolution', Regional Studies, 52, 6, 853–864.

Baldwin, D. A. (1985) Economic Statecraft, Princeton University Press: Princeton, NJ.

Baldwin, T. (2018) Control Alt Delete: How Politics and the Media Crashed Our Democracy, Hurst & Company: London.

Bamberger, L. and Katz, B. (2019) How Financial Innovation Can Enable Inclusive Opportunity Zones, https://drexel.edu/nowak-lab/publications/reports/voices-from-the-field/; Accessed: 24 November 2021.

Bank of England (1966) 'Local authorities and the capital and money markets', Quarterly Bulletin, Q4, Bank of England: London.

Bartley Hildreth, W. (1996) 'Financial management: a balancing act for local government chief financial officers', Public Administration Quarterly, 20, 3, Fall, 320–342.

BBC News (2018) 'Lib Dem Gerald Vernon Jackson wins Portsmouth council leadership', 15 May, https://www.bbc.co.uk/news/uk-england-hampshire-44129218; Accessed: 26 April 2022.

BBC News (2021) 'Councils' Libor legal action against Barclays bank thrown out', 23 February, https://www.bbc.co.uk/news/uk-england-56171741; Accessed: 19 November 2021.

BBC Radio 4 (2021) 'The hangover—COVID-19 and local government finances', BBC Radio 4, August, BBC: London, https://www.bbc.co.uk/sounds/play/m000yywf; Accessed: 13 October 2021.

Benjamin, J. (2018) Icelandic Bank Investments by UK Local Authorities, 10 September, https://www.whatdotheyknow.com/request/icelandic_bank_investments_by_uk; Accessed: 11 January 2022.

Beswick, J. and Penny, J. (2018) 'Demolishing the present to sell off the future? The emergence of "financialized municipal entrepreneurialism" in London', International Journal of Urban and Regional Research, 42, 4, 612–632.

Bhatti, S. and Manley, R. (2015) 'Dirty deals: how Wall Street's predatory deals hurt taxpayers and what we can do about it', Journal of Law in Society, 17, 1, Fall, 65–90.

Blyth, M. (2013) Austerity: The History of a Dangerous Idea, Oxford University Press: Oxford.

Boggero, G. (2017) Constitutional Principles of Local Self-Government in Europe, Brill: Leiden.

Bore, A. (2013) 'Time for a major rethink as Jaws of Doom widen', Birmingham Post, https://www.birminghampost.co.uk/news/local-news/albert-bore-time-major-rethink-5732576; Accessed: 4 November 2021.

Borja, J. and Castells, M. with Belil, M. and Benner, C. (1997) Local and Global: Management of Cities in the Information Age, Earthscan: Abingdon.

Bozeman, B. and Kingsley, G. (1998) 'Risk culture in public and private organizations', Public Administration Review, 58, 2, 109–118.

Brady, D. (2019) 'English councils at risk of exhausting reserves named', Public Finance, 29 May, https://www.publicfinance.co.uk/news/2019/05/english-councils-risk-exhausting-reserves-named; Accessed: 10 February 2023.

Brenner, N. (2004) New State Spaces: Urban Governance and the Rescaling of Statehood, Oxford University Press: Oxford.

Bridge, T. (2014) 'Councils recoup £1bn lost to Icelandic bank collapse', Local Government, 5 February.

Brill, F. (2020) 'Complexity and coordination in London's Silvertown Quays: How real estate developers (re)centred themselves in the planning process', Environment and Planning A, 52, 2, 362–382.

Brooks, R. (2018) Bean Counters: The Triumph of the Accountants and How They Broke Capitalism, Atlantic Books: London.

Brown, A., Passarella, M. and Spencer, D. (2017) 'The extent and variegation of financialisation in Europe: a preliminary analysis', Revista de Economia Mundial/Journal of World Economy, 46, 49–70.

Brown, M. and Jones, R. E. (2021) Paint Your Town Red: How Preston Took Back Control and Your Town Can Too, Watkins Media: London.

Buckley, J. (2016) 'Canada Life agrees £73m Wightlink Ferry Terminal deal', CoStar, http://www.costar.co.uk/en/assets/news/2016/December/Canada-Life-agrees-73m-Wightlink-Ferry-Terminal-deal/; Accessed: 29 August 2018

Bülow, J. (2004) 'Money for nothing from the USA—municipal authorities and cross-border leasing in Germany', Frontline, 19 February.

Bulpitt, J. (1983) Territory and Power in the United Kingdom, Manchester University Press: Manchester.

Burns, D., Cowie, L., Earle, J., Folkman, P., Froud, J., Hyde, P., Johal, S., Rees Jones, I., Killett, A. and Williams, K. (2016) Where Does the Money Go? Financialised Chains and the Crisis in Residential Care, CRESC Public Interest Report, March, CRESC: University of Manchester.

Byrne, M. (2016) '"Asset price urbanism" and financialization after the crisis: Ireland's National Asset Management Agency', International Journal of Urban and Regional Research, 40, 1, 31–45.

Campbell-Smith, D. (2008) Follow the Money: The Audit Commission, Public Money and the Management of Public Services, Duncan Allen Lane: London.

Carr, R. (2012) Credit Where Credit's Due: Investing in Local Infrastructure to Get Britain Growing, Localis: London.

Carr, R. (2015) Commercial Councils: The Rise of Entrepreneurialism in Local Government, Localis: London.

Centre for Public Scrutiny (2017) Written Evidence to the House of Commons Communities and Local Government Inquiry Effectiveness of Local Authority Overview and Scrutiny Committees, http://data.parliament.uk/writtenevidence/committeeevidence. svc/evidencedocument/communities-and-local-government-committee/overview-and-scrutiny-in-local-government/written/48723.pdf; Accessed: 12 October 2021.

Cheverton, S. and Sykes, T. (2016) 'Portsmouth's smeargate: dirty politics in the age of austerity', Red Pepper, 21 April, Red Pepper: London.

Chiapello, E. (2015) 'Financialisation of valuation', Human Studies, 38, 13–35.

Christophers, B. (2015a) 'The limits to financialization', Dialogues in Human Geography, 5, 2, 183–200.

Christophers, B. (2015b) 'Value models: finance, risk and political economy', Finance and Society, 1, 2, 1–22.

Christophers, B. (2019) 'Putting financialisation in its financial context: transformations in local government-led urban development in post-financial crisis England', Transactions of the Institute of British Geographers, 44, 3, 571–586.

Christophers, B. and Fine, B. (2020) 'The value of financialization and the financialization of value' in P. Mader, D. Mertens and N. van der Zwan (Eds.) The Routledge International Handbook of Financialization, Routledge: London, 19–30.

CIPFA (2018) CIPFA releases briefing on Financial Resilience Index, 20 December, CIPFA: London.

CIPFA (2019) The Guide to Local Government Finance, CIPFA: London.

Cirell, S. (2020) 'Lessons from local authority energy companies', Current, 29 September, https://www.current-news.co.uk/blogs/lessons-from-local-authority-energy-companies; Accessed: 23 November 2021.

Cirolia, L. R. and Robbins, G. (2021) 'Transfers, taxes and tariffs: fiscal instruments and urban statecraft in Cape Town, South Africa', Area Development and Policy, 6, 4, 398–423.

Clark, A. and Middleton, A. (2022) 'United Kingdom: diversity amid the Cinderella elections?' in A. Gendzwill, U. Kjaer and K. Steyvers (Eds.) Routledge Handbook of Local Elections and Voting in Europe, Routledge: London, 84–94.

Clarke, A. and Cochrane, A. (1989) 'Inside the machine: the left and finance professionals in local government', Capital and Class, 37, 35–61.

Clegg, N. (2014) Speech to the 'Northern Futures' Conference, Leeds, 6 November.

CLES (2021) Community Wealth Building: A History, CLES: Manchester.

Co-op and Locality (2020) In Community Hands: Lessons from the Past Five Years of Community Asset Transfer, Co-op and Locality: Manchester and London.

Coane, J. and Brown, O. (2020) 'The role of local authorities as a lender to boost the economy', Room 151, 26 November.

Cochrane, A. (1993) Whatever Happened to Local Government?, Open University Press: Milton Keynes.

Cochrane, A. (2015) 'So, how come local government is still around after all these years?', Regional Studies, 2, 1, 448–454.

Cockburn, C. (1977) Local State: Management of Cities and People, Pluto Press: London.

Communities and Local Government (2006) Developing the Market for Local Government Services, Communities and Local Government: London.

Communities and Local Government (2011a) A plain English guide to the Localism Act, Communities and Local Government: London.

Communities and Local Government (2011b) 'Armchair auditors are here to stay', 8 July, Communities and Local Government: London.

Communities and Local Government (2011c) Communities in the Driving Seat: A Study of Participatory Budgeting in England: Final Report, Communities and Local Government: London.

Communities and Local Government (2017) Self-sufficient Local Government: 100% Business Rates Retention, Communities and Local Government: London.

Communities and Local Government Committee (2009) The Balance of Power: Central and Local Government, Sixth Report of Session 2008-09, HC 33-I, House of Commons: London.

Competition Commission (2011) STS/Butlers Merger Inquiry Final Report: Appendices and Glossary, Competition Commission: London.

Conservative Party (2010) Control Shift: Returning Power to Local Communities, Conservative Party: London.

Copus, C. (2017) The Political and Governance Implications of Unitary Reorganisation, Local Government Association: London.

Copus, C., Roberts, M. and Wall, R. (2017) Local Government in England: Centralisation, Autonomy and Control, Palgrave Macmillan: London.

Cowper, F. (2018) 'Ferris Cowper: our aim is to abolish Council Tax in East Hampshire within four years', ConservativeHome, 27 February.

Crewe, T. (2016) 'The strange death of municipal England', London Review of Books, 38, 24, 6–10.

Cross, L. (2015) 'Warrington council issues first direct local authority bond in 10 years with CPI-index linked deal', Social Housing, 26 August.

Crouch, C. (2004) Post-Democracy, Polity: Cambridge.

Cumbers, A. (2012) Reclaiming Public Ownership: Making Space for Economic Democracy, Zed: London.

Cumbria County Council (2020) Medium Term Financial Plan, Cumbria County Council: Carlisle.

Curtis, P. (2010) 'Eric Pickles slams town hall for not dipping into "Fort Knox" reserves', The Guardian, 30 November, Guardian Newspapers: London.

Dagdeviren, H. and Karwowski, E. (2021) 'Impasse or mutation? Austerity and (de)financialisation of local governments in Britain', Journal of Economic Geography, 22, 3, 685–707.

Davidson, M. and Ward, K. (2018) Cities under Austerity: Restructuring the US Metropolis, State University of New York Press: New York

Davies, G. (2018) 'The public service gamble: councils borrowing billions to play the property market', Bureau of Investigation, 4 December.

Davies, G. and Smith, D. (2021) 'Year-long battle for the public's right to know about council investments has been won', Wales Online, 21 March.

Davis, A. and Walsh C. (2016) 'The role of the state in the financialisation of the UK economy', Political Studies, 64, 3, 666–682.

Debt Resistance UK (n.d.) Does Your Council Have LOBO loans?, http://lada.debtresistance.uk/debt-resistance-uk-investigation/who-are-the-major-borrowers-from-the-banks/; Accessed: 21 July 2022.

Department of Levelling Up, Housing and Communities (DLUHC) (2021a) Local government structure and elections, 19 October, DLUHC: London.

Department for Levelling Up, Housing and Communities (2021b) Live tables on local government finance, Borrowing and Investment Live Table Q2 2021–22, https://www.gov.uk/government/statistical-data-sets/live-tables-on-local-government-finance;   Accessed: 18 November 2021.

Department for Levelling Up, Housing and Communities (2021c) Exceptional Financial Support for Local Authorities, DLUHC: London.

Deruytter, L. (2022) The repurposing of utility companies in Flanders. Institutional bricolage by the local state under budgetary restraint and financialized capitalism, PhD Thesis, Vrije Universiteit Brussel: Brussels.

Deruytter, L. and Bassens, D. (2021) 'The extended local state under financialized capitalism: institutional bricolage and the use of intermunicipal companies to manage financial pressure', International Journal of Urban and Regional Research, 45, 2, 232–248.

Deruytter, L. and Möller, S. (2020) 'Cultures of debt management enter City Hall' in P. Mader, D. Mertens and N. van der Zwan (Eds.) The Routledge International Handbook of Financialization, Routledge: London, 400–410.

Detter, D. (2017) 'UK councils are taking huge commercial risks in trying to be hedge fund managers', The Guardian, Guardian Newspapers: London.

Detter, D. and Fölster, S. (2017) The Public Wealth of Cities: How to Unlock Hidden Assets to Boost Growth and Prosperity, Palgrave Macmillan: London.

Dhillon, A. (2017) 'Council setting "very bad example" by buying Birchwood Park offshore to "avoid tax"', says MP', Warrington Guardian, 25 September.

Dodd, R. (2010) 'Municipal bombs', Finance & Development, June, 33–35.

Dörry, S. (2022) 'The dark side of innovation in financial centres: legal design and the territoriality of law', Regional Studies, https://doi.org/10.1080/00343404.2022.2107629.

Duncan, S. and Goodwin, M. (1988) The Local State and Uneven Development, Policy: Cambridge.

The Economist (2010) 'Cities in the casino', The Economist, 18 May, The Economist: London.

Engelen, E., Fernandez, R. and Hendrikse, R. (2014) 'How finance penetrates its other: a cautionary tale on the financialization of a Dutch university', Antipode, 46, 4, 1072–1091.

Engelen, E. and Konings, M. (2010) 'Financial capitalism resurgent: comparative institutionalism and the challenges of financialization' in G. Morgan, J. L. Campbell, C. Crouch, O. K. Pedersen and R. Whitley (Eds.) The Oxford Handbook of Comparative Institutional Analysis, Oxford University Press: Oxford, 601–624.

EY and Oxygen Finance (2021) Local Government Third-Party Spend 2021–21, EY and Oxygen Finance: London.

Eyles, A., Machin, S. and McNally, S. (2017) 'Unexpected school reform: academisation of primary schools in England', Journal of Public Economics, 155, 108–121.

Farmer, S. (2014) 'Cities as risk managers: the impact of Chicago's parking meter P3 on municipal governance and transportation planning', Environment and Planning A, 46, 9, 2160–2174.

Farmer, S. and Poulos, C. D. (2019) 'The financialising local growth machine in Chicago', Urban Studies, 56, 7, 1404–1425.

Fastenrath, F., Schwan, M. and Trampusch, C. (2017a) 'Where states and markets meet: the financialisation of sovereign debt management', New Political Economy, 22, 3, 273–293.

Fastenrath, F., Orban, A. and Trampusch, C. (2017b) From Economic Gains to Social Losses: How Stories Shape Expectations in the Case of German Municipal Finance, MPIfG Discussion Paper 17/20, Max-Planck-Institut für Gesellschaftsforschung: Köln.

Fawcett Society (2019) 'New data reveals that women's representation in local government "at a standstill"', 2 July, Fawcett Society: London.

Fenwick, J. and Johnston, L. (2020) Public Enterprise and Local Place: New Perspectives on Theory and Practice, Routledge: London.

Ferry, L. and Murphy, P. (2018) 'Local government under austerity, narrowing the accountability landscape in England' in A. Farazmand (Ed.) Global Encyclopedia of Public Administration, Public Policy and Governance, Springer, 3829–3835.

Fields, D. S. (2018) 'Constructing a new asset class: property-led financial accumulation after the crisis', Economic Geography, 94, 2, 118–140.

Flyvbjerg, B. (2006) 'Five misunderstandings about case study research', Qualitative Inquiry, 12, 2, 219–245.

Ford, J. (2020) 'Local authorities need to be weaned off their debt addiction', Financial Times, 22 November, Financial Times: London.

Ford, M. (2021) 'Councils grapple with multi-million pound budget deficits, The Municipal Journal, 6 January.

French, S., Leyshon, A. and Wainwright, T. (2011) 'Financializing space, spacing financialization', Progress in Human Geography, 35, 6, 798–819.

Fuller, G. W. (2016) The Great Debt Transformation. Households, Financialization and Policy Responses, Palgrave Macmillan: Basingstoke.

George, M. (2020) 'Cabinet Office: 5% of councils "at high risk of financial failure"', Local Government Chronicle, 24 August, LGC: London.

Goldman, M. (2011) 'Speculative urbanism and the making of the next world city', International Journal of Urban and Regional Research, 35, 3, 555–581.

Gore, G. (2020) 'UK MBA finally makes much delayed bond debut', Nasdaq, 5 March, https://www.nasdaq.com/articles/uk-mba-finally-makes-much-delayed-bond-debut-2020-03-05; Accessed: 19 November 2021.

Government Finance Function (2021) Risk Appetite Guidance Note, Government Finance Function: London.

Gray, M. and Barford, A. (2018) 'The depth of the cuts: the uneven geography of local government austerity', Cambridge Journal of Regions, Economy and Society, 11, 541–563.

Greenhalgh, P. and Purewal, B. (2015) 'Challenging the myths: an investigation of the barriers to wider use of Local Asset Backed Vehicles in the UK', Journal of Urban Regeneration and Renewal, 8, 3, 260–278.

Greenhalgh, P. M., Muldoon-Smith, K. and Angus, S. (2016) 'Commercial property tax in the UK: business rates and rating appeals', Journal of Property Investment and Finance, 34, 6, 602–619.

Halbert, L. and Attuyer, K. (2016) 'Introduction: the financialisation of urban production: conditions, mediations and transformations', Urban Studies, 53, 7, 1347–1361.

Hall, C. (2020) 'Olympian task: stepping up at Newham', Room 151, 10 February.

Hall, S. (2018) Global Finance: Places, Spaces and People, Sage: Thousand Oaks, CA.

Hall, S. and Massey, D. (2010) 'Interpreting the crisis', Soundings, 44, 57–71.

Hammond, E. (2021) Audit Committees and Scrutiny Committees: Working Together, Centre for Governance and Scrutiny: London.

Hammond, G. (2020) 'UK local councils banned from making risky property bets, Financial Times, 25 November, Financial Times: London.

Hardingham, J. (2021) 'Is local government funding "broken"?', Room 151, 12 February.

Harvey, D. (1982) The Limits to Capital, Basil Blackwell: Oxford.

Harvey, D. (1989) 'From managerialism to entrepreneurialism: the transformation in urban governance in late capitalism', Geografiska Annaler. Series B. Human Geography, 71, 1, 3–17.

Harvey, D. (2015) Seventeen Contradictions and the End of Capitalism, Oxford University Press: Oxford.

Hastings, A., Bailey, N., Gannon, M., Besemer, K. and Bramley, G. (2015) 'Coping with the cuts? The management of the worst financial settlement in living memory', Local Government Studies, 41, 4, 601–621.

Hendrikse, R. and Lagna, A. (2018) State Financialization: A Multi-Scalar Perspective, https://ssrn.com/abstract=3170943; Accessed: 13 October 2021.

Hendrikse, R. P. (2015) The long arm of finance: exploring the unlikely financialization of governments and public institutions, PhD Thesis, Amsterdam Institute for Social Science Research: Amsterdam.

Hendrikse, R. P. and Sidaway, J. D. (2014) 'Financial wizardry and the Golden City: tracking the financial crisis through Pforzheim, Germany', Transactions of the Institute of British Geographers, 39, 2, 195–208.

HM Government (2011) Open Public Services White Paper, HM Government: London.

HM Treasury (2012) Review of HM Treasury's management response to the financial crisis, https://assets.publishing.service.gov.uk/government/uploads/system/uploads/attachment_data/file/220506/review_fincrisis_response_290312.pdf; Accessed: 10 February 2023.

HM Treasury (2015) 'Chancellor unveils devolution revolution', 5 October, Speech, HM Treasury: London.

HM Treasury (2020) Public Works Loan Board: Future Lending Terms—Response to the Consultation, HM Treasury: London.

Hood, J. and Young, P. (2005) 'Risk financing in UK local authorities: is there a case for risk pooling?', International Journal of Public Sector Management, 18, 6, 563–578.

Hooghe, L., Marks, G., Schakel, A. H., Chapman Osterkatz, S., Niedzwiecki, S. and Shair-Rosenfield, S. (2016) Measuring Regional Authority: A Postfunctionalist Theory of Governance, Volume I, Oxford University Press: Oxford.

Horton, A. (2021) 'Liquid home? Financialisation of the built environment in the UK's "hotel-style" care homes', Transactions of the Institute of British Geographers, 46, 179–192.

Housing, Communities and Local Government Committee (2021) Local Authority Financial Sustainability and the Section 114 Regime, Second Report of Session 2021–22, HC 33, House of Commons: London.

Institute for Government (2021) Local Government, IfG: London.

Jameson, H. (2020) 'EXCLUSIVE: No bail outs for commercial investments', The Municipal Journal, 22 May, The Municipal Journal: London.

Jennings, I. (1947) Principles of Local Government Law (3rd edition), University of London Press: London.

Jennings, W. and Stoker, G. (2019) 'The divergent dynamics of cities and towns: geographical polarisation and Brexit', The Political Quarterly, 90, S2, 155–166.

Jessop, B. (2016) The State: Past, Present, and Future, Polity: Cambridge.

Jessop, B. (2018) The Financialisation of Governments, the Public Sector and States, FINGEO Plenary Lecture, Brussels, May.

John, P. (2014) 'The Great Survivor: the persistence and resilience of English local government', Local Government Studies, 40, 5, 687–704.

Jones, G. W. (1975) 'Varieties of local politics', Local Government Studies, 1, 2, 17–32.

Kass, A. (2020) 'Working with financial data as a critical geographer', Geographical Review, 110, 1–2, 104–116.

Kass, A., Luby, M. J. and Weber, R. (2019) 'Taking a risk: explaining the use of contemporary debt finance by the Chicago Public Schools', Urban Affairs Review, 55, 4, 1035–1069.

Keating, M. (2001) Plurinational Democracy: Stateless Nations in a Post-Sovereignty Era, Oxford University Press: Oxford.

Kennett, P., Jones, G., Meegan, R. and Croft, J. (2015) 'Recession, austerity and the "Great Risk Shift": local government and household impacts and responses in Bristol and Liverpool', Local Government Studies, 41, 4, 622–644.

Kenyon, M. (2021) 'DLUHC engages with 150 councils over finances', Local Government Chronicle, 1 December.

Keynes, J. M. (1936) General Theory of Employment, Interest, and Money, Palgrave Macmillan: London.

Knight, F. H. (1921) Risk, Uncertainty and Profit, Houghton Mifflin: Boston and New York.

Knott, J. (2021) 'Turbulence ahead: how Covid and climate concerns have hit council-owned airports', Local Government Chronicle, 15 June, LGC: London.

Krippner, G. (2011) Capitalizing on Crisis: The Political Origins of the Rise of Finance, Harvard University Press: Cambridge, MA.

Kumar, N. (2019) 'Shuttered hedge fund Arrowgrass writes down fun fair bets by 70%', Bloomberg News Wire, 4 October.

Kutz, W. (2017) 'Municipalizing geo-economic statecraft: crisis and transition in Europe', Environment and Planning A, 49, 6, 1224–1246.

Ladner, A., Keuffer, N. and Bastianen, A. (2021) Local Autonomy Index in the EU, Council of Europe and OECD Countries (1990–2020), European Commission: Brussels.

Lagna, A. (2016) 'Derivatives and the financialisation of the Italian state', New Political Economy, 21, 2, 167–186.

Lagna, A. (2017) 'The financialisation of local governments: evidence from the Italian case' in I. Ertürk and D. Gabor (Eds.) The Routledge Companion to Banking Regulation and Reform, Routledge: London, 208–222.

Lai, K. P. Y. (2020) 'Refining the state-finance nexus through urban infrastructure', Environment and Planning A, 52, 4, 800–802.

Lai, K. P. Y. and Daniels, J. A. (2017) 'Financialization of Singaporean banks and the production of variegated financial capitalism' in B. Christophers, A. Leyshon and G. Mann (Eds.) Money and Finance After the Crisis: Critical Thinking for Uncertain Times, Wiley-Blackwell: Oxford, 217–244.

Larsen, P. T. (2009) 'Essex council opens its own bank', Financial Times, 25 April, Financial Times: London.

Laski, H. J. (1925) A Grammar of Politics, George Allen and Unwin: London.

Latham, P. (2017) Who Stole the Town Hall? The End of Local Government as We Know It, Policy Press: Bristol.

Lauermann, J. (2016) 'Municipal statecraft: revisiting the geographies of the entrepreneurial city', Progress in Human Geography, 42, 2, 205–224.

Leach, S., Stewart, J. and Jones, G. (2017) Centralisation, Devolution and the Future of Local Government in England, Routledge: Abingdon.

Leitner, H. (1990) 'Cities in pursuit of economic growth: the local state as entrepreneur', Political Geography Quarterly, 9, 2, 146–170.

Leong, L. (2016) The 'Rail plus Property' model: Hong Kong's successful self-financing formula, https://www.mckinsey.com/industries/capital-projects-and-infrastructure/our-insights/the-rail-plus-property-model; Accessed: 24 November 2021.

Local Government Association (2021a) LGA Data Pack: Local Government Workforce Summary Data, March, LGA: London.

Local Government Association (2021b) Shared Services Map, LGA: London.

Local Government Association (2018) National Procurement Strategy for Local Government in England, LGA: London.

Local Government Lawyer (2021) 'High Court strikes out bid by councils to rescind loans from Barclays following "LIBOR" rigging affair', 23 February 23, https://www.localgovernmentlawyer.co.uk/procurement-and-contracts/402-procurement-news/46273-high-court-strikes-out-bid-by-councils-to-rescind-loans-from-barclays-following-libor-rigging-affair; Accessed: 20 July 2022.

Localis (2017) Neo-localism: Rediscovering the Nation, Localis: London.

Lowndes, V. and Gardner, A. (2016) 'Local governance under the Conservatives: super-austerity, devolution and the "smarter state"', Local Government Studies, 42, 3, 357–375.

Lyons, M. (2007) Lyons Inquiry into Local Government—Place-shaping: A Shared Ambition for the Future of Local Government, The Stationery Office: London.

MacKinnon, D. (2021) 'Governing uneven development: the Northern Powerhouse as a "state spatial strategy"', Territory, Politics, Governance, 9, 5, 613–635.

Mader, P., Mertens, D. and van der Zwan, N. (2020) (Eds.) The Routledge International Handbook of Financialization, Routledge: London.

Marrs, C. (2017) '"Seamless transition" for clients says new owner of Capita Asset Services', Room 151, 29 June.

Marrs, C. (2018a) 'Portsmouth set to lose £2.5m over cancelled energy company', Room 151, 15 August.

Marrs, C. (2018b) 'Spelthorne nears £1bn in borrowing for property acquisitions', Room 151, 16 August.

Marrs, C. (2018c) 'PWLB money stokes bonfire of the LOBOs', Room 151, 5 December.

Marrs, C. (2019a) 'PWLB rate hike sends shockwaves through council finance sector', Room 151, 9 October.

Marrs, C. (2019b) 'Councils warned over 'son of LOBOs' income strip deals', Room 151, 4 April.

Martin, R., Gardiner, B., Pike, A., Sunley, P. and Tyler, P. (2021) Levelling Up Left Behind Places: The Scale and Nature of the Policy Challenge, Regional Studies Association: Falmer.

Massey, D. (1980) 'The pattern of landownership and its implications for policy', Built Environment, 6, 263–271.

McCann, E. J. and Ward, K. (2011) 'Introduction: urban assemblages: territories, relations, practices, and power' in E. J. McCann and K. Ward (Eds.) Mobile Urbanism: Cities and Policymaking in the Global Age, Minnesota University Press: Minneapolis, xiii–xxxv.

McCarthy, A. (2018) The changing role and structure of the local state in economic development, PhD Thesis, CURDS: Newcastle University

McGuirk, P., Dowling, R. and Chatterjee, P. (2021) 'Municipal statecraft for the smart city: retooling the smart entrepreneurial city?', Environment and Planning A, 53, 7, 1730–1748.

Mertens, A., Trampusch, C., Fastenrath, F. and Wangemann, R. (2020) 'The political economy of local government financialization and the role of policy diffusion', Regulation and Governance, https://doi.org/10.1111/rego.12285

MHCLG (2018) Statutory Guidance on Local Government Investments, MHCLG: London.

MHCLG (2020a) Addressing Cultural and Governance Failings in Local Authorities: Lessons from Recent Interventions, 16 June, MHCLG: London.

MHCLG (2020b) Local Authority Revenue Expenditure and Financing 2019–20 Budget, England, MHCLG: London.

MHCLG (2021) Live tables on local government finance, Borrowing and Investment Live Table Q1 2021–22, https://www.gov.uk/government/statistical-data-sets/live-tables-on-local-government-finance; Accessed: 17 August 2021.

Migozzi, J. (2020) 'Selecting spaces, classifying people: the financialization of housing in the South African city', Housing Policy Debate, 30, 4, 640–660.

Minton, A. (2017) Big Capital: Who Is London For?, Penguin: London.

Möller, S. (2017) Financializing town halls: Local councils, LOBO loans and the derivatives markets, Sheffield Political Economy Research Institute: Sheffield.

Möller, S. (2021) 'Connecting local government with global finance: professional service firms as agents of financialization' in C. Hurl and A. Vogelpohl (Eds.) Professional Service Firms and Politics in a Global Era: Public Policy, Private Expertise, Palgrave Macmillan: Cham, Switzerland, 175–194.

Moody's (2017) Moody's downgrades 54 UK sub-sovereign issuers and changes outlook to stable; universities and two local authorities retain negative outlook. Affirms University of Cambridge's Aaa rating with stable outlook, https://www.moodys.com/research/Moodys-downgrades-54-UK-sub-sovereign-issuers-and-changes-outlook-PR_372870; Accessed: 29 August 2018.

Moran, M., Tomaney J. and Williams, K. (2018) 'Territory and power in England: the political economy of Manchester and beyond' in M. Kennery, I. McLean and A. Paun (Eds.) Governing England: English Institutions and Identity in a Changing UK, British Academy: London, 189–206.

Morphet, J. and Clifford, B. (2017) Local Authority Direct Provision of Housing, Royal Town Planning Institute: London.

Muldoon-Smith, K. and Sandford, M. (2021) 'Grasping the nettle: the central-local constraints on local government funding in England', Territory Politics Governance, 1–18, https://doi.org/10.1080/21622671.2021.1924249

Murie, A. (2016) The Right to Buy? Selling Off Public and Social Housing, Policy Press: Bristol.

National Audit Office (2014) Financial Sustainability of Local Authorities 2018, HC 783, NAO: London.

National Audit Office (2015a) Code of Audit Practice, NAO: London.

National Audit Office (2015b) The Choice of Finance for Capital Investment, National Audit Office: London.

National Audit Office (2018a) Financial Sustainability of Local Authorities 2018, HC 834, NAO: London.

National Audit Office (2018b) PFI and PF2, HC 718, NAO: London.

National Audit Office (2019a) Local Authority Governance, HC 1865, NAO: London.

National Audit Office (2019b) Departmental Overview 2019—Local Authorities, NAO: London.

National Audit Office (2020) Local Authority Investment in Commercial Property, HC 45, NAO: London.

National Audit Office (2021a) Financial Sustainability of Local Authorities Visualisation: Update, NAO: London.

National Audit Office (2021b) Local Government Finance in the Pandemic, HC 1240, NAO: London.

Newton, K. and Karan, T. J. (1985) The Politics of Local Expenditure, Macmillan: Basingstoke.

Ó Riain, S. (2014) The Rise and Fall of Ireland's Celtic Tiger: Liberalism, Boom and Bust, Cambridge University Press: Cambridge.

O'Brien, P. and Pike, A. (2019) 'Deal or no deal? Governing infrastructure funding and financing in the UK City Deals', Urban Studies, 56, 7, 1448–1476.

O'Connor, J. R. (1973) The Fiscal Crisis of the State, St. Martin's Press: New York.

O'Dwyer, M. (2021) 'EY's UK partners handed record pay as deals boom', Financial Times, 2 November, Financial Times: London.

O'Neill, P. (2004) 'Bringing the qualitative state back into Economic Geography' in T. J. Barnes, J. Peck, E. Sheppard, and A. Tickell (Eds.) Reading Economic Geography, Blackwell: Oxford, 257–270.

O'Neill, T. with Hymel, G. (1995) All Politics Is Local: And Other Rules of the Game, Adams Media Corp.: Stoughton, MA.

OECD (2019) Making Decentralisation Work: A Handbook for Policymakers, OECD: Paris.

OECD (2020) Tax Revenue Trends 1965–2018, OECD: Paris.

Office for Budget Responsibility (2021) Departmental Expenditure Limits, OBR: London.

Office of Fair Trading (2011a) Completed acquisition by Sector Treasury Services Limited of ICAP plc's treasury consultancy services business known as Butlers, OFT: London.

Office of Fair Trading (2011b) Terms of reference and conduct of the inquiry, OFT: London.

Ogden, K. and Phillips, D. (2021) COVID-19 and English Council Funding: How Are Budgets Being Hit in 2020–21?, IFS: London.

ONS (2020a) Quarterly Public Sector Employment Survey (QPSES) England, ONS: London.

ONS (2020b) Trade Union Membership, UK 1995–2020: Statistical Bulletin, 27 May, ONS: London.

Operation Black Vote (2019) BAME Local Political Representation Audit 2019, OBV: London.

Ordnance Survey (2021) Boundary-line 1:10000, https://www.ordnancesurvey.co.uk/business-government/products/boundaryline; Accessed: August 2021.

Osborne, D. and Gaebler, T. (1992) Reinventing Government: How the Entrepreneurial Spirit Is Transforming the Public Sector, Penguin Books: New York.

Osborne, G. (2010) Financial Statement, 22 June, Hansard, Volume 512, Columns 167–181, House of Commons: London.

Ostry, J., Ghosh, A., Kim, J. and Qureshi, M. (2010) Fiscal Space, International Monetary Fund: Washington D.C.

Pacewicz, J. (2013) 'Tax increment financing, economic development professionals and the financialization of urban politics', Socio-Economic Review, 11, 413–440.

Pagano, M. A. and Hoene, C. W. (2018) City Budgets in an Era of Increased Uncertainty: Understanding the Fiscal Policy Space of Cities, Brookings Institution: Washington, D.C.

Parkinson, M. (1986) 'Creative accounting and financial ingenuity in local government: the case of Liverpool', Public Money and Management, 5, 4, 27–32.

Parr, J. B. (2020) 'Local government in England: evolution and long-term trends', Commonwealth Journal of Local Governance, 23, Id7382.

Patterson, A. and Pinch, P. L. (1995) '"Hollowing out" the local state: compulsory competitive tendering and the restructuring of British public sector services', Environment and Planning A, 27, 9, 1437–1461.

Pearson, B., Paul, F., Cumbers, A. and Stegemann, L. (2021) Public Futures Database Report, March, https://www.gla.ac.uk/media/Media_782991_smxx.pdf; Accessed: 3 November 2021.

Peck, J. (2012) 'Austerity urbanism: American cities under extreme economy', City, 16, 6, 626–655.

Peck, J. (2017) 'Transatlantic urbanism, part 1', Urban Studies, 54, 1, 4–30.

Peck, J. and Theodore, N. (2007) 'Variegated capitalism', Progress in Human Geography, 31, 6, 731–772.

Peck, J. and Whiteside, H. (2016) 'Financializing Detroit', Economic Geography, 92, 3, 325–268.

Penny, J. (2019) '"Defend the Ten": everyday dissensus against the slow spoiling of Lambeth's libraries', Environment and Planning D, 38, 5, 923–940.

Penny, J. (2022) '"Revenue generating machines"? London's local housing companies and the emergence of local state rentierism', Antipode, 54, 2, 545–566.

Pérignon, C. and Vallée, B. (2017) 'The political economy of financial innovation: evidence from local governments', The Review of Financial Studies, 30, 6, 1903–1934.

Peters, D. (2021) 'Future Forum: Whiteman accuses some councils of going too far', Public Finance, 30 September.

Phillips, D. and Harris, T. (2018) The Fair Funding Review: Is a Fair Assessment of Councils' Spending Needs Feasible?, Institute for Fiscal Studies: London.

Pickard, J. (2016) 'Local councils suffer after taking out exotic loans', Financial Times, 11 March, Financial Times: London.

Pike, A., Coombes, M., O'Brien, P. and Tomaney, J. (2018) 'Austerity states, institutional dismantling and the governance of sub-national economic development: the demise of the Regional Development Agencies in England', Territory, Politics, Governance, 6, 1, 118–144.

Pike, A., Kempton, L., Marlow, D., O'Brien, P. and Tomaney, J. (2016) Decentralisation: Issues, Principles and Practice, CURDS: Newcastle University.

Pike, A., Marlow, D., McCarthy, A., O'Brien, P. and Tomaney, J. (2015) 'Local institutions and local economic development: the Local Enterprise Partnerships in England, 2010-', Cambridge Journal of Regions, Economy and Society, 8, 2, 185–204.

Pike, A., O'Brien, P., Strickland, T., Thrower, G. and Tomaney, J. (2019) Financialising City Statecraft and Infrastructure, Elgar: Cheltenham.

Pike, A., O'Brien, P., Strickland, T., Thrower, G. and Tomaney, J. (2020) 'What and where next?', Environment and Planning A, 52, 4, 808–810.

Pilling, S. and Cracknell, R. (2021) UK Election Statistics: 1918–2021: A Century of Elections, House of Commons Library: London.

Pinch, P. L. (1995) 'Governing urban finance: changing budgetary strategies in British local government', Environment and Planning A, 27, 965–983.

Plender, J. (2017) 'A quirky and hazardous corner of British public finance', Financial Times, 17 February, Financial Times: London.

Portsmouth City Council (2018) Property Investment Fund (Information Report), https://democracy.portsmouth.gov.uk/documents/s20189/Property%20Investment%20Fund%20Information%20Report%20with%20appendices%201%202.pdf; Accessed: 26 April 2022.

PricewaterhouseCoopers (2006) Sub-optimal Markets, PwC: London.

Public Finance (2020) 'Whiteman slams Plymouth's interest rate swap move', Public Finance, 19 October.

Puviani, A. (1897) *Teoria della illusione finanziaria* (Theory of Financial Illusion), Unione Tipografica Cooperativa: Perugia.

Raco, M. and Souza, T. (2018) 'Urban development, small business communities and the entrepreneurialisation of English local government', Town Planning Review, 89, 2, 145–165.

Redmond, T. (2020) Independent Review into the Oversight of Local Audit and the Transparency of Local Authority Financial Reporting, MHCLG: London.

Ridley, N. (1988) The Local Right, Centre for Policy Studies: London.

Robson, W. A. (1931) The Development of Local Government, George Allen and Unwin: London.

Rudgewick, O. (2021a) 'Council appoints KPMG on £18m strategic partnership', Public Finance, 12 April.

Rudgewick, O. (2021b) 'Government announces new local audit leader', Public Finance, 19 May.

Rudgewick, O. (2022) 'Council's credit rating cut over debt concerns', Public Finance, 3 May.

Sandford, M. (2016a) 'Public services and local government: the end of the principle of "funding following duties"', Local Government Studies, 42, 4, 637–656.

Sandford, M. (2016b) Local Government in England: Capital Finance, Briefing Paper 05797, House of Commons Library: London.

Sandford, M. (2017) Local Government: Commercial Property Investments, Briefing Paper 08142, House of Commons Library: London.

Sandford, M. (2019) Local Audit in England, Briefing Paper 07240, House of Commons Library: London.

Sandford, M. (2020a) Local Government in England: Structures, Number 07104, House of Commons Library: London.

Sandford, M. (2020b) Reviewing and Reforming Local Government Finance, Number 07538, House of Commons Library: London.

Sandford, M. (2020c) Local Authority Financial Resilience, Number 08520, House of Commons Library: London.

Sandford, M. (2021a) Unitary Local Government, Number 09056, House of Commons Library: London.

Sandford, M. (2021b) Council Tax: Local Referendums, Number 05682, House of Commons Library: London.

Sanfelici, D. and Halbert, L. (2019) 'Financial market actors as urban policy-makers: the case of real estate investment trusts in Brazil', Urban Geography, 40, 1, 83–103.

Savini, F. and Aalbers, M. (2016) 'The de-contextualisation of land use planning through financialisation: urban redevelopment in Milan', European Urban and Regional Studies, 23, 4, 878–894.

Sawyer, M. (2022) The Power of Finance: Financialization and the Real Economy, Agenda: Newcastle Upon Tyne.

Sbragia, A. (1986) 'Capital markets and central-local politics in Britain', British Journal of Political Science, 16, 3, 311–339.

Sbragia, A. M. (1996) Debt Wish: Entrepreneurial Cities, U.S. Federalism and Economic Development, University of Pittsburgh Press: Pittsburgh, P.A.

Seitz, R. (1998) Over Here, Phoenix: London.

Singla, A. and Luby, M. J. (2020) 'Financial engineering by city governments: factors associated with the use of debt-related derivatives', Urban Affairs Review, 56, 3, 857–887.

Singla, A., Stritch, J. M. and Feeney, M. K. (2018) 'Constrained or creative? Changes in financial condition and entrepreneurial orientation in public organizations', Public Administration, 96, 769–786.

Skelcher, C., Weir, S. and Wilson, L. (2000) The Advance of the Quango State, Local Government Information Unit: London.

Steil, B. and Litan, R. (2008) Financial Statecraft: The Role of Financial Markets in American Foreign Policy, Yale University Press: Yale.

Stoker, G. (1989) 'Creating a local government for a post-Fordist society: the Thatcherite project?' in J. Stewart and G. Stoker (Eds.) The Future of Local Government, Macmillan: London, 141–170.

Strange, S. (1986) Casino Capitalism, Blackwell: Oxford.

Streeck, W. and Mertens, D. (2013) 'Public finance and the decline of state capacity in democratic capitalism' in W. Streeck and A. Schäfer (Eds.) Politics in the Age of Austerity, Polity Press: Cambridge, 25–58.

Strickland, T. (2016) Funding and financing urban infrastructure: a UK-US comparison, Unpublished PhD thesis, CURDS: Newcastle University.

Stubbington, T. (2020) 'Plymouth council makes first dive into swaps market 30 years after scandal', Financial Times, 8 October, Financial Times: London.

Stubbington, T. (2021) 'Foreign investors buy UK government debt at record rate', Financial Times, 3 June, Financial Times: London.

Swallow, M. (n.d.) Income Strips, Arlingclose, https://www.arlingclose.com/insights/income-strips; Accessed: 19 November 2021.

Tapp, R. and Kay, K. (2019) 'Fiscal geographies: "placing" taxation in urban Geography', Urban Geography, 40, 4, 573–581.

TaxPayers' Alliance (2020) Local Authority Commercial Property Investments, TaxPayers' Alliance: London.

TaxPayers' Alliance (2021) Council Energy Companies, TaxPayers' Alliance: London.

Tickell, A. (1998) 'Creative finance and the local state: the Hammersmith and Fulham swaps affair', Political Geography, 17, 7, 865–881.

Trampusch, C. (2019) 'The financialization of the state: government debt management reforms in New Zealand and Ireland', Competition and Change, 23, 1, 3–22.

Travers, T. (2017) 'Local government spending and taxation are now unsustainable', Local Government Chronicle, 21 February, LGC: London.

Travers, T. and Esposito, L. (2003) The Decline and Fall of Local Democracy: A History of Local Government Finance, Policy Exchange: London.

Treasury Committee (2009) Banking Crisis: The Impact of the Failure of the Icelandic Banks, First Report of Session 2019–20, HC 402, House of Commons: London.

Trowers & Hamlins (2013) Public Sector Commercial Local Asset Backed Vehicles, Trowers & Hamlins: London.

Turley, G., Robbins, G. and McNena, S. (2015) 'A framework to measure the financial performance of local governments', Local Government Studies, 41, 3, 401–420.

UK Municipal Bonds Agency (2020) Fixed Income Investor Presentation August 2020, UK MBA: London.

Unlock Democracy (2021) Local Government in England: Forty Years of Decline, Unlock Democracy: London.

van Loon, J., Oosterlynck, S. and Aalbers, M. B. (2019) 'Governing urban development in the Low Countries: from managerialism to entrepreneurialism and financialization', European Urban and Regional Studies, 26, 4, 400–418.

Wade, R. H. and Sigurgeirsdottir, S. (2011) 'Iceland's meltdown: the rise and fall of international banking in the North Atlantic', Brazilian Journal of Political Economy, 31, 5 (125), 684–697.

Waite, D., Maclennan, D. and O'Sullivan, T. (2013) 'Emerging city policies: devolution, deals and disorder', Local Economy, 28, 7–8, 770–785.

Wallis, W. (2022) 'One council's painful journey into investing', Financial Times, 7 February, Financial Times: London.

Wang, Y. (2020) 'Financialization and state transformations' in P. Mader, D. Mertens and N. van der Zwan (Eds.) The Routledge International Handbook of Financialization, Routledge: London, 188–199.

Ward, C. (2021) 'Contradictions of financial capital switching: reading the corporate leverage crisis through The Port of Liverpool's Whole Business Securitization', International Journal of Urban and Regional Research, 45, 2, 249–265.

Ward, C. (2022) 'Land financialisation, planning informalisation and gentrification as statecraft in Antwerp', Urban Studies, 59, 9, 1837–1854.

Ward, C., Van Loon, J. and Wijburg, G. (2018) 'Neoliberal Europeanisation, variegated financialisation: common but divergent economic trajectories in the Netherlands, United Kingdom and Germany', Tijdschrift voor Economische en Sociale Geografie, 110, 2, 123–137.

Ward, S. (2018) 'One Angel Square sale cost Northamptonshire County Council half-a-million in fees', Northamptonshire Telegraph, 28 September.

Weber, R. (2010) 'Selling city futures: the financialization of urban redevelopment policy', Economic Geography, 86, 3, 251–274.

Weber, R. (2015) From Boom to Bubble: How Finance Built the New Chicago, University of Chicago Press: Chicago.

Wendell Holmes O. Jr., (1927) Dissenting judgement on Compañia General de Tabacos de Filipinas vs. Collector of Internal Revenue, 275 U.S. 87, 100, 21 November; https://caselaw.findlaw.com/us-supreme-court/275/87.html; Accessed: 9 May 2022.

Whiteman, R. (2021) 'On the brink: reform of council finances needed more than ever', Public Finance, 4 June.

Whiteside, H. (2020) 'Historicizing financialization and the postwar "infrastructure ideal"', Environment and Planning A, 52, 4, 806–807.

Whitfield, D. (2010) Global Auction of Public Assets: Public Alternatives to the Infrastructure Market and Public Private Partnerships, Spokesman: Nottingham.

Whitfield, D. (2020) Public Alternative to the Privatisation of Life, Spokesman: Nottingham.

Williams, A. (2018) 'Haringey Council scraps £4bn property venture with Lendlease', Financial Times, 18 July, Financial Times: London.

Williams, S. (2020) 'Government to weigh up "moral hazard" of response to councils with "riskier" commercial assets', Social Housing, 6 May.

Willmott, H. (1986) 'Organising the profession: a theoretical and historical examination of the development of the major accountancy bodies in the U.K.', Accounting, Organizations and Society, 11, 6, 555–580.

Wills, J. (2016) Locating Localism: Statecraft, Citizenship and Democracy, Policy Press: Bristol.

Wilson, D. and Game, C. (2011) Local Government in the United Kingdom (5th Edition), Palgrave Macmillan: Basingstoke.

Wilson, P. (2018) 'Liverpool mayor defends city's £280m loan to Everton for stadium scheme', The Guardian, 10 January, Guardian Newspapers: London.

Women's Budget Group (2021) Local Government and Gender—A Pre-Budget Briefing from the Women's Budget Group, March, WBG: London.

Wu, F. (2023) 'The long shadow of the state: financializing the Chinese city', Urban Geography, 44, 1, 37–58.

Index

For the benefit of digital users, indexed terms that span two pages (e.g., 52–53) may, on occasion, appear on only one of those pages.